THE DYNAMICS OF EDUCATIONAL CHANGE:
TOWARD RESPONSIVE SCHOOLS

|I|D|E|A| REPORTS ON SCHOOLING
JOHN I. GOODLAD, *General Editor and Director*

EARLY SCHOOLING SERIES
Assisted by Jerrold M. Novotney

SERIES ON EDUCATIONAL CHANGE
Assisted by Kenneth A. Tye

THE DYNAMICS OF EDUCATIONAL CHANGE: TOWARD RESPONSIVE SCHOOLS

by John I. Goodlad

Introduction by
Samuel G. Sava
Executive Director |I|D|E|A|

A CHARLES F. KETTERING FOUNDATION PROGRAM

McGRAW-HILL BOOK COMPANY
New York St. Louis San Francisco
Düsseldorf London Mexico Sydney Toronto

Library of Congress Cataloging in Publication Data

Goodlad, John I
  The dynamics of educational change.

  (|I|D|E|A| reports on schooling. Series on educational change) (|I|D|E|A| reports on schooling. Early schooling series)
  "A Charles F. Kettering Foundation program."
  Bibliography: p.
  Includes index.
  1. School management and organization—United States. 2. Educational innovations—United States. I. Title.   II. Series: Institute for Development of Educational Activities. Series on educational change. III. Series: Institute for Development of Educational Activities. Early schooling series.

LB2806.G57   371.2   75-22314
ISBN 0-07-023762-X

|I|D|E|A| is the service mark for the Institute for Development of Educational Activities, Inc., an incorporated affiliate of the Charles F. Kettering Foundation.

|I|D|E|A| was established in 1965 to encourage constructive change in elementary and secondary schools. It serves as the primary operant for the Foundation's missions and programs in education.

As an institution committed to stimulating constructive changes for the benefit of mankind, the Kettering Foundation believes strongly in the potential of education to help bring about such changes.

Robert G. Chollar

President and
Chief Executive Officer
Charles F. Kettering Foundation

Acknowledgments for permission to use excerpts from copyrighted material include:

James B. Conant, *Modern Science and Modern Man.* Copyright 1952 by James B. Conant. Used by permission of Columbia University Press.

James B. Conant, *Slums and Suburbs.* Copyright 1962 by James B. Conant. Used by permission of Educational Testing Service.

James B. Conant, *Two Modes of Thought.* Copyright 1964 by James Bryant Conant. Used by permission of Trident Press, Simon & Schuster, Inc.

John Dewey, *The Sources of a Science of Education.* Copyright 1929, 1956 by John Dewey. Used by permission of W. W. Norton & Company, Inc.

Leon Edel, "Walden: The Myth and the Mystery." Copyright 1975 by Leon Edel. Used by permission of the author.

Loren C. Eisley, "Alternatives to Technology." Copyright 1969 by Loren C. Eisley. Used by permission of Columbia University Press.

Rudolf Ekstein, "Towards Walden III." Copyright 1974 by Rudolf Ekstein. Used by permission of the author.

Daniel E. Griffiths, "Administrative Theory and Change in Organizations." Copyright 1964 by Daniel E. Griffiths. Used by permission of Teachers College Press.

Joseph Heller, *Something Happened.* Copyright 1974 by Joseph Heller. Used by permission of Alfred A. Knopf, Inc.

Ernest R. House (ed.), *The Politics of Educational Innovation.* Copyright 1974 by Ernest R. House. Berkeley: McCutchan Publishing Corporation. Reprinted by permission of the publisher.

James G. March, "Model Bias in Social Action." Copyright 1972, American Educational Research Association, Washington, D.C. Reprinted by permission of the publisher.

Robert M. Hutchins, "The Great Anti-School Campaign." Copyright 1972 by Robert M. Hutchins. Reprinted by permission of Encyclopaedia Britannica, Inc.

Max Nicholson, "The Big Change." Copyright 1973 by Max Nicholson. Reprinted by permission of McGraw-Hill Book Company.

Carl R. Rogers, *Freedom to Learn.* Copyright 1969 by Carl R. Rogers. Reprinted by permission of Charles E. Merrill Books, Inc.

B. Othanel Smith, "The Anatomy of Change." Copyright 1963 by B. Othanel Smith. Reprinted by permission of the National Association of Secondary School Principals.

CONTENTS

ACKNOWLEDGMENTS

So far as I am able consciously to determine, the central thesis of this book had its genesis in the late 1940s or early 1950s and took on increased meaning over the succeeding quarter century. Consequently, it is not possible to identify and thank individually all those persons who contributed in various ways to its maturation. The best that can be done is to identify them in clusters. And so I express my appreciation to:

Those hundreds of teachers, dozens of school principals, and several superintendents in Atlanta, Georgia, and its environs who, from 1947 to 1956, invited me into their schools and classrooms and discussed their problems so freely and frankly

Colleagues in the Atlanta Area Teacher Education Service who helped form my thoughts through daily dialogue about schools during these nine fruitful years

The principals, teachers and friends of the Englewood School in Florida with whom I had the good fortune to be associated—again over a period of nine years, partly overlapping the nine in Atlanta—in reconstructing that school and restoring the community's faith in it

Colleagues at the University of Chicago who taught me the meaning of theory—not dogma, abstraction, or a theory but the importance of finding tentative explanations for phenomena and of testing them

Colleagues at the University Elementary School, UCLA, who were so patient with my questions and who helped me answer some of them

Visitors to the School who were willing to trade questions for questions

Educators across the country who let us into their schools and classrooms as part of our effort to learn something about the school as a workplace

Those superintendents, principals, and teachers of the eighteen schools and those staff members of the Research Division, Institute for Development of Educational Activities, Inc. (|I|D|E|A|), who created the League of Cooperating Schools

The Kettering Foundation for providing through its affiliate, |I|D|E|A|, financial support for the Study of Educational Change and School Improvement described on succeeding pages

The Center for Advanced Study in the Behavioral Sciences for a year to reflect and read as a Fellow there

My family and my administrative colleagues at both |I|D|E|A| and UCLA who kept many problems from me while I was getting the words down on paper.

Undoubtedly, there are many more to whom I am indebted, including those who disagreed with me, for what I learned during these years about schools and their functioning, relationships between people and institutions, and humankind. The temptation to try to name them is great but the list would be very long. Included would be those who came as students; I trust they are still learning. Some of them are listed in Appendix A.

The specific help of three people regarding this volume must be identified, however. Elisabeth Tietz faithfully typed the several drafts, the first from my notorious illegible handwriting, page by yellow page. Lillian K. Drag diligently tracked down fugitive references and compiled the bibliography, much of which constituted my reading. Judith S. Golub stayed with the manuscript to completion, suggesting, changing, always improving and demonstrating that almost-lost art of good editing.

Of course, for what is written only I am responsible. Officials of the Kettering Foundation always have left me completely free to carry on work through |I|D|E|A| and to write about it without intervening in any way. Royalties from this volume and the others reporting our inquiries into schooling go to |I|D|E|A| for the support of various activities in the field of education.

What follows is addressed to the problems and processes of personal and institutional renewal—the dynamics of educational change. To try to change something is to come to understand it better. The dividend is what one learns about oneself.

John I. Goodlad

INTRODUCTION

As a long-distance colleague (about 2,000 miles separate our respective offices) of John Goodlad since the beginning of my affiliation with |I|D|E|A| eight years ago, I have been privileged to watch the study on which this volume is based take shape. It has been a learning experience for me—one of a sort which, I suspect, few educators ever have the good luck to encounter. No matter how complete and accurate a research report is, the printed page cannot duplicate the human process by which ideas are conceived, tested, glumly rejected, or delightedly adopted; nor can it recreate the intellectual pleasure I enjoyed as, during our periodic meetings, I watched John worry his problems back and forth, declare certain avenues of investigation promising and cross others off as blind alleys, and ingeniously craft yet another approach to a stubborn problem. In short, I fully enjoyed my ringside seat at the making of this book, not only because the result is so excellent but because the rehearsals were engrossing, too.

Now that the result is in print, however, and any words of encouragement or discouragement can have no effect upon it, I must confess to a certain sense of amusement at having watched John and his colleagues bring the Study of Educational Change and School Improvement to a successful conclusion. It is an exaggeration—but a forgivable one, because pertinent and illuminating—to state that the greatest problem they encountered was giving this book (and others in the |I|D|E|A| Report Series) a title.

One early candidate in place of the present title of this volume was *The Ecology of Educational Change*. Though on balance I think "dynamics" is the right word, I am somewhat sorry that "ecology" lost out in the bidding, for this relatively new, financially undernourished discipline—and some of the tales emanating from it—seem to me to have something to tell us not only about the nature of past educational research but about the unusual significance of this volume.

An underlying motivation for the Study of Educational Change and School Improvement (SECSI)—a five-year research project on which this volume and its companions are based—was the continuing, frustrating failure of promising innovations to alter school practice in desired ways. An underlying stimulus for the environmentalist movement of the past ten years, and some recent impetus for the study of ecology, has been the major and minor disasters accompanying the application of technology to human needs or convenience. Applied technology has produced plenty of change—but, as we are learning to our grief almost weekly, many of the changes are undesirable.

The automobile, for example, has given us convenient, personal transportation, extending our mobility and liberating us from the scheduling of mass transit. But its exhausts, reacting with sunlight and other environmental factors in an unanticipated chemistry, have produced smog, potentially toxic concentrations of lead in the atmosphere, and even "acid rains" in some regions of the country. Prodded by promises of whiter, brighter clothes, Americans poured billions of pounds of synthetic detergents into their washers (and into municipal sewage systems) before it was learned that these detergents could not be broken down by bacterial action; hence "nonbiodegradable" chemical compounds have simply accumulated in water supplies. The completion of the St. Lawrence Seaway—an economic boon in that it permitted ocean-going vessels to enter the Great Lakes—proved an ecological disaster when it was learned that the sea lamprey, a singularly aggressive and hungry predator, had gotten into the Lakes with the ships. Within a few years, the sea lamprey virtually extinguished the lake trout and several other species on which a substantial commercial fishing industry had been based.

In his introduction to *The Careless Technology*,[1] Barry Commoner argues that these costly, unlooked-for byproducts of applied technology result from "a reductionist bias" in our science, our technology, and our modern ways of solving problems. He defines this bias as "the view that understanding of a real, complex system can be achieved by investigating the properties of its isolated parts." The problem with this bias is that:

> If, for the sake of analytical detail, molecular constituents are isolated from the smashed remains of a cell, or single organisms are separated from their natural neighbors, what is lost is the network of interrelationships which crucially determines the proprieties of the natural whole. (Farvar & Milton, 1972, p. xxiv.)

The reductionist approach works well when applied to purely mechanical systems, such as the production of an automobile, or the creation of a synthetic compound. Indeed, most of our technology—as

---

[1] *The Careless Technology*, by M. Taghi Farvar and John P. Milton (eds.), The Natural History Press, Garden City, N.Y., 1972.

reflected, for example, in mass-production operations—consists of breaking down complex tasks into single pieces. Such specialization and division of labor were essential to the development of technology, and unquestionably go far toward explaining the economic rise of the West during the nineteenth and twentieth centuries. This reductionist approach is similarly reflected in our pursuit of knowledge, in that we break the general endeavor of learning and research into analogous pieces called "disciplines": sociology, physics, chemistry, biology, psychology, and so forth. Such subdivision of investigation has been absolutely essential to the development and advance of modern scholarship.

The mischief comes when we forget that such disciplines do not exist in the real world—that they are man-made categories designed to aid us in investigating reality, not explanations or replicas of reality —and when we apply this reductionist approach to natural, as opposed to mechanical, systems.

In my view, based not only on my experience as a foundation official but also on earlier experience as a program officer with the U.S. Office of Education during that agency's most euphoric and busy days, most efforts at educational change have been based on a reductionist view of the schools. That is, if you wanted to understand the schools with a view toward changing them, you would begin by breaking them down into their various components: teachers, students, curriculum, financing, governance, facilities, and equipment. Once you had done this, you "understood" the workings of the schools and were prepared to start changing them.

If the researcher were of a simplistic or blunt turn of mind, he might select one of these components as his point of attack for change: improve teacher training, he might decide, and you improve all ... or improve curriculum, that's the key to everything. If the researcher were of a more subtle, patient turn of mind, he would produce a more complex program for change, involving several components and frequently illustrated by charts fitted out with bold lines, dotted lines, arrows going in several directions, and terms such as "input," "feedback network," and "evaluation-revision loop." No matter how simple or ingenious, the salient fact about these programs to produce change was that they did not seem to work.

In this volume, Goodlad puts his finger on a basic cause for the failure of change efforts in education: each school is a natural, not a mechanical system. Consequently, as the ecologist tells us, a school cannot be adequately understood in terms of its isolated components and their separate operation, but only as an interrelated whole; a school's operation as an ecosystem differs significantly from that of a mechanical system, whose operation can be broken down into discrete components that function in unvarying, predictable ways.

Goodlad is not the only thinker to conceive of the school in terms of a natural system; he has noted Seymour B. Sarason's description of the school as a "culture"[2]—a term which, especially as used by natural scientists, is generally synonymous with "ecosystem." But Goodlad and his colleagues have been the first, to my knowledge, to utilize this concept as a fundamentally new way of conducting educational research.

Their use of the concept of the school's "culture" or "ecology" led to two fundamental elements of the SECSI study. First, they focused their attention and research energies on the school as a whole functioning institution rather than as simply a sum of discrete parts. They made no attempt to introduce a specific innovation and then judge its effectiveness in terms of student achievement. Instead, the researchers encouraged schools to try to improve their own programs and studied the process (conceptualized as dialogue, decision making, action, and evaluation—DDAE) by which they went about it. Schools were encouraged to look at this process in order to improve their functioning as institutions.

The second element was the recognition that the school is a fragile, vulnerable organism that needs nurturing and encouragement if it is to cope with anything more than daily survival. Therefore, the research focused also on the League of Cooperating Schools which was made up of eighteen schools from eighteen districts in southern California. The League created a new culture from which the schools could derive moral support in their struggles to change and improve. Of equal importance was the fact that the personnel and material resources of seventeen other schools were available to each League School. The fundamental belief was that given the right atmosphere and mechanisms, schools already contain most of the resources needed to bring about improvement of their educational programs.

The first element should appeal to researchers and, hopefully, will lead to other studies which try to understand the school as an institution. The second element has already entered into a major effort to improve schooling identified as the |I|D|E|A| Change Program for

[2]Seymour B. Sarason, *The Culture of the School and the Problem of Change*, Allyn and Bacon, Boston, 1971.

Individually Guided Education.[3] Leagues of schools are now located in thirty-five of the fifty states.

The Dynamics of Educational Change was, after all, the better choice for the title of this book. As "dynamics" suggests—and "ecology" does not—this study goes beyond the passive, hands-off investigation of a natural system at work to the formulation of an active, interventionist strategy for producing change. This latter feature will, of course, particularly recommend The Dynamics of Educational Change to those charged with making our schools better—however they define "better."

Whether read as a blueprint for better education, as a corrective for reductionist educational research, or as a piece of scholarly detective work absorbing in its own right, this volume offers, I believe, a contribution to educational theory that will be remembered for decades to come. My only question is whether it will make a commensurate contribution to educational practice.

That question can be answered only by the readers of this volume.

Samuel G. Sava
Executive Director
|I|D|E|A|

---

[3]Information on the |I|D|E|A| Change Program is available from |I|D|E|A|, 5335 Far Hills Avenue, Suite 300, Dayton, Ohio 45429.

For Len

There are two kinds of fools: those who say, "This is new and therefore better" and others who say, "This is old and therefore good."

—William Ralph Inge

CHAPTER 1

STABILITY AND CHANGE IN AMERICAN EDUCATION

Institutions have histories or they are not institutions. . . . Over the generations, institutions slowly change but they have to have a certain amount of
stability to sustain societal order. Flickering and dancing in the play of our
great machines, however, and haunting our scientific establishment, is an
unseen invisible elf to whose whims we are subjected in an ever-intensifying
fashion—an elf we call change. . . . The question is how long man can adapt
to the rapidity of social change, and how well the single great society . . . can
sustain itself and at the same time sustain our human freedoms.

> —Loren C. Eiseley ("Alternatives to Technology," in
> Aaron W. Warner et al. (eds.), *The Environment of
> Change*, Columbia, New York, 1969, pp. 175–176)

In the short history of the United States of America as a nation, the
role of the schools looms large. The concerns of the schools have reflected the concerns of the nation, and the democratic experiment and
one of the most comprehensive mass educational systems in the world
have grown up together.

Ironically, as the schools have come ever closer to embracing that
classic duality of educational aim idealistically envisioned for the learning society—instilling an ever-widening concept of social and cultural
responsibility and promoting full development of the individual—
criticism of them has intensified. While schools have been attacked for
not changing, for being mired in the past, they also have been attacked
for embracing the new uncritically, for grasping at every passing fad.
There is little doubt that the accompanying tension has been productive of much constructive change as well as periods of despair regarding our schools.[1]

Although I challenge this rhetoric of despair, I set forth no
utopias. Schools make and have made a difference, but not as much as
many eloquent proponents would have us believe. Some of this dif-

ference is on the negative side, largely because the schools have mirrored too well the ills of an imperfect society. But they are not and never have been as bad as their most articulate critics have charged. The schools have not changed as quickly as some would like. On the other hand, they change much faster than others would prefer. They will not be nearly as good by 2001 as some futurists say they will, nor will they be nearly as bad as others predict. That there will be no schools is a provocative thought, but no doubt it is wrong. That they will be different probably is the only safe prediction.

This book is based on the premise that schools, *under certain conditions,* can become much more vital than they currently are. They can and must be reconstructed, just as most of our other institutions are in need of reconstruction. Though I believe that most of the reconstruction must be effected by those who work and live in them each day, they probably will not initiate and sustain such a task entirely on their own. A productive tension between inner-directed and outer-directed efforts to improve must be created and maintained. The elements essential to this productive tension constitute both the conditions under which schools can become more vital and much of the subject matter of this volume.

This book is concerned, then, with the process, the dynamics, of educational change and improvement—not with descriptions of what reconstructed schools should look like. Many such models are available (I have my own) and should be drawn upon in the process of reconstruction according to their relevance and usefulness. To prescribe one here would be to violate a critical subpremise: schools (which are a personification of the people who comprise them) must become responsive to their own problems and needs and to the rich array of resources, including alternative models, available for dealing effectively with these problems and needs.

The focus here is not, then, the prescription of utopias but the building of Waldens—not Thoreau's and not Skinner's but the Waldens that emerge when school communities address themselves seriously to the task of reconstruction. But here the analogy must end because schools must never be, can never be, idyllic ponds or communes, splendid in their isolation from the rest of society. Schools must be, to a degree, responsive to that society, just as they must be responsive to the exigencies of their own existence. This is why change, to be dynamic and productive, necessarily involves a certain state of tension between inner and outer forces. Many of the problems of improving schools have resulted from deficiencies in this tension—usually, a destructive imbalance weighted on the side of outer forces. This observation is explored later.

Although eschewing prescriptions with respect to school environments and practices, this volume takes a position both implicitly and explicitly with respect to certain substantive restraints governing the conduct of schooling. In recent times, there has been in my judgment a dangerous redefinition of the concept of community. Hutchins described the change succinctly: "The community became people of my race, my neighborhood, my economic class."[2] This definition leads to the conclusion that the role of the school is simply to serve the self-interest of each parochial community.

This is a far cry from the school's traditional responsibility to provide "a degree of education that would enable one to perform all social, domestic, civic, and moral duties." Further, it is an ironic corruption of the definition of education for social and cultural responsibility at the very time when schools must have a mankind perspective.[3] If the schools do not educate for this enlarged concept of community, who or what will?

It is my contention that the state, in the sense of the nation-state, must assure this transcendence of the local community on behalf of all the people. In this country, although the conduct of education is the responsibility of the fifty substates, this does not relieve the nation of its role as overseer. Brown v. Board of Education (1954) makes this point clear, although the Supreme Court recently has been ambivalent in its support of ". . . that most vital civic institution for the preservation of a democratic system of government."[4]

One way for this responsibility to be dispatched is the periodic articulation of what our schools are for. This is done in a variety of ways: through presidential and various governmental commissions, White House conferences on education, Supreme Court decisions and, at the state level, the formulation and issuance of goal statements. New commitments and fresh interpretations of old ones almost invariably are presaged in the writings or reports of influential leaders working alone or in groups. Official commitments lag well behind and are frequently behind changing public opinion as well.

It is my contention that these goals must be taken seriously by schools at all times and must guide the process of reconstruction. These, along with criteria pertaining to the needs of pupils and the immediate community, provide guidelines for the process of renewal.

The conditions and processes deemed to be minimally essential for reconstructing schools, discussed in succeeding chapters, are not the result of mere speculation. An hypothesis regarding them began to form in my mind in the 1950s and was strengthened in importance by subsequent experiences (Chapter 3). This hypothesis was tested in the late 1960s and early 1970s (Chapters 4 and 5). The observations about and the strategies for school improvement presented in the later chapters are derived from these experiences and both concomitant and subsequent testing. The balance of this chapter and all of Chapter 2 are devoted to analyzing the context within which reconstruction must occur. This chapter concludes with an explication of some assumptions that affect my views throughout.

AIMS, GOALS, FUNCTIONS, AND REGULARITIES

It has been said about schools, as about many things, that "nothing changes but the appearance of change." Usually, the statement is made pejoratively. But if schools were predominantly educational institutions, it could be interpreted as a commendation. Since the aims of education, as differentiated from schooling, do not change, for the schools to remain true to unchanging educational aims over the passing decades and centuries would be a good thing.

The goals, functions, and regularities of schools change. The direction of change, how schools change, and whether they change fast enough give rise to much frustration and the derisive comment, "The more things appear to change, the more they remain the same."

Clearly, if it is deemed desirable for some aspects of education and schooling to remain stable and other aspects to change, the problems of understanding and effecting change are vastly complicated. It becomes necessary to look into the question of what is best reaffirmed and what is best changed. Herein, it would seem, lies at least a partial explanation for those recurring alternating waves of concern over whether the schools are changing too quickly, too slowly, or not at all.

Educational Aims and School Goals

From the time of the Greeks to the contemporary era, the most thoughtful statements of educational aims in the Western world have been fundamentally alike. They have affirmed and reaffirmed the inquiring, self-understanding individual of wisdom and compassion living in harmony and justice with his fellow man—the good person in the good society. The words may change but the ideas remain essentially the same.

From such ends, it is an easy step, for some persons, to the means. Those great, expressive works of art, literature, and science to have best survived the test of time because of the truths they reveal become the subject matter for successive generations. Dialogue enlightened by familiarity with such works becomes the method. Aims, subject matter, learning processes, and pedagogy blend harmoniously in a learning society.

Probing the rhetoric of today's reform polemists, whether neo-behaviorist or neo-humanist, reveals at the core little disagreement with these classical aims. The concern almost invariably proves to be some perceived neglect or excess with respect to the desired balance between individual and societal welfare. It is not that man's best visions have been found wanting but that men and women have lost sight of them, perhaps seduced by false prophets. All will be well if only they will now listen to the new prophet!

If, then, we keep coming back to the same truths, why all this concern with the glacierlike slowness of educational change, epitomized by the sardonic comment, "Nothing changes but the appearance of change?" Should we not rejoice if this is, indeed, the case? "The more things appear to change, the more they remain the same," should be a reassuring observation.

The reason this is not so is that events in their changing and perceptible forms can be distinguished from the permanent essence of things. Events, conditions, and even the concepts used both to describe them and to project ideal alternatives are not everywhere and at all times the same. Consequently, both the roles ascribed to our institutions and the meanings attached to our concepts change with time and place.

The aims of education are long-term and stable. The goals of schooling are oriented to living generations, to the here and now. Consequently, one's view of change depends not only on the perspective of time and place but also on whether one is talking about education or schooling. Most of us like the implied verity of basic educational concepts, ever subject to fresh interpretations. They can reassure us in times of uncertainty. They can be used as a formidable bulwark against change or, for that matter, against doing anything whatsoever. They have the potential for taking us back to first principles. We aren't adrift after all! "Education is at all times and in all places the same" becomes both an affirmation and an ultimate criterion for judging the worth of educational activities here and now.

But schooling is something else again. It is the institutionalization of certain functions and tasks seen as at least minimally essential to the community (and perhaps the individual) and, consequently, not safely left to the vagaries of family life or institutions created for other functions and tasks. Whatever the rhetoric of justification, schools are called upon to perform what is only minimally educational: protecting the adult labor force, providing custodial care, and assuring continuity in certain religious or nationalistic rituals. Before change agents rush in to do away with all this, they would be well advised to lend an attentive ear to those working mothers who say about the custodial role, "Don't knock it." Goals for schooling also take on a sociopolitical character as schools are charged with the task of improving society. Of course, what are perceived as needed improvements change as society itself changes. In one era the schools are viewed as the melting pot. In another they are expected to promote ethnic awareness and identity.

Education is almost inevitably direction-oriented. Webster's defines it as "the act or process of providing with knowledge, skill, competence or *desirable* qualities of behavior or character..." (italics mine). Implied are present and desired conditions and special processes of moving from the former to the latter. Ends and means arise out of consideration of the nature of humans, humankind, the good person, and the good society. Normative postulates and scientific inquiry live together, quite comfortably, each gathering strength from internecine intellectual squabbles.

Perhaps because educational aims are direction-oriented—toward some better human condition—some subgroups in society apparently conclude that schools are goal-oriented, too. At any rate, fresh statements of goals for schools are formulated from time to time. But schools only rarely are consciously goal-oriented, much to the frustration of those change agents who conceive of them differently or would have them behave differently.

When school personnel occasionally do pay serious attention to goals, especially when these goals are derived from analysis of educational aims, they often get into serious trouble with segments of their community. Many citizens are afraid of open inquiry, expressive children, and creativity, whatever the expressed aims or goals about such matters. They speak of the dangers in "progressive education" and point to the better ways of the past. But note that it is usually to the better "ways" that they point, not to any divergence from educational aims. It is questionable, in fact, whether society wants its schools to be goal-oriented.

Educational aims, then, potentially provide for stability in schooling. They speak to things worth sustaining, calling continuously for fresh interpretation of individual welfare, social justice, and what is good for humankind. School goals speak to needed changes, usually calling for correcting some imbalance between individual welfare and the common good. Frequently, because they are sociopolitical in character, the goals sought for in schooling are themselves out of balance, representing only the interests of some groups currently in power. And so educational aims must be sought, and often fought for, if balance is to be achieved.

The National Commission on the Reform of Secondary Education recommends that every secondary school should formulate and post in school buildings a statement of goals for students.[5] I would want to balance this recommendation with another: that the aims of education as stated by Aristotle and restated by Whitehead, Dewey, and a few contemporary thinkers become standard fare for school and community discussion groups. And, for good measure, I would add *The Saber-Tooth Curriculum*,[6] that classic reminder of what happens when tribes come to revere outmoded goals and activities well-suited to a bygone era of saber-toothed tigers and fish-filled streams, neglecting to reinterpret more fundamental ends in the light of changed circumstances.

School Functions and Regularities

We have seen that educational aims arise out of ideas pertaining to the long-term human condition. They are essentially apolitical, seeking to define a better life in a better world. To the extent that goals for schooling result only from fresh interpretations of the duality comprising both individual and group welfare, they are educational in character. Too often, however, such goals are little more than window-dressing, to be produced on demand or to occupy a momentary discussion or flight of idealism (as when listening to the keynote speaker at a convention).

Schools are activity-oriented. Means and ends are virtually synonymous. The goals of nursery schools, for example, are what is done in them—playing, coloring, singing, resting, expressing.[7] The staff quite probably will be able to produce a list of better-sounding goals, but these are not what guide daily behavior. Those who would change schools from the outside by giving them new goals seem not to realize that even to become goal-oriented is a significant change for school personnel.

Pervasive in the expectations for and conduct of schooling are the functions to be performed: prepare for college; contribute to the GNP; keep an age bracket out of the job market; produce a labor force; instill a competitive drive; maintain a certain homogeneity of values; curb juvenile crime. These are not stated as explicit aims or goals. They are functions more or less assumed. Performing these functions justifies schools in the eyes of many policy makers and groups. Schools are to serve these functions.

Schools derive a good deal of their stability and support by performing some exclusively educational functions in such way that these are both visible and understood. Innovation is accepted and even applauded when it is designed and carefully explained (over and over) as a way of performing these basic functions better. The wise "change agent" stresses not the forms of the new but the merits of doing established things even better. As a beginning teacher during one phase of the progressive era, I was told by a perceptive school inspector, "Your activity-centered social studies program is just fine, but remember always to stress a solid math program."

A goal is something intended; a function is performed. One would not find the above functions posted in school buildings. But they are more pervasive in the conduct of schooling than any list of lofty aims or goals. Several years ago, I asked a visiting educator from Western Europe who or what determined the curriculum of the secondary schools in his country. He responded immediately, "Why, the universities and the business world, of course." Presumably, the function of the schools was to prepare for both. In the United States, too, influences from both spread through the very fabric of schooling.

It is in recognition of this fact that Illich and others recommend that society be deschooled.[8] Their concern, unlike that of critics in other camps, is that schools are overly faithful to the surrounding society; they perform these functions too well; they reflect and perpetuate a class society in which the many are exploited for and by the few. We must get back to basic educational aims pursued in a variety of existing settings and away from schools serving the dominant class.

Look how quickly the schools are taken over by those who effect a coup, they say. They charge that schools inhibit rather than promote educational ends and processes.

To the degree that these critics are right—and it is difficult to deny a great deal of what they say—schools inevitably are placed in an unenviable dilemma. The functions to be performed are imbedded in the very structures of schooling; the aims of education and even the goals of schools are ephemeral—something to be pursued. Many sensitive, insightful young men and women who enter teaching with education in mind find themselves in a classic Catch-22 situation. The more they try to adhere to the educational principles they believe in and think the institution exists to uphold, the more they come into conflict with the regularities which uphold (or are thought to uphold) those functions imbedded in the school simply because of the fact that it is an agent of the state. The frustration, disillusionment, and ultimate disenchantment of such teachers are vividly portrayed in Bel Kaufman's sometimes funny, sometimes sad *Up the Down Staircase.*[9]

Those who believe the schools can and must be reconstructed so that they become much more educational in the conduct of their activities, and, therefore, in their functions, probably have responded too little from the cerebrum. Even though we may dislike or reject the deschoolers' solution, there is much to be learned from their analyses. The implicit agenda of the schools pertaining to their sociopolitical functions overshadows their educational agenda. The reconstruction of schooling calls for the balance to be shifted in the other direction. Clearly, this is a task the schools cannot do alone. Conceivably, this may be a task that cannot be done at all.

A contemporary example helps to unveil the problem. The Watergate break-in and subsequent events shook the American people. The aftermath, inescapably tied in to the Bicentennial and accompanying nostalgia for virtues thought lost, focused attention on the responsibilities of the schools for moral development. Proposals for the teaching of moral values popped up everywhere, especially among those legislators who naïvely perpetuate the myth that a prescribed weekly period in a given subject matter somehow possesses the power to correct deeply ingrained ills (and the even greater myth that what they prescribe ends up behind the classroom door in its intended form).[10]

Since moral values are learned, it is possible that they can be taught. And so, some class time on their teaching, properly spent, might make a little difference, if it were not for the fact that all day long young people are internalizing—accepting and rejecting—values pervasive in the structures and regularities of the school, to say nothing of those inherent in their lives at home and in the community. One of these values is achievement—and in most schools that means a particular kind of academic achievement best demonstrated in tests. Achievement becomes more important than how one demonstrates achievement. It is an easy step to cheating and, in time, to the justification of cheating (and from there to Watergate and all the rest).

I remember with chagrin one of my own most flagrant periods of reinforcing this insidious process. As the only young male teacher in an elementary school, and one who participated in all the children's games and sports, I was a somewhat idolized rarity. I used the accompanying power to spur the children to even greater heights of academic achievement—until, to my sorrow and enlightenment, I realized the amount of cheating I was diligently reinforcing.[11] Unfortunately, there no doubt have been many, many occasions when I sought to promote idealistic ends while unwittingly reinforcing quite contradictory lessons of successful survival in school or college.

When certain expectations for schools become pervasive in the surrounding community and society, schools begin to take on what appear to be relevant tasks, not as goals but as activities and conditions. These, in time, become regularities or givens in the operation of schools and are recognized as such by successive generations. Certain regularities in home and community life tend to grow up around school customs, such as the times for beginning and ending the school day. Innovations in these customs, especially those already regulating home patterns to some degree, are suspect or even taboo. It may be easier in some communities, for example, to instill a new science program for the upper elementary years than to send children home an hour early on Thursday afternoons so as to provide time for teachers to plan together.

In time, some of these regularities become equated with school. They become what school is for. Long-established ways of fulfilling functions become the *proper* functions and, indeed, often are defended by school and community alike as desired educational goals. Thus, teaching all six-year-olds to read simultaneously, regardless of how many children year after year fail to learn, becomes a virtue rather than what it more accurately is—a blind anachronism ignoring the facts of individual differences and the realities of children's learning. So blind is it, in fact, that children who come to school speaking

Spanish often are labeled "slow learners" or "retarded" when they fail to read in English by the end of the first grade!

When ways of doing things become rituals and maintaining these rituals in turn becomes a function of schools and this function becomes reified in a body of traditions (purported to fulfill some of our most revered educational goals), we have a cult. Cults are not amenable to the persuasion of alternative experience or scientific evidence. The questioning of a cult alerts the cultists to possible attack and (perhaps because of intuitive awareness of vulnerability—what dares not be spoken by the true believers has been spoken by outsiders!) to the more vigorous practice of cultism. The system's defenses are alerted. Even cults built on the rhetoric of love and compassion for others become bloodthirsty, and the Ten Commandments are reinterpreted so as to apply only to the faithful. It is important to remember that cultism is not confined to maintaining established rituals. Those who promote the new, exhorting its virtues over those of what is to be replaced, frequently are equally addicted to single answers and equally hostile to contrary viewpoints. Alternative schools can become cultist in their ritualistic adherence to the single alternative they endorse.

Even though history is replete with examples of this phenomenon, the lessons for contemporary life tend to be obscured by our cultural blinders. Educators chuckle over the story of primitive tribes increasing the frequency and intensity of their rain dances on being "shown" by outsiders that no rain results. But there is little or no concomitant transfer of insight to our own sacred rites. Certain practices of marking, grading, grouping, and otherwise classifying children are "right," evidence to the contrary notwithstanding.

School regularities which intrude into and support home and community regularities are particularly pervasive, subtle, and in the face of attack, resilient or intransigent. They serve not goals but unexamined habit. Often, they become what sociologists sometimes refer to as latent or residual functions. They come into existence not because of what schools are supposed to do but simply because schools exist. Sometimes they are brought into being with construction of the school. The schoolhouse is the place to hold town meetings, socials, or dances. Or, although the subject matter of Parent-Teacher Association meetings is regarded as irrelevant (the program chairman slavishly follows a list of topics handed down by the national body), they provide a time and place to meet friends or a forum for launching a political career. Then, there are graduation exercises, glee clubs, oratorical contests, and, of course, interschool athletics as well as the baby-sitting functions mentioned earlier. Until recently, school was regarded as a safe place for one's child, away from perverts and perversions in general. Homework assured a certain household peace and quiet in the evening. The culture of the school as part of the culture of home and community participates in complementary regularities and thus performs many latent functions having little to do with education.

James B. Conant encouraged the school consolidation movement when he specified the minimum size of a graduating class to encourage adequate depth and breadth in a high school's curriculum, an educational value.[12] He ignored certain latent functions inherent in the small high school in a self-contained community. Although we have a few studies into the effects of such consolidation, most of them the story of individual schools and communities, the full impact on American life is not at all clear. Were old ways eroding anyway or might the retention of local schools, however small, have provided some stability during recent years of high population mobility? Were schools grown apart from homes anyway or did consolidation cause not only a physical separation but also a certain attitudinal irritation among parents because of early morning bus schedules, the elimination of after-hours' play on the schoolgrounds, and other inconveniences imposed by a centralized bureaucracy grown faceless like city hall? Change agents, take note!

THE PROBLEM OF CHANGE

We have seen, then, that aims, goals, functions, and regularities, although all characteristics of schools, are differing phenomena springing from different roots, dependent on varying sources for nourishment and subject to differing forms of blight and deformity. Aims grow out of the recorded wisdom of humankind. They reflect the well-articulated insights of wise observers of the human scene who are able to project a better state for humankind in an improved society at some future time.

Goals for schools are more of the here and now. They reflect much of what is extant in the surrounding society and are designed to be corrective. Something is lacking (scientific understanding) or out of balance (not enough attention to the aesthetic). Because they are sociopolitical as well as educational, they frequently promote special interests (an uncritical unit on the value of milk in the diet of *all* children). As already noted, the overt goals of schooling are more educational, less sociopolitical, and less influential than those frequently unexamined expectations for schooling embedded in its intended functions (contribution to the GNP) or in its latent functions (keeping children off the streets and out of their homes for five or six hours each day).

Functions are what schools actually do. If the goals state the importance of teaching moral and spiritual values but the students are cheating more and more each day under the reinforcing influence of the school, then the school's function is the promotion of cheating. The educational ends stated in overt goals for schooling and the functions schools perform probably always are in varying degrees of conflict; often, they are in direct conflict. Each day of schooling in some settings actually moves many children a few more steps away from what is intended in the puerile goals perhaps posted somewhere in the building.

Regularities are the fixed or recurring routines by means of which schools conduct their daily business, day after day, week after week. Institutions must regularize their activities; innovations propose to change regularities in some way. Then, today's innovations become tomorrow's regularities. This is not bad, if tomorrow's regularities are better than today's: more aesthetic, more efficient, more productive of satisfaction.

Given these fundamental differences among aims, goals, functions, and regularities, it becomes clear that change is no unitary phenomenon for which single innovations or strategies can be effectively devised and implemented. It should become clear, also, that the desirability of change and the pace at which change might be expected to occur depend on which of these realms one is talking about. Likewise, regarding educational institutions, whether productive change is likely to come more from without than from within, or the reverse, depends on whether one has in mind aims, goals, functions, or regularities. And which of these one has in mind goes a long way toward determining whether one responds negatively or positively to the statement, "The more things change, the more they appear the same."

Attacking the Problem of Change

Whenever the schools come under fire and appear to be in need of substantial improvement, there rarely is any effort to determine in which of these realms the trouble lies. Have they lost sight of educational ends because they are called upon to perform so many community functions such as large-scale baby sitting? Has the state failed, by way of not providing resources, to convey the message that the arts, once considered a frill, are now a desired part of the curriculum? Are the teachers required to use a prescribed method of teaching reading even when they perceive it not to be working with some children? Questions like these suggest not only a possible problem but also an entry point for a solution. They have some chance of suggesting criteria for correcting even trial-and-error approaches. Of great importance, they could lead to relatively early determination of whether there are adjustments to be made outside of schools, things to be done to them, or corrections to be effected from within.[13]

Usually, reformers simply assume that things are to be done to the school. Schools and the people in them become objects of and for reform and often are referred to as "targets." Not surprisingly, change models and strategies are derived primarily from the military. Our system of producing missiles provides an example. Rough estimates and predictions are made, requiring detailed knowledge of our assumed adversaries. Is it better to gamble that hostilities can be held off for a decade or more, perhaps by a show of prepared belligerency, in order to have exceedingly advanced weaponry by that time? Or is it better to have on hand a smaller but continuously updated arsenal? With the necessary inquiries (including "intelligence" operations) completed and the basic policy decision made, specifications are prepared for the research and development required for the actual production of missiles. Completed missiles must then be delivered to and mounted on the launching pads.

It is an exceedingly rational and seemingly efficient process. Little wonder that it is seen by some as having great relevance for tidying up the messy processes of schooling. Indeed, why not plan and develop a new generation of schools designed for conditions two or three decades from now, just as one plans successive generations of missiles? Interestingly, even with something as apparently straightforward as moving those missiles from conception to delivery, there are human problems all along the way. At the outset, the military wants both immediate preparedness and long-term superiority and so it favors both alternatives rather than making a deliberate choice. The battle of the budget proceeds at the highest levels of government, using rhetoric that is difficult to ignore.

At another level, there are disagreements among researchers, designers and developers over specifications. And there is rumbling from the receivers who, in turn, disagree over whether the changes from the previous generation of missiles are too great or too little, with human resistance to change being a factor in satisfaction and dissatisfaction. Behavioral scientists work hard at trying to smooth "the people part" of the process.

Business and industry have borrowed and adapted a good deal from these methods. Products coming off the production line are akin to the missiles. But these products are not simply to be shot at a target. There are clients to be persuaded, and so a work force must be trained in the techniques of persuasion. Increasingly, advertising is becoming the main technique, forcing out small competitors, increasing the costs of competition among those remaining, and enlarging what is at stake. There is considerable disagreement over whether the public is well served, necessitating a government role in assuring a modicum of diversity.

During the late 1950s and 1960s, the impact of all this on school reform, especially of the curriculum, was substantial (see Chapter 2). Under the heading "The Failure of Federal R&D Policy," House provides an intriguing description and analysis of the penetration of the "research, development, diffusion" (R,D&D) model of change into Federal educational policy and practice.[14] Those employing the system, being outside of the schools and oriented elsewhere, have control over the R&D segments and declining power and understanding as they move outward to diffusion. House notes that the practitioner operates in a context essentially foreign to the developer.

Reading the literature advocating the R,D&D strategy, I was struck by the declining concern for difficulty or complexity regarding the consumer or target end. National priorities were set, and specific goals were distributed among mission-oriented projects (funded first by the National Science Foundation and later by the United States Office of Education as well). R&D needs were intuited; products were to be developed. Then, went the rhetoric, they were to be put into the system (the school district, school, or classroom). The slighting of this last step suggests both a lack of understanding of its true complexity and, perhaps a dangerously naïve assumption, put well by House:

Use of the paradigm is justified on the basis of the belief that the practitioner is passive and will not initiate innovation on his own. The teacher is seen as slightly resistant, though someone who can be induced through persuasion to accept the new innovation. ... Such a depiction justifies acting upon these people.[15]

The educational reform movement of the 1960s was heavily dominated by this model of change and innovation. From the perspective of those at the planning level, it was eminently rational. There were national priorities (goals) to be achieved. The infusion of large sums controlled by the NSF and the USOE and distributed through curriculum project centers, regional laboratories, and R&D centers in universities would assure the creation of attractive answers to perceived needs. Unfortunately, much of what was developed and diffused turned out to be answers in search of problems. Practitioners perceived their problems differently and, frequently, did not see these answers, however elegantly packaged, as relevant.

The R,D&D model appears not to be, in its functioning, a strategy for change. It is simply what the letters stand for: research, development, and diffusion, with what comes out to be diffused being more or less adrift, requiring some other force to pull it into close juxtaposition with persons who might have some use for it. A productive change strategy requires the inclusion of this latter element.

The fact that the model is not an adequately comprehensive change strategy does not rule out completely its potential usefulness for educational improvement. Obviously, it can and does produce good products from the perspective of many criteria pertaining to quality control. In the curriculum field, for example, much more care went into research and development than can be afforded, apparently, by commercial publishers. However, perhaps it is a more appropriate role for the federal government to conduct the necessary research into needs at many levels of the educational enterprise, drawing upon the perceptions of practitioners as well as other groups, leaving the ultimate production of resources to the private sector.

The idea of planning and conducting efforts to improve the schools from the outside certainly did not originate with the events and procedures just described. However, the massive nature of this effort and the amount of money made available, in relative terms at least, tended to obscure other rationales and activities. Also, the fact and nature of federal intervention were unique—and, indeed, controversial. The reader uninformed on these matters might want to consult some of the general references included in the bibliography with which this volume concludes.

Concentration on the R,D&D model during the 1960s and early 1970s tended to obscure and diminish long-standing, more inner-oriented approaches to educational improvement. Most of these involve some kind of partnership or change agent–client relationship but concentrate on the interests of persons inside the institution. The approach is as old as the concept of teaching.

In modern times, the use of "expert" consultants has been and continues to be popular and constitutes a major use of money for in-service education. Since World War II, there has been accelerating interest in approaches designed to relate to school personnel less as targets or clients and more as temporary partners, with the role of the outside agent diminishing over time. The group dynamics movement, although fluctuating in popularity, appears and reappears in various forms and has a solid following.[16] A wide array of aproaches focuses on helping teachers acquire new insights, knowledge, and skills. Most of the curriculum reform projects of the 1960s counted heavily on training teachers in the new content and pedagogy. Recent approaches seek to help teachers formulate and teach to precise behavioral objectives or according to a learning theory involving conscious utilization of reinforcement mechanisms with children.

It is fair to say that the dominant assumption in the improvement of schooling has been that the most direct route is to change the behavior of the teacher. The most common index of success is pupil achievement. Some approaches have simply assumed this relationship; others have sought to test it. The results are discouragingly inconclusive. I shall have a good deal to say about the general model later.

The literature of planned change suggests two formidable sets of obstacles frustrating the whole array of change strategies from those seeking to mount and diffuse large-scale innovations to those with modest goals focused on small groups of teachers.[17] An obvious one has to do with the drives, needs, and personalities of individuals. Teachers' needs for survival and, indeed, satisfaction do not necessarily match up with the rational goals of change agents. Rationality is a matter of perception. Teachers presumably see what they do as rational and, if not, at least as required of them. The goals from outside are seen as puerile and in conflict with the functions perceived as necessary. Or, they are seen as threatening existing regularities. Often, a staff which probably would be unable to agree on goals effectively closes ranks to block out or sabotage the intrusion.

Entering more recently into the educational literature is a body of research and analyzed experience on organizations, including school systems, schools, and classrooms. It reveals, among other things, that much of what individuals do in organizations is governed by what has evolved in the institution to give it a character, a way of surviving and behaving—in Sarason's words, a culture.[18] This culture is not immune to change. Indeed, schools have evolved considerably in appearance, functions, and regularities and have responded to new goals communicated to them by the surrounding society. But they also are survival-oriented, more than change-oriented or goal-oriented, unless we call survival and the maintenance of stability a goal.

The culture of the school sets certain limits on teacher behavior. Teachers possess or potentially enjoy a great deal of freedom behind the doors of their own classrooms, until what they do interferes with other teachers and the established ways of the school. Innovations calling for collaboration, such as nongrading and team teaching, strain the system and so appear to be more difficult to establish than pedagogical innovations. But to bring about instructional changes may be far more difficult to achieve than many reformers assume. Implicitly, most schools support controlled, quiet, total group practices (frontal teaching), for example, and do not reinforce noisy small-group learning. It takes a relatively autonomous teacher to buck the system and gain satisfaction from inner rewards.

Griffiths questions the ability of organizations to effect significant change on their own:

> Since the tendency of organizations is to maintain a steady state, the major impetus for change comes from outside rather than inside an organization. Since organizations are open systems, they have a self-regulating characteristic which causes them to revert to the original state following a minor change made to meet demands of the supra-system.[19]

Wide-scale acceptance of this proposition has supported repeated prodding of the schools to become more responsive to what is expected of them. But what is expected of them is not at all clear. Are they to become truly educational institutions adhering closely to those stable aims of education? That would be innovative, indeed! Which among all the contemporary goals proposed for them should they espouse? Whatever the choice, dissatisfaction will be little diminished. Should they weed out the noneducational functions and regularities now characterizing their daily conduct? Even to recognize these for what they are will be difficult because they conform so much with what many inside the schools perceive as rational.

We seem to be caught in an irreconcilable dilemma. Change arising from without usually is foreign to the system for which it is intended and is rejected like an unsuitable transplanted kidney. But a system afflicted with diseased kidneys cannot help itself. There must be some way for outside resources and inside needs to come together productively and, ultimately, harmoniously. The thesis explored in this volume is that *an effective change strategy is one through which the alternative best suited to the needs of a given institution come to the attention of those in it and are used in a continuous process of improvement.* Or, stated differently, an effective change strategy is one through which those within a given institution become responsive to what is required to assure institutional renewal and to outside resources most likely to expedite that renewal.

Such a proposition recognizes the necessity of inner and outer processes proceeding simultaneously. It will not appeal to those who know what others need and already have the solutions; to those who have given up on any capacity for self-renewal organizations; or to those who see change arising only from within. As Ekstein points out:

> Ideas about change have always seemed to divide men into two polarizing groups. Some believe that in order to change man must change his outer reality—society. Others say that regardless of how much one changes the culture, the external world of men, unless one can make that change reach the inner man, one will not succeed.[20]

But there is a growing realization that the proposition stated above makes sense and must be put to work, especially in such a way that various efforts designed to implement it are documented so that we profit from their failures and successes. The short history of planned change in schooling suggests that we tend to reject alternative concepts when strategies developed from them supposedly fail, without checking the adequacy of either the interpretation or the implementation. The literature and practice of schooling are replete with this error. There is danger now that various combinations of inner- and outer-directed approaches to change will be combined into change strategies which are inadequately conceived and executed. The concepts are likely to be discredited along with or perhaps even beyond the instance of defective use.

There is evidence of growing interest in placing greater stress on what has before been the target for or intended recipient of changes and innovations. There has now been time to gain some introspective wisdom from the emphases of the 1960s. Summaries of research and evaluation conclude that individual and institutional factors were neglected. The National Institute of Education has commissioned position papers which draw the same conclusion and has funded several projects designed to test new models and gather data about promising projects. Perhaps there are grounds for hope that some solid reconstruction of schools will take place.

But, for this to occur, there must be a good deal more faith in the desire and ability of those working in schools to participate productively in designing their own workplaces. That faith will be tested when it is accompanied by the allocation of authority and resources designed to facilitate the self-renewing part of the change process in the way previous allocations have supported forces from without. For this to occur, unaccompanied by the usual restraints of "those who know what is best," will be in the nature of a miracle. In effect, it would mean legitimatizing the right to fail as well as to succeed and, indeed, even providing money for the former. But a staggering amount of money already has been spent on failures by "those who knew what was best" in the military and business worlds, in particular, and, recently, in education. Perhaps at least a small fraction of this amount spent in the name of faith in people and the support systems they need to help themselves would be a good investment.

ORGANIZATION AND ASSUMPTIONS

As stated earlier, this book is organized around the premise that schools, *under certain conditions,* can become more vital than they currently are and that most of the reconstruction must be effected by those who work and live in them each day. The reconstruction must occur school by school. This means that it will move forward on a broken front and not as part of a national grand strategy. But there must be help and support from outside. There must be created a productive tension between inner- and outer-directed forces.

This volume describes and analyzes a field project which sought to create and foster such a relationship. The inner process, supported and encouraged from outside, took place in individual schools. But this is a rather lonely odyssey for which one needs the corrective influence of peers. Otherwise, one begins not to trust the validity of one's judgments. And so, from the beginning, each school had seventeen peer or sister schools available for interaction when wanted. They could be ignored, but they were there.

Until one is ready to enjoy peers, in the way individuals enjoy one another after they transcend narcissism, there is need for feedback—indeed, acceptance and encouragement—from some trustworthy source, some source whose praise is valued. And so there was, from the beginning, a center to which schools could relate on a one-to-one basis before and while peer-school bonds strengthened and matured. This center not only provided support but also observed and studied what was going on, feeding back information to be used in the process of self-examination and change.

The whole was called the League of Cooperating Schools and comprised each of the eighteen schools and a linkage system—center-to-school, school-to-school, and center to the entire network of schools. It promoted no particular innovations. It was itself an innovation, suddenly existing in embryonic form and then taking on shape in response to its own experiences and interpretation of those experiences. Descriptions and analyses of the League as a strategy for school change take up several chapters in this volume.

Chapter 2 describes elements of recent educational reform in the United States, with special attention to the form and substance of some of the change processes briefly described on preceding pages. Chapter 3 is an account of personal experience with much of what is described in Chapter 2 and of the hypothesis regarding change which arose out of this experience and which became virtually a guiding principle. Chapters 4 and 5 describe the testing of this hypothesis through the creation and study of the League of Cooperating Schools. Chapter 6 reflects on the effectiveness of the hypothesis at work, problems encountered in its utilization, the people in the process, and some of the things about change that were learned. Chapter 7 attempts to relate this entire experience to some of the existing realities of the schooling enterprise in seeking to come up with a more comprehensive strategy for change than the one embedded and tested in the League or, for that matter, elsewhere. The volume concludes with some comments on the development and maintenance of effective school ecosystems.

Many assumptions are built into what follows. As far as possible, I endeavor to make them explicit, but my most fundamental beliefs probably will remain implicit and unexamined. Two assumptions pertaining to the earlier discussion of aims, goals, functions, and regularities and, in turn, to change call for brief exposition here.

First, every possible effort should be made to maximize the educational and minimize the sociopolitical functions of schools. To do this, schools must rise above the parochial concerns of their immediate communities in seeking to serve a much larger constituency—a democratic society, if you will. This assumption flies in the face of much current rhetoric regarding citizen involvement but in no way denies the right of the people to determine what their schools are for. Likewise, it flies in the face of current efforts by many educators, especially union and association leaders, to politicize the process even more. The issues of who should make what educational decisions and how are extraordinarily complex. They may be settled by power groups fighting power groups in ways ultimately destructive of the schools before the processes of reconstruction described and proposed here even begin to function on any large scale. No process of change is immune from the sociopolitical process of schooling.

Schools must take their direction from the *educational* goals articulated for them by the state and nation and, with their communities, interpret their meaning and implications. In spite of change, there is rather broad agreement on educational goals. And, in spite of their broad generality, they are meaningful. These are the appropriate goals to be used by schools to explain their public responsibility and to be used as guiding criteria in seeking to examine their functions and regularities. In effect, such goals, with a few concessions to individual welfare, articulate the responsibility of schools to the societal side of the classic duality in educational aims. Those pertaining .more to the welfare of the individual and humankind are carried into the school by pupils and teachers.

Second, the extent to which the schools actually serve the goals set for them and the welfare of both individuals and humankind is determined by their regularities. The values actually subscribed to are embedded in the forms and activities by which the schools conduct their business. These regularities determine what functions actually are fulfilled and, in large measure, what children are taught in schools. To examine the regularities of schools carefully is to encounter their goals and functions.

The one place, then—the only place—where aims, goals, functions, and regularities become one is the individual school. Consequently, the place to begin reform in all of these is the individual school. All four of these elements, in turn, become one in the regularities of the school. When one looks closely at the regularities, one finds the school's real functions, and from these one deduces its real goals, regardless of what may be posted on the principal's door. And when one knows these, one knows something about the extent to which it is an educational institution rather than, for example, merely a custodial one. Consequently, when the school changes significant regularities to some considerable degree, it changes both its functions and the ends it serves. The people in schools, by changing these regularities, can change the fundamental elements of schooling. This can be done when there is a productive tension with significant external forces.

These assumptions and their far-reaching implications for reconstructing the schools are the subject matter of this book. Whether or not they can be put to work productively has much to do with the quote from Eiseley with which the book begins and with the future of schooling.

NOTES

1 For elaboration of this point, see John I. Goodlad, "An Emphasis on Change," *American Education*, vol. 11, no. 1, pp. 16–21, 24–25, 28, January–February 1975.

2 Robert M. Hutchins, "The Great Anti-School Campaign," *The Great Ideas Today*, Encyclopaedia Britannica, Inc., Chicago, 1972, p. 174.

3 See John I. Goodlad, M. Frances Klein, Jerrold M. Novotney, Kenneth A. Tye, and Associates, *Toward a Mankind School: An Adventure in Humanistic Education*, McGraw-Hill, New York, 1974.

4 Robert M. Hutchins, "Two Fateful Decisions," *The Center Magazine*, vol. 8, no. 1, pp. 7–13, January/February 1975.

5 The National Commission on the Reform of Secondary Education, *The Reform of Secondary Education: A Report to the Public and the Profession*, McGraw-Hill, New York, 1973.

6 Harold R. W. Benjamin [J. Abner Peddiwell], *The Saber Tooth Curriculum*, memorial ed., McGraw-Hill, New York, 1972.

7 See John I. Goodlad, M. Frances Klein, Jerrold M. Novotney, and Associates, *Early Schooling in the United States*, McGraw-Hill, New York, 1973.

8 See Ivan Illich, *Deschooling Society*, Harper & Row, New York, 1970. For a discussion of the *pros* and *cons* of deschooling society, see Daniel U. Levine and Robert J. Havighurst (eds.), *Farewell to Schools???*, Charles A. Jones, Worthington, Ohio, 1971.

9 Bel Kaufman, *Up The Down Staircase*, Prentice-Hall, Englewood Cliffs, N.J., 1964.

10 Hill's study of one state legislature revealed that the vast majority of teachers is blissfully unaware of legislative enactments designed to affect their instruction, just as legislators generally are unfamiliar with what has been enacted previously into the education code. See Henry W. Hill, "Curriculum Legislation and Decision-Making for the Instructional Level," unpublished doctoral dissertation, University of California, Los Angeles, 1971.

11 For an insightful portrayal of many such contradictions and hypocrisies, see Carl Weinberg, *Education Is a Shuck*, Morrow, New York, 1975.

12 James B. Conant, *The American High School Today*, McGraw-Hill, New York, 1959.

13 Until relatively recently, these questions and various suggestions and strategies designed to respond to them were relatively unstudied. Now, a substantial body of literature dealing with them is available. To summarize it here would be a diversion. Only the broader issues dealt with in some of this literature are relevant here. Readers interested in pursuing strategies in depth are referred to the annotated bibliography at the end of the volume, which, in turn, opens the door to a much larger body of material. For a brief but useful summary of the various major approaches to educational change, see a companion volume in this series, Kenneth A. Tye and Jerrold M. Novotney, *Schools in Transition: The Practitioner as Change Agent*, McGraw-Hill, New York, 1975.

14 Ernest R. House, *The Politics of Educational Innovation*, McCutchan Publishing Corporation, Berkeley, Calif., 1974, pp. 214–226.

15 Ibid. p. 223.

16 Dorwin Cartwright and Alvin Zander (eds.), *Group Dynamics: Research and Theory*, 3d ed., Harper & Row, New York, 1968.

17 See particularly Warren G. Bennis, Kenneth D. Benne, and Robert Chine, *The Planning of Change*, 2d ed., Holt, New York, 1969; Ronald G. Havelock, *Planning for Innovation*, University of Michigan, Ann Arbor, 1971; and Richard A. Schmuck and Matthew B. Miles, *Organization Development in Schools*, National Press Books, Palo Alto, Calif., 1971.

18 Seymour B. Sarason, *The Culture of the School and the Problem of Change*, Allyn and Bacon, Boston, 1971.

19 Daniel E. Griffiths, "Administrative Theory and Change in Organizations," in Matthew B. Miles (ed.), *Innovation in Education*, Teachers College, New York, 1964, p. 431.

20 Rudolf Ekstein, "Towards Walden III," *Reiss-Davis Clinic Bulletin*, vol. 11, no. 1, p. 13, Spring 1974.

CHAPTER 2

THE SCHOOLING DECADE AND ITS AFTERMATH

Nobody has a kind word for the institution that was only the other day the foundation of our freedom, the guarantee of our future, the cause of our prosperity and power, the bastion of our security, the bright and shining beacon that was the source of enlightenment, the public school.

—Robert M. Hutchins ("The Great Anti-School Campaign," *The Great Ideas Today 1972*, Encyclopaedia Britannica, Inc., Chicago, 1972, p. 155)

It would be a mistake to assume that dissatisfaction with our schools is a new phenomenon. Recently, however, dissatisfaction has been so widespread and run so deep as to connote disaffection with schooling itself, even to the point of giving serious attention to the idea of deschooling society. That's about as far as disaffection can go.

In the years following World War II, there was some dissatisfaction but little disaffection with schools. Returning veterans wanted a better life for their children and for themselves—for the whole world, in fact. Education was seen as important to the attainment of that life and all levels of schooling were viewed as central to the educational process. Under the provisions of the GI bill, tens of thousands of veterans went back to school, living with their English, French, Dutch, and American wives and their children in hastily assembled barracks on college and university campuses. It was a relatively simple, solid, satisfying life in many ways, filled with gratitude over being alive and with hope in what lay ahead. Then on to jobs, paychecks of a size never before considered possible, and a house in the suburbs where new cottage-type schools were springing up all over.

There were problems with the schools, of course. Construction could not keep up with expanding enrollments, and the new schools were on double sessions; good teachers were few and hard to hold; it was difficult to find out what went on in schools and whether they were any good. But, time and money would take care of the problems; the schools would provide the best education any generation ever had. For some people, change and improvement meant mostly more of what they thought schools had once been.

The educational literature of 1953, however, implied that the schools needed a great deal more. Books by Bestor, Hutchins, and Lynd[1] got under the skins of teacher educators, particularly in those teachers colleges that were rapidly becoming general colleges and universities. They hastened the demise of the Progressive Education Society, seen as the villain in "soft" life-adjustment education of preceding decades. This was an intense round in the feud between the "tender" and the "tough" in American education.[2] The excess had been tenderness; the need now, critics argued, was toughness, particularly in the high schools. Although a good deal of the rhetoric spilled over into the larger community, this was an internecine battle in the long war between academic adversaries, who knew each other and each other's arguments rather well. The schools were pawns, but their existence was not at stake.

Flesch's hastily put together polemic (the author derisively reported that he had been able to review all the research on the subject in a few hours in the library at Teachers College, Columbia University) was of a different order, as its title, *Why Johnny Can't Read*, suggests.[3] It hit directly at the growing frustrations of those ambitious parents whose children were entering the first grade by the hundreds of thousands. Newspapers across the country published large segments in syndicated versions; few published rebuttals. Neighborhood coffee klatches provided ready-made forums.

Flesch was an expert on readability analysis, a technique pioneered and developed primarily by Edgar Dale and Jeanne Chall for determining the reading difficulty of subject matter. Flesch used the technique to keep his book at the reading level of most citizens. He espoused no new philosophies of education and no complex schemes for renovating the schools. He supported his argument that Johnny couldn't read with enough documentation to be impressive to the layman and offered an explanatory hypothesis and a simple, direct, "common sense" remedy which touched the experience and accompanying nostalgia of millions of adults. His was a strong cry for return to the fundamentals. Certainly, his book did much to arouse suspicion regarding "modern" schools with their supposed new ways and to make innovation suspect. Also, it reinforced the notion that a method of teaching, such as almost exclusive attention to phonics in reading, is sufficient to assure whatever learning in children is desired by those supporting the schools.

But Bestor, Hutchins, Lynd, Flesch, and other critics to follow did not shake our basic faith in schooling—only in some schools, some principals, some teachers, and, especially, teacher educators. Further, there were other things to do and think about: getting a promotion, moving to another job and suburb, and whether or not to trade in the two-year-old Chevrolet (another steel strike threatened). Also, in the South particularly, the implications of a 1954 Supreme Court decision were becoming increasingly clear. Life was changing very rapidly. It soon would be hard to argue convincingly that schools should return to the imagined good old days.

SPUTNIK AND THE EDUCATIONAL REFORM MOVEMENT

Years later, it is difficult to comprehend the impact of a small capsule circling the earth at a distance as close as the distance between Los Angeles and San Diego. The date was October 1957. The school year was settling in. During the preceding decade, Americans had been enjoying the sudden emergence of their nation as an undisputed world power—probably *the* world power—basking in the misconception that they were loved almost universally for their role in World War II and taking pride in becoming philanthropist to the world.

Suddenly, there it was—Sputnik! Sputnik—unheralded, unannounced, unwanted, and yet as compelling as a good horror movie. Look up there and you can see it—almost.

For reasons that are difficult to sort out, a good deal of the resulting sadomasochistic behavior on the part of Americans focused on the schools, particularly the secondary schools. The faith that we had had in our schools began to crack a bit, as did some of the dreams about that personal and family future envisioned in the affluent fifties. We were now growing accustomed to having the world in our living rooms by way of television, and cameramen readily unveiled that "foundation of our freedom, guarantee of our future, cause of our prosperity and power, the bastion of our security . . . the public school." The whole country saw able-bodied young men in home economics classes, hardly a reassuring scene for a nation with rather clear alternative perceptions of the "tough" education thought to be required.

It was still a time for heroes. The hero of the hour became James B. Conant, distinguished former president of Harvard University, postwar High Commissioner for West Germany, and, in many ways, champion of the public schools. In his widely read report, *The American High School Today*,[4] addressed primarily to school boards, he endeavored to put together the major strengths of what he had observed across the country in several dozen "exemplar" secondary schools. Diverse segments of the schooling enterprise were ready for what he had to say.

Conant came out unequivocally for the comprehensive high school, that unique and at times controversial American invention designed to provide education for all members of the age group. Then, he spelled out a tough program of mathematics, science, foreign languages, English, and history with differentiation for the more and less able students. In a sense, there was to be an intellectual elitist track within a heterogeneously populated school. Conant summarized his recommendations before large audiences of professional educators, administrators, teachers, and laymen; his specifics became a check list for judging a good school.

It is important here to note a significant milestone in an accelerating shift of emphasis in the United States on the role schooling plays in the development of the individual. Intelligence tests had served to slow this shift somewhat because they were based on the assumption of the unchanging character of the IQ and, therefore, of sharp limits on the potential for school attainment. But now these companion assumptions were breaking down. Johnny's failure to read was not low intelligence but the failure of the school to use the proper method. The onus of failure, to some considerable degree, shifted from the child to the school. Almost everyone is an able student. All we need are better motivators, better school structures, better programs, better instruction. The locus for change, it would appear, became the school, although "try, try, and try again" was not completely discarded as a desirable disposition for the learner.

If we take Sputnik in 1957 as the beginning marker and 1967—when the high expectations of the Elementary and Secondary Education Act of 1965 were rapidly fading—as the concluding one, we have ten years of trying to do almost everything to and through the schools. It was the "Schooling Decade."[5] One of its characteristics was failure to differentiate appropriate and inappropriate expectations for schools. At the outset and for several years subsequently, the focus was on substance and process in the conduct of schooling: those regularities of curriculum, organization, and instruction (tied more and more closely to growing insights into the nature of learning) which characterize schools as educational institutions. Toward the end of the decade, however, concern shifted more and more to the functions being performed by schools, with particular attention to human rights, equity, and socioeconomic reform.

REFORM IN THE REGULARITIES OF SCHOOLING: CURRICULUM

Jerome Bruner's much-quoted thesis about children's learning capabilities was as seminal as Conant's recommendations for secondary schools and made the latter seem even more plausible and attainable. His statement that ". . . any subject can be taught in some intellectually honest form to any child at any stage of development" became justification for solid fare in the curriculum, extended downward to the early years.[6] In some ways, Bruner's little book was for academics what Conant's was for the interested layman. Conant whetted the public appetite and gave it voice; Bruner stimulated a new crop of chefs. There were menus here for professional educators as well as scholars in the disciplines. His "spiral curriculum" is reminiscent of Whitehead; his concern with humanizing knowledge for popularization links up with Dewey. Concepts such as intuition (not previously popular with psychologists), discovery or inductive learning, and structure of the disciplines have a certain abstract, esoteric quality appealing particularly to those academicians who are suspicious about orderly learning principles and particularly pedagogical precepts presumably derived from them. Such terms became as central to the jargon of the new era as "the whole child" and "life adjustment" had been to the progressive era.

Bruner's concepts fit nicely into an approach to curricular reform already taking shape under the leadership of an M.I.T. physicist, Jerrold Zacharias. He challenged academicians, especially in mathematics and the natural sciences, to exercise their responsibilities in a concerted effort to improve secondary-school curricula, meanwhile effectively exhorting the newly formed National Science Foundation to provide extensive funding. Bruner's involvement assured legitimacy on the "process" side. Although professors of education and schools of education were ruled out of the partnership, Zacharias was astute enough to recognize the importance of some accumulated wisdom regarding schooling, and so a few prominent professional educators were on the "resource" list. Jerrold Zacharias, a man of considerable wisdom, commitment, and charisma, wanted the best for America's young people that money and talent could provide. And he wanted it quickly.

The substantive threads of this discipline-centered curriculum reform movement go back farther, however. One is able to pick up some of the elements in a small group of mathematics professors working in the mid-forties with Ralph Tyler, then director of the board of examiners at the University of Chicago, who sought through evaluation to identify something more fundamental in learning than mere arithmetic manipulations. This thread appeared later in the work of Max Beberman at the University of Illinois where the Committee on School Mathematics was formed in 1951. Emphasis on discovery learning and on certain structural ties between language and mathematics concepts became central to this and other ensuing projects. Soon, a half-dozen major mathematics projects were blossoming around the country. Reform quickly spread to physics, biology, chemistry, and elementary-school science and, somewhat abortively, to modern languages. The social sciences, humanities, and arts were poor, starving second-cousins. Reform ultimately hit them, too, but much later and to a lesser degree.

The assumptions and methods of curriculum development in perhaps a dozen and a half major projects were essentially alike. The ends and means of schooling are *educational* in character and are drawn from man's accumulated experience as expressed in the organized disciplines of knowledge—not general science or social studies but physics, biology, and chemistry, or history, geography, and civics. Scholars in these fields, aided by classroom teachers to assure appropriateness for students, plan the curricula; students are to learn to think like these scholars—at any age, in accordance with the Bruner thesis.

Curriculum builders sought to organize curricula in spiral fashion around the concepts, key ideas, principles, and modes of inquiry constituting the structural elements of the disciplines. Understanding these elements, rather than merely possessing facts, would give the student the intellectual power to tackle unfamiliar problems and intuit relationships. Teachers were inducted into this approach and the means to its implementation through a "hands-on" process of actually developing instructional units during summer workshops and, occasionally, all-year institutes. The amount of such involvement declined as the movement matured. There seemed to be the implicit assumption that, as curricular materials improved in quality, they would more and more do the necessary job, without recourse to much teacher education.

From the beginning, the movement was directed at students in the classroom. It did not seek to change the traditional function or the basic structure of American schools. Nor was it directed at administrators. In fact, during my visits to project headquarters, directors sometimes spoke complainingly and even peevishly of mutton-headed administrators who were not really interested in education and who frequently got in the way. "How does one do end-runs around them?" paraphrases the query heard more than once.[7]

With the exception of the Biological Sciences Curriculum Study in its green, yellow, and blue versions, there was virtually no evaluation other than some trial-and-error reworking of materials on the basis of limited, formative use. As stated earlier, goals were rather sharply focused on learning subject matter; there was little rhetoric pertaining to the traditional dual aims of education. These, presumably, were assumed, as was the near-certainty that the new curricula would be better for education, the schools, students, and the country than anything served up before.

At the outset, what was proposed smacked very much of a return to the fundamentals—if one did not listen too carefully. It took a few years for parents to begin to suspect that what they had taken for the tried-and-true in new dress was anything but. When they ultimately did find out, they had some allies in those teachers without benefit of the year-long institutes and summer workshops who were now being held responsible for improvement in those skills of figuring, reading, and writing that had been either assumed or were somewhat peripheral to the "structure of the disciplines" during preceding years of reform.

The scholars most centrally involved were prototypes of these who earlier were saying, "The schools are too important to be left to the educators." But now it might well have been said that the schools are too important to be left to the academicians. With the exception of a very few who stayed on to become students of the educative process—physicists-become-educators, for example—the academicians went back to their more familiar kitchens in the university, where the rewards lie.

REFORM IN THE REGULARITIES OF SCHOOLING: SCHOOL AND CLASSROOM ORGANIZATION

Curriculum reform came almost exclusively from outside of what has sometimes been described as the interlocking education establishment, from persons more traditionally concerned with academic standards and the quality of preparation received by young men and women entering college than with direct involvement with schools. Attack on the locked-in structures of schooling and on the regularities of how pupils are classified and advanced through the grades and how teaching resources are distributed came more from within and especially from teachers of teachers. The data sources and the data extracted from them to rationalize the proposed reforms are those most commonly taught in educational psychology classes. These are data on individual differences, grading and various promotion practices, the effects of ability and achievement grouping, and so on.

Educationists were not left out of the post-Sputnik reform period. They simply had a different part of the action. This helps to explain why curriculum reform and organizational or structural reform, which should have had much to derive from and give to each other, simply failed to join. Even the reformers in learning and instruction—who more and more came to dominate curriculum reform as the discipline-oriented scholars drifted back to their basic work—and the structural reformers barely reported to, let alone communicated with, each other. For the most part, they published in different journals and went to different meetings. Reform, then, was piecemeal. Teachers and administrators were subjected to several unorchestrated players, none of whom heard or understood the others' rhythms and lyrics. The schools suffered but were not the only losers. The players lost, too.

Reform in the organization of schools sought to open them up conceptually, programmatically, and physically. There were two dominant unshackling sets of ideas. One had to do with raising the ceilings and lowering the floors of pupil expectancy in any given class to conform more accurately with the realities of variability increasingly becoming apparent. This set led to proposals for multigraded, multiaged, and nongraded classrooms. The other had to do with breaking out of the self-contained classroom so as to create more varied patterns of grouping pupils and using adult resources. This set led to a variety of cooperative or team-teaching plans and to more extensive use of aides and other helpers in the expanded classroom. Both took a good deal of their credibility from data on inter- and intra-individual variability. Both sets of ideas enjoy a relatively long family tree in educational thought, and both contributed significantly to the emergence of open schools and classrooms and family grouping plans in the seventies. They seriously threatened those previously unchanging elements referred to in Chapter 1 which give considerable credence to the charge that nothing about schools changes but the appearance of change.

These were "in-house" ideas; that is, they came from educators for educators. Consequently, at least at the beginning, they enjoyed no community pressure groups, no public endorsement as answers to Johnny's reading problem. However, they threatened some of the sacred cows of school keeping and called for teachers to both think and behave differently: no more grades (and most advocates recommended accompanying elimination of conventional marking systems) and no more promotion/nonpromotion. What was not fully realized at the time was that such changes took away some of the familiar crutches and, indeed, negotiating strength of teachers with their pupils. Much of what goes on in classrooms is, indeed, very basic human negotiation.[8] There are tacit agreements which are made early in the pupil-teacher relationship and, in general, maintained. The tyrant-teacher carries tyranny only so far; troublesome pupils engage in only so much disorderly behavior. The teacher who is unable to set and maintain a consistent orientation to tasks or a consistently warm, friendly relationship and who vacillates in expectations is soon in serious trouble. Recourse to the marking or passing system becomes an important equalizer in the form of an ever-present club.

Reorganization of adult resources was also threatening to long-standing regularities which had been reinforced by the Child Study Movement. Emerging immediately after World War II and flourishing well into the fifties, it stressed unity in the learning process and hitched to this the long-standing concept of a single elementary school teacher working almost exclusively with a class of children. Consequently, the Bay City, Michigan, experiment involving aides and the Harvard team-teaching projects with Lexington and Newton, Massachusetts, were seen as very threatening to the traditional, well-established self-contained classroom. These and other similar projects, many of them supported by the Ford Foundation, smacked also of being subterfuges for merit salary schemes, thus threatening the profession of teaching as defined by organized national associations.

Although the advocates of such troublesome innovations were

invited to the speakers' platforms of various national education associations, their presentations seldom went without intense criticism by frequently hostile reaction panels. Clearly, less than subtle efforts were made to filter and blunt the ideas to which principals and teachers were being exposed. But such attempts were of little avail. Later use of the age-old technique of co-opting undoubtedly was far more effective in reducing the impact of troublesome ideas.

Given the fact that ready-made, community coffee klatch forums of the kind enjoyed by Flesch were not early adopters of these ideas, that they threatened many sacred cows and required new ways on the part of teachers, and that there was open opposition from powerful segments of the teaching profession, why and how did these ideas come to gain considerable currency? Several alternative hypotheses come to mind. The first—and the one an educational reformer would most like to believe—is that many teachers were ready for these ideas, just as many laymen were ready for a curriculum reform movement appearing to offer promise of toughening the American fiber. Basically, teachers are interested in what bears directly on their daily practices— witness the tens of thousands annually attending conferences on the teaching of reading. They are only too acutely aware of individual learning problems, an awareness which plagues them and which frequently causes them to feel guilty about personal inadequacies in coping. Therefore, many teachers were ready to listen: it was some of their professional leaders and some professors of education who saw deeper threats to the teaching profession.

Next, some of the major proponents were seen by teachers as friends—coworkers in schools of education—who appeared sincere in their belief that there were data to support the concepts and that proposed reforms would be beneficial for schools, teachers, and children alike. As with curriculum reform, identification of several of these reformers with prestigious universities such as Harvard and Chicago helped to legitimize their ideas. Also, as in curriculum development, money was available, particularly from the Fund for the Advancement of Education of the Ford Foundation, for innovations designed to shake up old structures and concepts. And more than one Ford Foundation official was astute enough to recognize leverage for change in situations where school districts and personnel had their backs to the wall.

Many school superintendents were in precisely that predicament. Demand for reform was growing. At the same time, school expenditures were perceived to be outstripping the growth of the Gross National Product; meanwhile, rapid increases in enrollments and the need for facilities were making it exceedingly difficult for administrators to demonstrate acceptable educational value for dollars spent. The theme of the National Commission on Teacher Education and Professional Standards, "a fully certified teacher in every classroom," accompanied by a strong drive for significantly higher salaries, intensified the cost-of-schooling issue in the public eye. And it was hard for many to believe that those new "carpeted palaces" still called schools were anything other than an extravagance. So-called differentiated staffing, with differentiated salary scales for persons doing differing work, was promoted, in part, as an economy measure and, therefore, was seen by some beleaguered superintendents as at least worth considering. Some other organizational innovations appeared to offer either economic advantages or improved learning (tailor-made instruction to meet individual differences in a nongraded plan) or both.

Unfortunately, the implementation of proposed organizational change was more apparent than real. It was easy to apply the labels of the new practices and everyone employed the rhetoric of change. One could talk in such a way as to convey being avant garde, implying without actually stating that the practices associated with the terms already were under way in one's school or district. It is not surprising, therefore, that the impression of change far surpassed the reality of change.[9] By the mid-1960s, there probably were only a few dozen thoroughly non-graded or team-taught elementary schools in the United States, and such innovations scarcely touched the high schools in spite of popular books on these subjects.[10] But most educators knew about them and many, many school districts reported consideration of them. Acceptance of these ideas frequently became confused with implementation of plans. A common occurrence was adoption without implementation or adaptation within existing structures—that is, a bending of the new to the old. For example, the old practice of interclass achievement grouping often was described as nongrading, which it is not. In essence, this was an effort to innovate without really changing anything.

These nonevents and retitled old events of the 1960s notwithstanding, there is evidence that the central ideas of organizational and structural reform are still gnawing away at the innards of schooling in the United States. They are compatible with certain elements in the neo-humanism flourishing in the late sixties and early seventies. Thousands of educator visitors to England have seen in some British Infant Schools at least parts of the models seemingly desired and in short supply in this country. Certain of the concepts fit forward-looking work in the realm of instruction begun in some federally supported R&D centers, as we shall see below. And, although modified buildings are exceedingly helpful, large sums of money for development are not required so that the ideas seemed to retain considerable currency even after the coin of the realm was in short supply. At any rate, much of the ongoing thrust of school reform in the seventies draws substantially from the ideas guiding organizational and instructional reform in the sixties.

REFORM IN THE REGULARITIES OF SCHOOLING: INSTRUCTION

Studies in human variability have provided a rather substantial core of knowledge for educators, knowledge which in general has substantially outrun our ability to make productive use of it. During the Schooling Decade this knowledge spurred the work of such scholars as Patrick Suppes and Robert Glaser, who sought to use and expand it in searching for improved instructional strategies. Coupled with the notion of self-directed learning, it led to the development of teaching machines and computerized instruction. The work of Pressey during the thirties had been seminal and, of course, the popularization of Skinner's work contributed significantly to the idea of orderly, self-reinforcing "programmed" instruction.

The model guiding research and development in instruction put together several elements in the reform movement already discussed, although these were not always recognized as closely related in their curricular and organizational forms. At its heart is the idea of arranging learning "sets"—identifiable and rather discrete segments— in such a way that each builds precisely on the one preceding. If a learner fails to go through a sequence of such sets successfully, the problem lies with the nature or arrangement of the sets, and the set should be broken down into subsets or more intervening sets should be added. Properly developed and arranged, the perfect sequence is one that can be learned by everyone, with time the only variable. Carried to their logical conclusions, the underlying assumptions lead nicely to Bloom's concept of mastery learning—everyone achieving a predetermined performance level deemed to be mastery.[11] These ideas, in turn, fit the Bruner hypothesis and the growing expectation, mentioned earlier, that almost everyone could achieve; for one not to do so was the fault of the school and its program.[12]

The ordering of substance in the instructional process continues to intrigue researchers, particularly psychologists. Not only has it been advanced in its own right, particularly by Gagné, but it has been hooked to some degree with Piaget's stages of learning and, notably by Glaser, with the notion of responsive learning environments, waiting and ready to respond to the learner's quest for knowledge. We come to see the tangible possibility of shifting away from the much criticized but nonetheless hypnotic "telling and questioning" pedagogical paradigm to one in which the student is the active participant and the teacher an interested helping resource. The latter paradigm has attracted generations of reformers but has been implemented rarely, perhaps because the necessary technology has been lacking.[13]

Fundamental work toward new models of instruction during the Schooling Decade, like much other good work on schooling, suffered from unrealistic expectations and inflated press notices. Most children, it was predicted, would have access to a programmed computer terminal by 1970. One starry-eyed commissioner of education went so far as to predict that Individually Prescribed Instruction (the self-pacing instructional program developed by Glaser and his associates at the University of Pittsburgh)[14] would be in every school in the country by 1971 or 1972. Curriculum planners included programmed modules in multimedia learning packages and spoke of "teacher-proof" materials from which pupils would learn without benefit of adult intervention. It is scarcely necessary to observe that these predictions fell somewhat short of realization. More than one fledgling firm went broke trying to peddle teaching machines to homes and schools. The gadgets were briefly intriguing to children, bust most of the subject matter to be propelled through them was pap because expertise in the writing of programs was spread thin.

In retrospect, it appears that certain practical aspects of the solid work then and still underway suffered both from being oversold and from being not practicable within the then-ongoing regularities of schools. The teacher was and, for the most part, still is "front and center" in the classroom. Classroom procedures are geared to class groups, not individuals. For example, I have observed teachers stop more rapid pupils from advancing in programmed workbooks and have these pupils sit idly and unproductively while slower ones caught up.

These were, presumably, teacher-proof materials. In several experimental classrooms, I saw children waiting for the results of computer printouts until the teacher could get around to interpreting them. The innovations in school and classroom organization which were being recommended by quite another group of reformers and which would have helped to accommodate these instructional changes had not yet been implemented.[15] The old regularities of classroom organization effectively nullified instructional reforms, while regularities of classroom instruction cancelled out organizational reforms.

At least two offspring of the instructional reform movement were gaining momentum toward the end of the decade. One is virtually "applied Skinnerian" learning theory for teachers. A precise definition of what the student is to learn or be able to do is held clearly in the mind of the teacher. The teacher then leads the individual or group through the learning tasks, reinforcing correct responses and generally ignoring incorrect ones so that they are not repeated. These are, of course, essentially the same principles as those used in programmed textbooks or machines, but the teacher and, therefore, teacher education are key.

The other, a close cousin, involves breaking down the required learning into "behavioral" objectives, each objective representing a precise, single behavior which, when learned, is elicited in an accompanying reinforcing evaluative process. The acts of conditioning mentioned above are regarded as appropriate for reinforcing the desired learning. Interestingly, this is a shift away from breaking down and sequencing the subject matter toward breaking down the criterion behavior and leaving the teacher to provide the sequence of contingencies necessary to elicit each behavior.

The emphasis in both of these spin-offs is on the teacher and teacher education. Curriculum, evaluation, and, indeed, schooling are virtually equated with the operations involved; there is not much else of importance in schooling from this viewpoint. Teacher education, pre-service and in-service, becomes, virtually exclusively, a process of training teachers to carry out the operations. From performing them in a number of subject matter contexts, they learn to transfer them to parallel situations.

Clearly, there is merit here, and teachers would benefit from acquiring such pedagogical repertoires. There is growing evidence to suggest, however, that this is not enough. Neither the complexity of schools and classrooms nor the pedagogical lives of teachers can be encompassed within such a neat format. Even when teachers learn the necessary operations, the press of their work environment may inhibit exercise of them. And there are, of course, strongly opposing pedagogical models evolving primarily out of humanistic as opposed to behavioristic thought.

Sharp focus on the learning act and the teacher's responsibility for it, leads naturally to pinpointing accountability for school achievement. The teacher is, indeed, front and center and is to be held accountable. The so-called accountability movement of the second half of the sixties, backed by legislative acts in some states, required precise delineation of school and classroom goals and implied or explicit teacher responsibility for fulfilling these goals and providing corroborating evidence. Needless to say, this was dismaying to many teachers who knew not where to turn for the safe-and-sure method of upgrading a class of readers scoring well below the mean. Learning how to define objectives behaviorally does not provide such assurances, but many school districts settled for it anyway. Because the science of pedagogy is not yet sufficiently advanced and because ongoing school regularities have a strange way of nullifying what threatens the old, an approach to accountability requiring certain teacher behaviors that, in turn, guarantee certain pupil behaviors appears to be ahead of its time. Unfortunately, some of the positive elements involved may be considerably retarded in their development because sharp delineation of accountability for teachers may have turned many of them, in self-defense, toward union power rather than toward teacher power based on professional, pedagogical competence. Ultimately, movements are set back by their own excesses, which often cause undue lapses of time before some of their elements return to visibility, usually in different dress. One of the challenges to progress is to utilize the residue of past excess while moving on to what usually become the new excesses.

CHANGING EXPECTATIONS FOR SCHOOLS

It will be recalled that the United States entered the post-Sputnik period with concern about the quality of schooling but with little loss of faith in what our schools were capable of doing. They simply needed to be redirected from their soft progressive ways and toughened up, especially by returning to some good old-fashioned learning. One might have expected schools to narrow their focus, concentrating on their traditional functions of teaching the three R's, as Bestor, Lynd, and the Council for Basic Education exhorted them to. But this was not to be the story of the era.

Cracks in fulfillment of the American Dream had been apparent to perceptive analysts for some time but were obscure to, ignored, or covered up by public officials, politicians, economists, business moguls, and others enamored of the explosively expanding GNP and obsessed by the possibilities of more—more of almost everything to unlimited degree. The ensuing decade was to open up these cracks. And it was to assign to schools the impossible task of supplying a good deal of the mortar to hold the pieces together. In the process, we lost much of our faith in schooling.

Some of the data regarding the cracks were old. The tax base required to support schools had been eroding for years in the inner city. It was into urban schools in Detroit, for example, that more and more blacks came in their migration toward jobs. Lloyd Allen Cook, an exponent of community schools, had spoken early on the inherent problems and dangers of the inner-city school situation. But whites, who had the power to change things, weren't listening; they simply moved or put their children into private schools. The black voice was still muted, though the NAACP became more visible and audible after 1954. The law added right to fingers pointing at what was wrong.

James B. Conant already was well known and respected when he published *Slums and Suburbs* in 1962. It was his reference to "social dynamite" accumulating in the large cities that caught the attention of the press and the public. His contrast of educational opportunity in the city to that of the suburb presaged court decisions of the seventies designed to right glaring inequities:

> The contrast in money available to the schools in a wealthy suburb and to the schools in a large city jolts one's notions of the meaning of equality of opportunity. The pedagogic tasks which confront the teachers in the slum schools are far more difficult than those which their colleagues in the wealthy schools face. Yet the expenditure per pupil in the wealthy suburban school is as high as $1,000 per year. The expenditure in a big city school is less than half that amount. An even more significant contrast is provided by looking at the school facilities and noting the size of the professional staff. In the suburb there is likely to be a spacious modern school staffed by as many as 70 professionals per 1,000 pupils; in the slum one finds a crowded, often dilapidated and unattractive school staffed by 40 or fewer professionals per 1,000 pupils.

The contrast challenges any complacency we may have about our method of financing public schools.[16]

These school-based inequities were and are, of course, one expression of deep-seated disparities in the general quality of life. It has been pointed out many times, worldwide, that the ultimate struggle is not based on color or creed but on socioeconomic class. But the focus of that struggle recently in the United States has been color and race, in part because of prejudice and, closely related, because those of a color other than white got a slow start on their share of the American Dream. On the first page of *Slums and Suburbs,* Conant put the matter bluntly: "This republic was born with a congenital defect—Negro Slavery." Later, the U.S. National Advisory Commission on Civil Disorders had a good deal more to say about deep-seated racism in American Society.[17]

More and more, the frequently militant drive for human equity and civil rights found its way into school policies and practices. The long stall in responding to court orders to integrate black and white in the South and the stubborn realities of de facto segregation in the North dominated much of school life throughout the Schooling Decade. For many superintendents, the cry for substantive curricular, organizational, and instructional reform was muted by complexities of bussing, confrontations with various interest groups, vandalism, and general erosion of the community from what it had been. The school, it turned out, was expected not merely to cope with and adapt to these changes; it was to become an active force in remedying social ills.

To say that the innovations designed to reform school regularities did not work is to miss the central point. For city superintendents, confronted with the harshest realities ever confronted by school administrators, reforms could be given only fleeting attention before turning them over to associates and rushing off to crises for which there were no recommended innovations. In many of these environments, either the reforms were not seriously tried or they were mustered as part of the armament to throw into a battle for which they had little firepower. The problems only got worse.

Federal action to improve education was delayed by long-standing reservations and controversies regarding the proper federal role in education, separation of church and state, states' rights, and the Horatio Alger notion that success is waiting for everyone willing to make the necessary early sacrifices and work hard enough. Nonetheless, far-reaching legislation was on the books before the sixties reached the halfway point. The eighty-eighth Congress passed legislation for vocational and technical education, higher education facilities, teaching handicapped children, preventing juvenile delinquency, medical education, college and public community libraries, graduate schools, technical institutes, public community colleges, student loans, guidance counseling, schools in federally impacted areas, educational media, educational research, manpower development, and instruction in science, mathematics, and foreign languages.

Through the Equal Educational Opportunities Program of the Civil Rights Act of 1964, this Congress provided special assistance to public schools seeking to effect desegregation and instructed the Commissioner of Education to report on "the lack of availability of equal educational opportunities for individuals by reason of race, color, religion, or national origin in public educational institutions at all levels. . . ." The Economic Opportunity Act of 1964 provided assistance to students of low-income families in their pursuit of higher education by promoting work-study programs; opportunities for persons over the age of eighteen to assume their adult responsibilities by initiating for them basic programs of instruction in reading and writing; and encouragement to school systems to provide early educational opportunities for the disadvantaged to offset the disabling effects of their restrictive environments.

In passing President Johnson's precedent-setting recommendations for what became the Elementary and Secondary Education Act (ESEA) of 1965, the eighty-ninth "Education Congress" responded as though education—in its ends, substance, and processes—was, indeed, a vital system in, if not the heart of, our national corpus. The President stressed this centrality in his message to Congress: "If we are learning anything from our experiences, we are learning that it is time for us to go to work, and the first work of these times and the first work of our society is education."

The lion's share of ESEA—almost 1.2 billion—was to assist school districts with their momentous tasks of keeping children from low-income families in school and giving them there the kind of education they need (Title I). Title II provided for books and authorized $100 million for the purchase of educational materials for children in both public and private nonprofit elementary and secondary schools. Titles III and IV, carrying broad implications for ultimate patterns of federal involvement in education, provided funds for linking the total educational resources of communities in ways scarcely conceived before and for comprehensive programs of research, development, and dissemination of knowledge through the collaborative efforts of universities, public schools, private nonprofit education agencies, and state departments of education. Title V put money directly into state departments of education for strengthening their ability to fulfill increasingly more compelling leadership responsibilities.

The rhetoric surrounding the federal education commitment was even more unprecedented than the ESEA itself. One startling juxtaposition of cause-and-effect relationships was the view that the economy was dependent on education, rather than the reverse. Also, the concept of education as a force for the welfare of all mankind was finding its place in official statements. Said President Johnson: "Education as a force for freedom, justice and rationality knows no national boundaries—it is the great universal force for good." At the 1965 White House Conference on Education, Vice President Hubert H. Humphrey added:

> The American educator and the American citizen need to think in larger terms, more ambitious terms, than we have ever yet begun to contemplate. The lessons we learn at home, therefore, must be applied in other places. We of this generation have the chance—oh, what a wonderful chance—to be remembered, as Toynbee said, not for crimes or even for astonishing adventures, but as the first generation that dared to make the benefits of civilization available to the whole human race.

The schools, then, were to do almost everything: prepare well for further schooling, provide for work experience, fight prejudice, mitigate the ravishes of inequity, improve the quality of urban life, relieve joblessness and poverty, and even bring about peace—all the things the larger society apparently could not do for itself. These are tasks for social engineering, perhaps using the fruits of education and schooling, but they are hardly realistic tasks for schools. In voting money for schools, there can be no short-term payoffs as in the building of roads and dams. Therefore, after a few years in office during the sixties, a legislator had little to show his constituency by way of tangible return for his support of education bills.

The Schooling Decade began with concern and curricular reform to assure that schools would perform their traditional functions well.

It ended with the expectation, fast fading by 1967, that they would assure everything ever envisioned in the American Dream. Monumental disillusionment, so effectively captured by Hutchins' words in the quote beginning this chapter, was inevitable.

But, of course, loss of faith in schools was only part of a larger cynicism. The Vietnam war strained the patience and faith of our people, particularly youth, and drained the vitality of this nation to a devastating degree.[18] Students at secondary and, especially, higher levels of education vented their frustration in disruption of campus life.[19] The war was not the only cause of tension, but it certainly exacerbated it and provided a ready rallying ground for widespread dissatisfaction and dissent ranging from irritations over rising costs to pockets of near-revolution.

The Vietnam war certainly turned down the spigot of the federal government's domestic money barrel and, with it, a good deal of the momentum for reform in the schools. The heady period was over. Grants were hard to get. Researchers and developers turning to private sources found stiff competition for funds and often were greeted by statements from foundation officials to the effect that the foundation was rethinking its policies.

The Schooling Decade did not come, suddenly to an inglorious end; it just faded away. For some the grave marker was the so-called Coleman Report on equality of educational opportunity.[20] A popular interpretation of the report is that schools don't make much difference; the critical factor in pupil achievement is what a student brings from home and encounters in school from other homes. This conclusion is still used frequently to justify curtailing expenditures for schools. It also is used to imply that the problem before us is not simply one of making local schools better but that schooling itself is fruitless. This is the ultimate loss of faith.

There are some signs in the seventies that schools are returning with vigor and even occasional joy to more realistic goals, now that we have plummeted to earth in regard to our expectations for them. It is somewhat reassuring to hear educators, instead of crawling away defensively from Jencks's somber conclusion to the effect that schools do not produce equality,[21] respond with the comment, "Who ever claimed they do or should?" An impossible struggle becomes a challenging venture when the call for continuing reconstruction includes rededication to the principle of equality of *educational* opportunity and reexamination of ends and means in the light of that principle.

THE SCHOOLING DECADE IN RETROSPECT

There can be no doubt that the Schooling Decade was an extraordinarily innovative period in American education. That it ended in considerable disillusionment regarding the potency of schools was in large part the result of unreasonable expectations for them. But our schools have been so much part and parcel of the hopes and ambitions of successive generations that dissatisfaction with them must be viewed in the context of a more general malaise. The period under review was one in which what had been normal schedules of social reform no longer were acceptable. Similarly, normal schedules of school reform no longer sufficed. In the short run, even accelerated schedules appeared insufficient.

The verdict in the long run regarding the effectiveness of schools may be quite different. The fact that at least the ideas of change and innovation penetrated the system at so many levels of decision making speaks optimistically for a future in which our expectations for schooling no doubt will be less grandiose.

It is fair to say, I think—and I shall endeavor in Chapter 3 to establish a case for this generalization—that failure to see the school as a social system in its own right and as the focal point for educational improvement constituted the greatest shortcoming of the Schooling Decade. There is virtually nothing in either the rhetoric or substance of federal intervention to connote that policy makers had a clear image of such a place or of its potential in the community. As we have seen, curricular, organizational, and instructional reform proceeded separately and disparately, hardly anyone providing a synthesis of what all this might add up to in a given school. And even each of these components was subdivided into single subjects (e.g., mathematics), part of the school's organizational fabric (e.g., team teaching), or a single, instructional panacea (e.g., programmed instruction). The Coleman Report averaged the data, ignoring possible differences among schools. The new infrastructure for improving the educational system proposed by ESEA included almost every component but schools and how the anticipated reforms were to get to them. Much of what went on was a little like seeking to improve the quality of family life without either an image of a family and what it might look like or any way of reaching it as an entity.

This apparent failure to see the school as a unit for change is further substantiated by the way teachers were involved. In both curricular and instructional reform, the focus was on the teacher as an individual, practically without reference to the social context of regularities within which teachers work. Perhaps this was because so many "university types" were involved in reform; perhaps they saw teachers in the schools as having the autonomy enjoyed by professors. Something of the same viewpoint was embedded in the so-called accountability movement as it matured during the late sixties and early seventies. With schooling not rising to expectations and most of the reformers moving offstage, teachers again moved front and center. But, to repeat, what teachers do is determined largely by the culture of the school. The degree of separation of teachers from one another and of administrators from teachers probably was increased more than reduced by much of what went on during the Schooling Decade, thus effectively reducing the capacity of the school as a whole to heal itself.

Many hypotheses regarding the conduct of change and innovation in schooling might be drawn from an analysis of the late fifties and sixties period of excitement in American education. I close this chapter with just three of these which appear to me rather significantly related to what follows.

First, *the kind of reform likely to be advocated and the principal actors in the process will tend to shift in relation to the ratio of nonregular funds to regular funds available.* The greater the proportion of nonregular money, the greater the likelihood that the locus of reform will be remote from schools and that the actors will be nonschool types. Change will tend to be "outer-directed." Usually, this will be short run, relatively expensive reform accompanied by excessive exhortative rhetoric and equally excessive but unsubstantiated claims. The tenacity of school regularities will tend to be ignored. When nonregular money is in short supply, the change process will be at the local level, school personnel will be the prime (perhaps sole) actors, and the focus is more likely to be on classroom organization and instruction. The substance of the curriculum is likely to remain untouched, although there is likely to be experimentation in arranging or presenting it. Change becomes "inner-directed."

Second, *the estimated significance of a proposed change (to society, for example) has little bearing on ease or difficulty of implementation in the school setting.* More important, it appears, is the extent to which the change is seen as threatening to long-standing regularities. Usually, threat is increased when the consequences are unknown or when uncertainty leaves ample room for critics to relate the proposal to what already has been tried and failed or to otherwise obfuscate the possible consequences. Aware of all this, canny change agents sometimes deliberately introduce a benign but controversial proposal in order to create a smokescreen under which significant change is implemented. Or, the "camel-in-the-tent" approach is used whereby what is intended is exposed only a little at a time.

Third, *the greater the focus of accountability on teachers and the greater their isolation from the whole of schooling in the rhetoric and processes of being held responsible, the greater the likelihood that teachers will seek protection and succor in large professional, probably unionized, organizations.* Unless strong countervailing influences are mobilized, this process will separate what increasingly will be seen as "management" from "the workers." Teachers' and principals' organizations, for example, will grow in power and influence over individual behavior at the possible expense of the school as a social organization. The more established these organizations become, the greater the necessity of including them in any processes of planned change, *whatever the intent and locus of what is proposed.* Further, because these organizations will not go into any significant change enterprises without knowing the consequences and since the consequences usually can be only speculative, almost all such efforts in the future will require multilateral agreement that they be "experiments," at least initially. While this will be an inhibiting concept to those who view change and innovation as a largely intuitive process, cloaked in charisma, it could well result in building in some much-needed analytical research-oriented activities at the outset. Educational change might then become other than the largely unstudied process which it now is.

NOTES

1 Arthur Bestor, *Educational Wastelands*, University of Illinois Press, Urbana, 1953; Robert M. Hutchins, *The Conflict in Education*, Harper, New York, 1953; and Albert Lynd, *Quackery in the Public Schools*, Little, Brown, Boston, 1953.

2 The characteristics of these alternative views of what education and schooling should be like, together with the manifestations of both in practice, have been described and analyzed effectively by Philip G. Smith, "The Philosophical Context," in John I. Goodlad and Harold

G. Shane (eds.), *The Elementary School in the United States*, Seventy-second Yearbook of the National Society for the Study of Education, Part II, University of Chicago Press, Chicago, 1973.

3   Rudolf Flesch, *Why Johnny Can't Read*, Harper, New York, 1955.

4   James B. Conant, *The American High School Today*, McGraw-Hill, New York, 1959.

5   Emphases and reforms of the decade are treated in some detail in John I. Goodlad, "Schooling and Education," in Otto Bird (ed.), *The Great Ideas Today*, Encyclopaedia Britannica, Inc., Chicago, 1969, pp. 101–145; and in John I. Goodlad (ed.), *The Changing American School*, Sixty-fifth Yearbook of the National Society for the Study of Education, Part II, University of Chicago Press, Chicago, 1966.

6   Jerome S. Bruner, *The Process of Education*, Vintage Books, New York, 1960, p. 33. Bruner's thesis was to be joined later with Bloom's (Benjamin S. Bloom, *Stability and Change in Human Characteristics*, Wiley, New York, 1964) to provide substantial support for early childhood education. This field blossomed during the sixties and today demonstrates considerable, solid progress. Space limitations prevent much attenion to it here, but for a summary of developments, see John I. Goodlad, M. Frances Klein, Jerrold M. Novotney, and Associates, *Early Schooling in the United States*, McGraw-Hill, New York, 1973.

7   During 1963–64, I conducted a review of most of the extant major projects at the invitation of the Ford Foundation, updating this work two years later. See John I. Goodlad, *School Curriculum Reform in the United States*, Fund for the Advancement of Education, New York, 1964; and Goodlad, Renata von Stoephasius, and M. Frances Klein, *The Changing School Curriculum*, Fund for the Advancement of Education, New York, 1966.

8   See C. Wayne Gordon and Leta McKinney Adler, *Dimensions of Teacher Leadership in Classroom Social Systems: Pupil Effects on Productivity, Morale, and Compliance*, University of California, Los Angeles, 1963.

9   In trying to secure data about the operation of nongraded schools in the early 1960s, Robert H. Anderson and I began our search for such schools by following up claims made or implied at a national conference. We found that many of the schools or school districts where such a practice was supposed to be in existence were unable to provide any information as to actual plans in operation. However, an NEA survey (John I. Goodlad, *Planning and Organizing for Teaching*, NEA Project on the Instructional Program of the Public Schools, Washington, D.C., 1963) which simply asked respondents if they had

nongrading or team teaching in operation revealed such plans to be in more than one of ten schools in the country. Then, a doctoral study which succeeded in isolating twenty nongraded, exemplar schools reported that, on visitation, only a half-dozen met a reasonable list of criteria for nongrading and only two of these met the criteria to a high degree. See, Maria T. Delgado-Marcano, "The Operation of Curriculum and Instruction in Twenty Nongraded Elementary Schools," unpublished doctoral dissertation, School of Education, Indiana University, Bloomington, 1965.

10 Frank Brown, *The Nongraded High School*, Prentice-Hall, Englewood Cliffs, N.J., 1963; Sidney P. Rollins, *Developing Nongraded Schools*, F. E. Peacock, Publisher, Itasca, Ill., 1968; and James Lewis, Jr., *A Contemporary Approach to Nongraded Education*, Parker Publishing Co., West Nyack, N.Y., 1969.

11 See, James H. Block (ed.), *Mastery Learning: Theory and Practice*, Holt, New York, 1971.

12 Perhaps the ultimate in such thinking is the suit, in the early seventies, charging a San Francisco school with negligence for failing to teach a youth to read by the time he graduated from high school.

13 Recently, Atkinson has developed a computer program for optimizing the sequencing of material to be presented to the student. See, Richard C. Atkinson, "Adaptive Instructional Systems: Some Attempts to Optimize the Learning Process," Technical Report No. 240, Psychology and Education Series, Institute for Mathematical Studies in the Social Sciences, Stanford University, Stanford, California, November 20, 1974.

14 Education U.S.A., *IPI: An Individualized Approach*, Special Report, National School Public Relations Association, Arlington, Va., 1975.

15 I clearly recall an animated discussion with Robert Glaser at an evening social affair when he talked about his growing realization that nongrading was eminently compatible with individually prescribed instruction. We should do more about bringing the two together, we said. In the course of time, they did come together, to considerable degree; perhaps ideas have to be seen in their compatible relationship for quite some time before a synthetic implementation will occur.

16 James B. Conant, *Slums and Suburbs: A Commentary on Schools in the Metropolitan Area*, McGraw-Hill, New York, 1961, p. 3. Data drawn upon a decade later in court cases challenging the legality of extant arrangements for supporting schooling from property taxes suggest the need for even *more* money to support in the urban environment schools equivalent to those maintained in the suburbs.

See, for example, H. Thomas James et al., *Determinants of Educational Expenditures in Large Cities of the United States*, Stanford University School of Education, Cooperative Research Project No. 2389, Stanford, Calif., 1966; and J. S. Berke, "The Current Crisis in School Finance: Inadequacy and Inequity," *Phi Delta Kappan*, vol. 53, pp. 2–7, 1971.

17   Otto Kerner et al., *Report of the National Advisory Commission on Civil Disorders*, Government Printing Office, Washington, D.C., 1968.

18   One becomes even more acutely aware of the strain and burden in reviewing the long, sad story of our involvement for so long a period in the affairs of Indochina. One is acutely reminded of those lines. "Of all the words of tongue and pen, the saddest are these, 'It might have been.' " See, for example, David Halberstam, *The Best and the Brightest*, Random House, New York, 1969, for a vivid picture of how this involvement ultimately affected the whole fabric of American life.

19   Analyses of the causes, course, and results of student unrest during the 1960s are numerous. Some of the retrospective views probably are the best balanced. See, for example, Carnegie Commission on Higher Education, *Dissent and Disruption: Proposals for Consideration by the Campus*, McGraw-Hill, 1971; and David Riesman and Verne Stoldtman (eds.), *Academic Transformation: Seventeen Institutions under Pressure*, McGraw-Hill, New York, 1973.

20   James S. Coleman et al., *Equality of Educational Opportunity*, U.S. Department of Health, Education, and Welfare, Office of Education, 1966.

21   Christopher Jencks et al., *Inequality: A Reassessment of the Effect of Family and Schooling in America*, Basic Books, New York, 1972.

CHAPTER 3

IMPROVING SCHOOLING: TWO MODES OF THOUGHT

Special investigations become barren and one-sided in the degree in which they are conducted without reference to a wider, more general view.... No matter how these are obtained, they are intrinsically philosophical in nature. But if a philosophy starts to reason out its conclusions without definite and constant regard to the concrete experiences that define the problem for thought, it becomes speculative in a way that justifies contempt.

—John Dewey (*The Sources of a Science of Education*, Horace Liveright, New York, 1929, p. 54–55, 56)

The phrase "two modes of thought" in the title of this chapter is taken from the title of a little book by James B. Conant, published in 1964.[1] In it, he develops several observations having enormous implications for the study and practice of education and for the necessary relationship between the two.

Conant argues that advances in the natural sciences have been a consequence of the collaboration of scientists with two different outlooks: the empirical-inductive method of inquiry on one hand and the theoretical-deductive on the other:

The empirical-inductive is by itself insufficient to generate advances in scientific theory. On the other hand, the theoretical-deductive mode by itself is too often barren; for advances in the practical arts, it has been in the past quite unnecessary.[2]

He refutes the popular view of Darwin's work as an example of how the accumulation of empirical facts leads to generalizations. Darwin had been unable to explain how each species fits its environment until he chanced to read Malthus's *Essay on Population,* and as he reported it, "the idea of natural selection suddenly rose to my mind." Conant comments: "Such are the flashes of genius that result in a great scientist's conviction that a working hypothesis is far more than a

51

hypothesis—that it is a principle, that it is correct."[3] Dewey, too, employed the term "working hypotheses": "They are *working* ideas; special investigations become barren and one-sided in the degree in which they are conducted without reference to a wider, more general view."[4]

In stressing the importance of generating working hypotheses, Dewey warned against the emptiness of thinking which is remote from the source of intellectual supplies. For him, educational practice provided the data. Similarly, he decried practice-related research devoid of big ideas. He felt that working hypotheses were necessary to guide and justify the laborious testing of the deductions from the generalizations:

> The lack of an intellectually coherent and inclusive system is a positive warning against attributing scientific values to results merely because they are reached by means of recognized techniques borrowed from sciences already established and are capable of being stated in quantitative formula. . . . Educational practices provide the data, the subject matter, which form the *problems* of inquiry. They are the sole source of the ultimate problems to be investigated.[5]

What follows is an attempt to recount the interplay between the two modes of thought described by Conant, in the context of educational practice as seen as essential by Dewey, for the purpose of revealing the development of an idea which ultimately found its locus in a strategy for improving schooling in the United States. The time period encompasses that covered in Chapter 2. Consequently, in Dewey's terms, the educational practices providing the data and context are those of the Schooling Decade and preceding years. The working ideas are my own, although the credit for much of their shaping, reshaping, and testing in practice belongs to my colleagues, primarily in the University Elementary School, UCLA, and the Institute for Development of Educational Activities, Inc. (|I|D|E|A|), the education arm of the Charles F. Kettering Foundation.

In effect, then, the Schooling Decade is revisited, this time to trace the genesis and maturation of a personal conviction and a strategy regarding the improvement of schooling *within the extant regularities of our federal, state, and local educational enterprise.* There is no attempt here to conjure up visions of a different kind of world or human species, either as a goal for or condition of educational reform. The most general, implicit working idea is directed to the possibility that schools can and must become better, more humane work settings, sustaining both the individuals in them and those institutional elements representative of what we are striving for in the larger society. Simultaneously, the best possibilities for schools must be viewed critically against the virtues of other educational alternatives. Before abandoning schools, we should be sure we have tested them fully, if only because the alternatives have scarcely been tested at all.

The idea of two modes of thought interweaving in the improvement of educational practice has intrigued me for some time. Several years ago, I noted the hollowness of empirical research on innovations which measures pupil effects under two supposedly different sets of circumstances without first either analyzing the conceptualizations differentiating control and experimental groups or determining whether the alternative circumstances exist.[6] Such research subsequently has been dubbed the study of nonevents.[7]

Properly conducted to include assurance that discrete circumstances have been both conceptualized and implemented, short-term inquiry, accumulated with other such inquiry, can be exceedingly useful, especially in checking the validity of claims for this or that alternative practice. But such work is of little or no use *in and of itself* in challenging the basic assumptions underlying specific pieces of inquiry. That is, the principle guiding the inquiry is not, itself the subject of inquiry in most empirical research. Consequently, in a field such as the teaching of reading, study after study rejects this or that method as showing no significant differences, but whether pedagogical method is the key differentiating factor in reading achievement is not often questioned. It may take a sociologist looking at the problem from the perspective of teachers' classroom leadership styles to place the problem in fresh prospective and trigger a new line of short-term inquiry.

A good many critics of the Schooling Decade have concluded that most of the innovations were ineffective. This conclusion has some research findings and a much more extensive body of opinion to support it. It is fair to say, however, that the research and evaluation available are almost exclusively within a single guiding principle or paradigm: the model of differentiated instructional circumstances providing differing sets of pupil outcomes.

There is also some research and a great deal of experiential evidence to suggest that most of the so-called ineffective innovations were installed only partially or not at all.[8] This hypothesis leads to inquiry and paradigms of research quite different from the well-known model of comparing pupil effects in supposedly differentiated circumstances. The guiding question is no longer whether the innovation produced effects but why it was not installed. This question, in turn, leads us into analysis of the theories supposedly guiding the change strategies of the period. This kind of inquiry is characterized by what Schwab calls "long-term syntax."[9] It postulates alternative principles which ultimately are rejected or come to replace, stand beside, or combine with other principles to provide new explanations of phenomena and guide subsequent research and practice.

Change during the Schooling Decade, as we have seen in Chapter 2, was largely outer-directed—financed from nonregular funds and led by scholars and enterprising innovators, with teachers and pupils as the target. The prime model was linear: from concept to development and testing to delivery and installation. I was an active participant and critic. Early on, I became uneasy about implementation and sensed that the model might be inadequate in this stage. This uneasiness joined and strengthened what I view today not so much as an alternative model but as elements of an infrastructure within which other, perhaps more limited and sharply focused, strategies might find nourishing soil.

It seems to me that this personal process, while lacking the flash of genius referred to by Conant, represents virtually a case study of his two modes of thought in action. Further, it seems to represent the interplay of working hypotheses within the practical context of critical educational problems which Dewey saw as crucial in the development of educational science. This return visit to the Schooling Decade is to gain increased insight, then, into problems and processes of educational change. Perhaps the account will be of some use to those scholar colleagues who, too, are caught in the vexing, often nonproductive, jousting between empiricists and theoreticians. And perhaps it will reveal to practitioner colleagues how two interweaving modes of thought can be productive in the practical affairs with which they are engaged.[10]

To the former group, Conant had this to say: "Just as man needs two legs to walk on, the social sciences need two types of thinkers if the advance is, as it should be, to meet the needs of a free and highly industrialized society."[11] To both, let me simply say that thought and action must go hand-in-hand if schooling is to be improved and so, too, must scholar and practitioner.

GENESIS OF A WORKING IDEA

For a nine-year period from the late 1940s through the middle of the fifties, I had the good fortune to be associated with a unique entity, the Atlanta Area Teacher Education Service (AATES), involving an almost unprecedented collaboration among six school districts and an equal number of institutions of higher learning.[12] The AATES was an early, comprehensive effort to recognize and meet the in-service education needs of teachers. There had been only limited recognition of what now is being increasingly accepted: pre-service teacher education provides little more than survival skills; a teacher's education must continue throughout a career.

The focus was almost entirely on the individual teacher. Annual surveys identified teachers' felt needs (an early, informal approach to today's "needs assessment"); courses were organized whenever there appeared to be a cluster of interests; instructors were recruited (usually from Emory University or the University of Georgia, the two major institutions offering graduate work, although not all the teachers held first-level degrees); and the courses were offered at convenient locations in the field. Higher education was brought to teachers, rather than the reverse.

The AATES, still operating and still largely unstudied, offers both a rich resource for students of educational change and a unique strategy, elements of which resemble certain elements of current much publicized "teacher centers." Operational aspects, in particular, should be of special interest to metropolitan areas where the record of collaboration between school districts and institutions of higher learning is not impressive and yet is of much potential significance. However, an analysis of strengths and weaknesses here must be eschewed.

The strategy from the beginning was to improve the understandings (particularly), skills, and attitudes of teachers; it follows that many of the courses offered for thirty years or so have emphasized the teaching of reading and other school subjects. There have been courses for administrators, especially principals, and guidance counselors, too. Occasionally, a course has been made up for a district-based group to deal with some general problem such as improving the system of reporting pupil progress to parents. At no time during my nine-year association with the AATES, however, did an entire staff, including the principal, organize and request a course cutting across the school's functioning as a social institution, although such may have occurred since.

This involvement and the pursuit of certain other interests brought me into rather intimate association (for a university professor) with dozens of school principals and many hundreds of teachers. As director of teacher education at Emory University, I reviewed professional preparation plans with hundreds of teachers and prospective teachers each year. And I visited a great many classrooms. It became obvious in all of this that larger numbers of school personnel in the greater Atlanta area were becoming relatively well informed about, for example, ranges of individual differences in their classrooms, and that a considerable drive to reform practices was emerging. It is doubtful that any section of the country offered such a large smorgasbord of in-service offerings so conveniently located and at such low cost to participants. (Participating school districts and universities directly subsidized the program, the latter particularly in counting instructor time, the cost of which AATES tuition did not fully cover; as part of a regular teaching load.)

It became equally obvious that substantial numbers of teachers also were becoming frustrated over real or imagined restraints in their school settings. For example, on invitation I visited the classroom of a teacher who immediately poured out her frustration over what to do with the advanced group who already, in February, had completed the assigned second-grade readers. She did not dare go on with third-grade material because the teacher in the next grade would be very upset! What should she do? She was butting up against those institutional regularities to which Sarason referred so insightfully.[13]

One of the best conceptualized and organized activities of the AATES operated as a center of the Child Study Program developed by Daniel Prescott at the University of Chicago in the mid-forties and subsequently moved to the University of Maryland.[14] Prescott saw the child at the heart of the educative process and the child-teacher relationship as critical. He believed that the teacher placed a predetermined curriculum as a screen in front of her, obscuring and distorting her view of the child. This screen could be removed, not quickly or easily, but ultimately, first by prolonged in-depth observation of the child—a single child as a functioning entity within the context of home, school, and peer group—to see the person becoming in all realms of development. Then, the lens could be widened to see children functioning together. The technique for data gathering was anecdotal, requiring special skills and an attitude of objectivity and withheld judgment.

Prescott's plan was to bring together successive cohorts of teachers for three years of child study and group discussion (a procedure very carefully worked out, following rather nondirective nonjudgmental lines which the teachers were themselves to use in their own class discussions with children).[15] Each year of the program had a rather sharp focus (e.g., study of a single child during the first year, involving conducting a comprehensive anecdotal case study and formulating tentative hypotheses about a bit of behavior). Increasingly, Prescott trained levels of leadership, as graduates of a three-year program, some of whom acquired doctorates, carried others through it, and these, in turn, became leaders for new centers springing up around the country.

But the Child Study Movement, too, smacked up against the regularities of schooling. During a period of my association with the AATES, I teamed with Lynn ("Pat") Shufelt, one of the most able veteran members of the Prescott group, in leading an experimental fourth-year class of educators, some of whom were themselves instructors of first- or second-year classes. The intent was to use our child-centered insights in constructing classroom environments—for example, to meet the challenge of designing learning opportunities around children's development tasks as set forth so clearly by Lilienthal and Tryon.[16] Months after we began to meet, in spite of our efforts to direct the discussion otherwise, the nagging theme continued to be the impossibility of doing anything much different, given parental expectations, district requirements, administrative controls, misunderstanding and lack of interest on the part of colleagues, and on and on, perceived and probably actual obstacles.

Suggestions that these limitations be tested directly—bringing in principals to meet with us, for example—were turned aside; they tended to cause discomfort. Discomfort was elicited, too, on those occasions when we did manage to get seriously into instructional and curricular matters. Much of the restructuring needed (regarding grade barriers, less primitive marking systems, expectations for pupil behavior, and the like) seemed to require collaboration with peers in one's own school. Just how to secure this was not at all clear. There were not, apparently, existing mechanisms for initiating dialogue and taking action.[17]

Principals were not excluded from this Child Study Program. However, studying a single child seemed to most of them not to relate to their needs; they enrolled primarily in classes labeled "administration" or "supervision." (Perhaps child study classes should have carried titles like "Administering Children in School Settings" and then simply proceeded as always!) However, there were a few strong "believers" among the principals who enrolled, some of whom ultimately became group leaders. Several of these worked diligently to interest their staffs, a very few ultimately turning out almost in full force. Some of their schools, in turn, began to gain "lighthouse" reputations. One, in particular, was almost in the inner city and had an energetic believer in child study as principal who managed to involve most of her staff. The school became exemplar in its ability to deal constructively with children from broken homes and unusually deprived environments. It, too, should have been studied.

SCHOOLS AS SOCIAL SYSTEMS

As the years went by and I moved increasingly freely among the schools, it appeared to me that they were not alike. Yes, they resembled each other in many outward ways, although at least three layers in the history of building construction were clearly in evidence.[18] A school is a school is a school. Or is it—necessarily? The atmospheres were not at all alike. For some, one phoned ahead, came at a precise time, went directly to the principal, and rarely was invited into classrooms. Some told you about "spooky" children who "laughed at you behind your back." In such schools, many things seemed a little "tight," from the principal's pursed lips to the constrained passage of children down hallways to the precise choice of polite words of greeting and departure. On leaving, one had a feeling of "hear no evil, see no evil, speak no evil" and of a lot held under control just below the surface. The appearance of a few black faces might just blow the lid off—and 1954 was just a few short years away.

In other schools, the climate was like a benign evening breeze across a Florida key. The principal was glad to see you; and she really meant it when, on departure, she said "Come see us, hear?" Access to classrooms was easy and visits expected. (I often was chided later for not visiting a teacher who had heard of my stopping by.) Teachers seemed not afraid that the class would blow up during a few minutes of chatting together. Frequently, there would be an invitation to come back some afternoon, "when you have time to meet with the entire staff—any day but Friday and some of us will be available even then, if that's the best you can do." It was more than friendship based on several years of association. It was a truly different climate—an open climate without an open building. No "tightness" here. Other schools seemed not to be systemic in any sense of the word—just collections of cells, with some differences among cells.

There should be no need to recount more of these experiences with school systems, schools, classrooms, principals, and teachers. Clearly, a working hypothesis was taking shape, a working idea about the locus and processes of improving the educational enterprise we know as schooling. Schools are social systems, albeit sick and mal-functioning or alive and well and enjoying their existence, in which people and things interact, ways of regularizing these interactions are formed, roles are determined and played out, activities arise and are sanctioned or snuffed out, personal and group behaviors are shaped and rewarded and, in the process, strengthened or weakened. The school, in turn, shapes toward the already established regularities of its character whatever intrudes into it—modifying, distorting, or ac-commodating according to the degree of compatibility between the system's view of the intruder and both the system's view of itself and its functioning character. Nothing of any importance or potential sig-nificance enters a school to become a permanent part of it and re-mains there in its original form. Those few things which enter a school and remain there unchanged probably are either of little significance or are walled off effectively and almost immediately from school life. (A dictatorial school superintendent who liked to tell one and all that every school in his district had a motion picture projector probably never found out how quickly the pick-up reels disappeared—and there was no rash of reordering!)

This is true, too, of adults coming to work in the school, and children also know much of what is expected even before they come. What all come to learn later is derived not just from formal teaching but simply from internalizing the system—socialization is a common word for it. It is to this subtle socialization of children and teachers into the many ways of the school that ardent critics usually object.

Principals and teachers are so socialized. Early in my own career, the first day on a new job, I discovered to my considerable em-barrassment, after choosing and moving from four successive chairs in the lunchroom, that there was a pecking order in the system's assignment of tables and seats to the staff. In frustration, I started my own table but, like many innovations, this bold act simply regularized the behavior of subsequent newcomers. Jackson's work suggests that teachers tend to grow toward an attitudinal mean over ten years of service, with initially divergent views either changing or disappearing through attrition in the system.[19] The work of Sorenson and his students suggests a general cleavage between the more open, inquiring attitudes desired by teacher educators in their students and the expectations of the social entities which they later join as faculty members.[20] But the possibility that schools themselves differ or could differ to any considerable degree in how and toward what they socialize remains a less studied question.

Whatever interest and knowledge there may be in the proposition that schools under certain circumstances are or could be different is not yet cast in a very useful form for improving the educational enterprise, as Dewey points out:

> ... educational practices provide the data, the subject-matter, which form the *problems* of inquiry. ... The educational practices are also the final *test of value* of all researches. ... Actual activities in *educating* test the worth of scientific results. They may be scientific in some other field, but not in education until they serve educational purposes, and whether they serve or not can be found out only in practice.[21]

Our purpose is improving schooling. In this regard, an embryonic working hypothesis directs us toward the proposition that the school in its total functioning as a social system must be taken into account in any process of change. But "taken into account" is a weasel phrase. Curriculum reformers of the sixties would say that they took the schools into account—by seeking to go around intractable administrators, by using expertise not available in schools, by developing teacher-proof materials. Clearly, this cannot be what is meant. If the school is seen as a target for reform—and my serious reservations about this view will come out explicitly later—then its inner workings must be understood.

We have seen in Chapter 2 that innovative strategies for creating an infrastructure for change and innovation fell short of or bypassed the school as an entity. Change elements finding their way into the school were fragmented, uncoordinated, and lacking synthesis. Reforms directed at the school's formal structure did not take account of the school's informal structure—its ways of functioning and resisting. Studies of the real world of the public schools are few, limited in size and scope, and as yet only suggestive of what goes on there day after day. It comes as a surprise to many otherwise well-informed persons to learn that no adequately definitive study exists.[22]

But even accepting the proposition that schools are social systems which wrap themselves around what comes into them and recognizing the importance of understanding them and this process thoroughly points us only to a kind of academic inquiry and not yet to change processes. Thus, a third proposition is added: the school is itself an agent of and for change. Accepting this proposition means that for the curriculum of a school to change and to go on changing there must be a kind of momentum in that school. It must have a disposition toward making such a change, to remaking it, and to making it once again. Without such momentum, layer upon layer of so-called reform will be laid upon the school, weighing it down and more and more encumbering its very ability to change. Teachers may be good, obedient automatons, learning all the right words and even exhibiting a little spirit of the intended reform, but they will go right on doing what they have always done. Nothing changes but the appearance of change.

Clearly, this is the most controversial part of the working hypothesis, although there are trends to suggest that it is more acceptable today than it could or would have been just a few years ago. There is little in the history of American education to suggest much expectation for or, for that matter, the granting of much authority to schools "to heal themselves." Principals have not been expected to be leaders nor, in general, have they been trained in leadership. Expectations have run to maintaining a tight ship and keeping community dissatisfaction at a minimum; training has run more to routine management. Communities have seen little need to provide more than the bare essentials for public school teachers: rarely are they provided with offices or secretarial help; frequently, there is no place to meet other than a classroom where chairs are for "little bears." Teachers are supposed to go into their classrooms, close the door, and teach. Children are to come home and speak a little algebra.

The more one thinks about it, the more one realizes that there has been very little expectation in American precollegiate education for the school to behave as a cohesive, organized entity. "School is what my child and his teacher do." In general, this seems to have been the image subconsciously held by most of the reformers during the Schooling Decade. And it seems even to be the image of teachers themselves.

It would not be at all surprising, then, to find that planning by those responsible in and for the school—the principal, teachers, students, and parents associated with it, "responsible parties," Joyce calls them[23]—in order to determine its present strengths and weaknesses and to set a course for its future is a near nonevent. I recall the consternation of my own small staff, several years before the experience with the AATES recounted here, when I proposed, as a first-year principal, that we meet to discuss and improve the total school environment. And although, in connection with my AATES involvement, I referred earlier to invitations to meet with total staffs, they were very rare, coming from those few schools where faculty groups actually did meet from time to time to discuss schoolwide concerns. By contrast, most teachers spoke favorably of principals who placed no demands on them for affairs beyond the confines of their own classrooms. In the League of Cooperating Schools, which occupies center stage in much of what follows, group processes in League schools were regarded with hostility by some other principals and teachers. Self-improvement activities of this kind apparently threaten certain regularities in schools; those involved are regarded as rate busters whose efforts, if institutionalized, will create new expectations for everyone else.

My first primitive formulation of this working hypothesis that the single school, with its principal, teachers, pupils, parents, and community links, is the key unit in educational change was set down briefly in 1955.[24] The statement said little or nothing about the school's systemic functioning and malfunctioning, the need to understand and take it into account, or the necessity of its developing a continuing propensity for and ability to change. These propositions were too ill-formed for any written formulation. They and others became clearer and were fleshed out by what might loosely be called the empirical-inductive work which followed these extrapolations from experience and the beginnings of what might be termed an intermediate theory —that is, a theory tentatively formed for empirical testing which might lead to a more firm and encompassing theory at a later time.

What that 1955 statement did deal with, however briefly, was the notion of the principal's key role in the school's becoming a dynamic self-renewing place. Supreme among the components of his or her "span of control" was intellectual or conceptual management—that is, the ability to conceptualize the whole so as to visualize other possibilities and how specific steps and innovations might lead to them.

This is not necessarily a personal thing; in fact, it virtually necessitates team effort and argues for the staff processes referred to above. But it is the leadership responsibility of the principal to see that such management occurs, not now and then but as a continuing vital element of the school's functioning. Without some reasonably well-formulated conceptualization and articulation of the school's character and sense of direction, it lies vulnerable to those entrepreneurs, most of them well-meaning, who would pile on another layer of something "good because it is new."

It is quite to be expected that the working hypothesis so far explicated would be treated with considerable skepticism in many quarters. And it most certainly was when it was put to work, so to speak, in 1966, in a research and intervention project involving eighteen schools called "A Study of Educational Change and School Improvement." Schools as social systems with responsibility for and capability of their own self-improvement have not been established part of the lexicon of American education. And the Ichabod Crane stereotype of the teacher has been commonly transferred in modern times to the principal. Putting the two together, conceptually and operationally, in a working hypothesis would appear to be counter-productive, if not downright countervailing.

In regard to the former possibility, judgment must be suspended at least until the data of this report are in hand. In regard to the second —of course! This is what a working hypothesis characterized by Schwab's concept of long-term syntax is all about. It seeks, among other things, to provide alternatives to hypotheses or principles recently or presently guiding short-term inquiries and interventions. We have followed up other alternatives, spending millions upon millions of dollars on some of them; why not this one?

But merely to try something because it has not been seriously tried before does not bring with it either the knowledge base derived from some sort of empirical testing or the belief that the hypothesis in Conant's words, a principle, that it is correct. Without the latter, there will be no empirical testing. Without the former, putting the skepticism in one's own mind, let alone in the minds of others, becomes improbable.

Of course, supporting a working hypothesis in the arena of educational practice requires a great deal more than data. The very fact that it has not been followed up seriously will be, for some people, part of its appeal. Innovation seems to be characterized by this quality.

An hypothesis embracing the local school and those immediately associated with it may be just right for this era of decentralized authority, low level of nonregular funds, and citizen involvement—an idea whose time has come. This certainly was not the case in 1955, nor in 1965.

But a caveat is in order. The hypothesis is not put forward as all-encompassing with respect to the improvement of schooling. It merely addresses itself to a neglected part and, therefore, must be coupled with others if a comprehensive strategy for reconstructing our schools is to be designed.

REFINING THE WORKING HYPOTHESIS

The time period covered in the preceding section carried us almost to Sputnik. What follows coincides precisely with the Schooling Decade, beginning just before Sputnik and coming up to 1966, a year after ESEA. Again, the discussion is unavoidably highly personal.

The Englewood Project

Toward the end of my rewarding association with the AATES, I was invited to be continuing consultant to the Englewood School and Project on the Gulf Coast of Florida. The charge was to upgrade in every way possible the total functioning of this little public school, which was at the time in dire trouble. Some funds for the purpose were to come from private sources.[25] In spite of the formidable obstacles clearly inherent in the situation, how lucky could one be, given the personal orientation and hypothesis-brewing already described!

Located some miles off the main highway near the southernmost end of Sarasota County, the Englewood School was relatively isolated from other schools and the central office. Supervisors and other district personnel did not just drop in, as they frequently did with other schools; they planned a special trip. Consequently, their visits were rare. Teachers and parents perceived their school to be somewhat neglected and seemed little motivated to do much about it.

Although the miles of virtually unpeopled sandy beach, semitropical vegetation, and benign climate offered idyllic outdoor recreation, cultural facilities did not offer even a movie house. There was little disposition on the part of teachers or parents to make the school a community center, perhaps in part because school already occupied a large part of teachers' lives and because many residents of Englewood had left other climes to get away from community involvement. It was sufficient to send children to school and to teach the daily classes. In languid communities like Englewood, doing it tomorrow is a line of least resistance to which one adapts easily.

But when I first saw the unprepossessing Englewood School in 1955, the situation was anything but benign or languid. Although the privately funded proposal for school improvement had been presented to the Sarasota County superintendent of schools, the staff, and the community with some care, it was nonetheless threatening. Perhaps differences in parental views regarding the school soon would have come to the surface anyway. At any rate, they exploded at a community meeting where some strong charges were leveled against members of the staff and particularly the principal. These tended to bring together teachers and principal in a defensive posture. A semiconfidential survey report by an outside consultant, approved by the superintendent and paid for by the project donors, recommended transfer of the principal and transfer or dismissal of most of the teachers, partly on the grounds that existing school-community tensions could not now be readily separated from individual personalities. Subsequent discussion among the several parties most directly involved produced the suggestion that I be brought in as continuing advisor.

The project was appealing, mostly because so much was wrong. But, there was at least as much chance of success as of failure. I asked for and got a relatively free hand but with clear understanding of my various responsibilities to the district, the school and community, and the donors.

The staff and I went to work together, my bimonthly visits serving primarily to initiate staff dialogue about school problems. Teacher distrust of certain community elements and individuals was high. Considerable tension surrounded meetings with the community, the teachers arriving self-protectively en masse. It became clear that more relaxed school-community relations were basic to any widespread attack on school problems.

At the end of that first year, the principal was promoted to a supervisory post. The new principal was picked for skill in human relations more than for pedagogical or supervisory skills in elementary schooling. She set for herself two priorities: to become acquainted on a person-to-person level with parents and others in the community and to address vexing school problems cutting across individual teachers and classrooms. The former was accomplished primarily through personally picking up the school's mail, an act providing an hour or two of casual conversation at the post office over what was for most people in the community the major event of the day. The second proved to be a long-term enterprise only well begun by the time another principal arrived two years later.

Work on the second set of problems revealed profound diffi- culties in creating and maintaining a process of staff decision making. Teachers simply are not accustomed to working together in this way. Their span of control encompasses little more than the management and instructional problems of coping with thirty or more children in a classroom. School problems, if considered at all, are for the principal and are merely something one gripes about. Getting these, too, within each teacher's span of conceptual and functioning control presents formidable difficulties.

Chaos on the playground was of more than passing concern, however, and clearly required group action if anything was to be done about it. Likewise, the influx of dozens of new pupils for the winter months was beyond the control of individual teachers who experi- enced temporary increases in class size of 50 percent or more. Further, the school had an unusually large number of children with special learning and behavior problems, perhaps because of their itinerant lives, perhaps because of nutritional deficiencies. These were problems of con- cern to all that could be resolved only by decisions and actions of all, including the small nucleus of parents soon attracted to a study group focused on human development, individual differences, and the like. The study group provided a nonthreatening opportunity for the teach- ers, too, to become familiar with data and concepts which they should have known but did not.

Rapid growth in pupil population—regular and temporary— confounded the neat one-teacher-per-grade pattern of organization which had prevailed for years and with which the school had stabilized for a time. More and more, the teachers had to cope with classes made up of more than one grade and with classes growing rapidly in size from December to March (class sizes of fifty pupils by mid-February were not uncommon). The teachers experimented over a period of years with multigrade, then multiage, and finally nongraded plans to deal with the first problem, and with "surplusing" a teacher to work with a nongraded class of widely varying ages which grew in size and then declined after winter months. This procedure left most other classes stable in size. But, soon, the school outgrew this device and a variety of team-teaching possibilities emerged as solutions. By 1958, the staff had developed a relatively sophisticated nongraded, team-taught school.[26]

As already indicated, the staff processes were not easy. Even the idea of meeting regularly together was foreign and the necessary skills of problem identification, seeking alternative solutions, arriving at some working consensus, and then taking action were lacking. The third principal saw this set of problems as crucial and set out to be introspective regarding it.[27] Continuous monitoring revealed that pinpointing the problem in a memo and engaging in some preliminary analysis of possible approaches focused discussion and resulted in productive, more satisfying meetings. The ordering of items on the agenda also was important; if trivia were placed at the beginning, it was easy to postpone more difficult, important issues. Soon a bulletin was used to take care of announcements and a cycle of meetings was employed to assure attention to both long-term problems and more immediate concerns.

It became clear that faculty meetings must be taken very seriously and planned carefully or they would quickly deteriorate into gripe or social sessions, with dialogue lacking in depth, scope, and significance. It was important to close each session with a short summary of areas of agreement and disagreement, suggested items for the next meeting, staff work to be done, and, frequently, specific jobs for a small task force. Subsequently, this summary was distributed in writing. A preplanning, postplanning cycle emerged, with in-between activities. Firm timetables and meeting schedules were established; attendance at and participation in these staff processes became a value internalized in the school's socialization processes. The school became increasingly responsive to its problems and to the need for and availability of resources to deal with them.

This responsiveness increasingly turned the staff outward from what had been a defensively introverted posture. Efforts were made to involve citizens meaningfully, and school-community activities ranged from picnics and socials to provisions for a family crafts program and a local library created cooperatively and integrated with the school's instructional program. Although isolated from other schools at the outset and openly criticized during beginning years of innovation, Englewood School personnel increasingly participated in countywide activities. By 1960, the impact of the school's program on other schools was clearly evident, and it, in turn, began to benefit from a spirit of change pervading the county. Its principal was elected president of the newly formed Elementary School Principals' Association. There is little point in endeavoring to ferret out what caused what; the interrelationships are too complex. Suffice it to say that the Englewood School had become a place to visit, even though accessibility was difficult, during the rash of visitation accompanying the Schooling Decade. Sarasota County was a rather exciting place to be an educator.

The University Elementary School

In 1960, I became director of the University Elementary School (UES) at UCLA. Although enjoying a considerable reputation as a showplace for supposed progressive education practices and known for its relatively well-trained teaching staff, many elements of the situation were not unlike those found initially at Englewood. The retirement, several years before, of a strong principal had precipitated cleavages in the parent body and much criticism of the school. Teachers were on the defensive; some had entered into alignments with parent factions. Happenings and rumored happenings within the school were on the telephone grapevine almost at the moment of creation. There was little sense of direction to be found anywhere within the school but considerable devotion to past greatness and to whatever anyone chose to associate with that past. Myths can be formidable obstacles to change, especially because the perceptions involved are so immune to scrutiny.

At our first staff meeting together, the teachers sat at alert, pencils poised, ready to write down whatever I said, whether or not it made any sense. They particularly wanted to hear about nongrading (my book on nongrading written with Robert Anderson had been published for a little more than a year).[28] Launching into the concepts and rationale was a temptation for all of us; we might easily have put off for a few years any serious attack on problems capable of destroying the school and we might have avoided developing any processes of real staff responsibility for and involvement in decision making. But we resisted the temptation and put aside both the pencils and nongrading—although we got around to serious implementation of the latter about two years later.

The cycle of reform was not unlike that initiated and refined at Englewood over the preceding five years. It included parental involvement in evening sessions on extant data on child development and learning together with analyses of traditional school regularities and emerging recommendations for reform.[29] No effort was made to secure parent agreement on or approval of a course of action. Emphasis was on developing a common body of understandings and the realization that there existed a staff responsibility to come up with better ways of arranging and conducting the school environment for living and learning.

We went through all aspects of staff development: initiating, refining, and regularizing total and small group processes; analyzing problems such as pupil variability, playground behavior, and the like; launching trial-and-error approaches; looking outside for relevant solutions; sharing experiences with parents; analyzing instructional processes. It was Englewood revisited but in a more complex setting—especially since UES carries functions of research, innovation, teacher education, and dissemination in addition to teaching functions—and had both the Englewood experience and a much richer array of resources to draw from. But, in many ways, it is more difficult to reconstruct a school with a distinguished reputation.[30] After all, why tinker with what already has worked? The trouble was that UES was a great school of the 1930s and 1940s, now woefully inadequate in the light of knowledge and opportunities of the 1960s.

It was a very exciting time to direct a laboratory school, especially on the campus of one of the fastest developing universities in the country. We struggled with fascinating problems; we traveled down many roads; we innovated quite a bit.[31] By 1963, thousands of people were visiting us each year. Early in the decade, they were skeptical, sometimes hostile. Later, they expressed both great interest and frustration over not being able to do much "back home." There was nobody to talk with seriously about what they had seen. "My principal won't understand," said teachers; "My superintendent wouldn't let me," said principals. There was a curious sense of impotence, of futility, on their part, in regard to doing what we were doing. Why? I wondered.

As we talked with our visitors, we became increasingly aware of a considerable gap between us. We took for granted so much that they perceived to be beyond attainment. Many simply departed with the almost angry statement that they could never do what we were doing. Those who stayed to talk inquired into the smallest detail of our operation and were frequently awed by our familiarity with the literature and our willingness to try, even in areas of little staff experience. By the mid-sixties, it was apparent that our effectiveness as agents for change necessitated gaining a better understanding of the settings from which many of our visitors came and the perspective from which they viewed their own schools and schooling generally.

Behind the Classroom Door

As described so far, the working hypothesis arose mainly from my own observations and experiences and was based in the theoretical-deductive mode. However, at much the same time, I was strengthening the hypothesis through work in the empirical-inductive mode. For example, during the first half of the 1960s, I had the good fortune to be associated with James B. Conant in his study of the education of teachers[32] and to conduct two studies of national curriculum reform projects.[33] In the course of these, I visited a good many schools across the country. Gradually at first and then at an accelerating pace, I became aware of a formidable discrepancy between the post-Sputnik rhetoric of school reform and the actuality of practice in schools and classrooms. My curiosity was whetted once again. It was not merely the fact of the gap between rhetoric and reality. Rather, it was, on one hand, the question of why concepts developed in curriculum projects and R&D centers were transformed or lost so completely in passage to classrooms and, on the other, the question of why teachers felt so helpless, so lacking in direction and confidence, even in the face of their own desire to adopt innovations or otherwise to change, a query growing largely out of conversations with visitors to UES.

My curiosity led to three rather comprehensive studies of the phenomena of schooling. Two were initiated in the mid-1960s. One of these was a study of what was going on in the first four grades of sixty-seven elementary schools in fourteen population centers in the United States.[34] The second was much more complex and involved a five-year study of educational change and school improvement in eighteen schools in Southern California.[35] The third set of studies surveyed practice in preschools in England, Israel, and eight countries of Asia and described the ongoing activities of 201 nursery schools in nine cities in the United States.[36] The results provided some insights into the institutions we call schools and strengthened in my mind the emerging hypothesis regarding their key role in educational reform.

Although the first of these studies emerged out of my growing curiosity about the seeming difficulty of inserting reforms into the daily functioning of schools, the more tangible, specific purpose was to gain some better insight into the settings from which our visitors to UES frequently came. Although we employed techniques common to field studies (such as agreeing on categories for the observation of classrooms and classification of data, training observers to a point of relatively high-level agreement, and the like), we did not have in mind a formal research study to be transmitted to others. However, the apparent significance of our tentative findings increasingly warranted the preparation of a report for broader consumption.

Since the results of this look behind the classroom door have been in print since 1970, I shall skim over the findings. The observations of trained observers in classes of the sixty-seven schools were put up against a value screen comprising reasonable expectations for schooling in this country. These expectations were derived from some of those most commonly heard and defended admonitions to schools: individualize instruction, use a variety of pedagogical techniques and a wide array of instructional materials, evaluate before and after teaching, employ principles of learning such as transfer of training and reinforcement, and so on.

Our general finding was that there was a considerable gap between these expectations and what was going on. Practice did not nearly match the rhetoric for change; the list of expectations appeared not reasonable. Most classrooms and teachers were generally supportive of children and certainly not inhumane in any physically punitive sense. But they were not exciting and the content of instruction appeared to us not to warrant even the amount of involvement generously displayed by the pupils.

But this gap between the rhetoric of reform in American schooling and reality as we perceived it was not our most important finding. What bothered us most was the apparent absence of processes by means of which the schools and the people in them might have some reasonable prospect for self-renewal. With the possible exception of four schools among the sixty-seven, they simply did not contain groups of responsible parties diligently at work on the problems teachers and principals said they faced. And there was not in any school, so far as we could see, a critical mass of people—principal, teachers, parents, children—committed to continuous analysis of what their school was for and what should be done to make it a better place of study and work today, next week, and in the years to come.

The study of 201 nursery schools referred to earlier was conducted simultaneously with the study of change briefly described below and recounted in considerable detail in later chapters. The nursery school study substantiated at the beginning level of schooling many of the findings summarized on preceding pages. Once again, there appeared not to be in these schools groups of faculty members continuously engaged in questioning what they were trying to do and how well they were doing it. We found practically nothing to suggest that nursery school personnel are engaged in a dialogue about such things as early childhood development, functions of early schooling, how to match functions and activities, or, for that matter, anything else of an intellectual nature likely to lead to self-criticism and institutional improvement.

Although the hypothesis regarding the school's centrality in educational reform had been formed initially in my mind out of personal experience and my confidence in it limited accordingly, these empirical studies strengthened it considerably. The question emerging was whether the school could become a potent force for its own improvement, given the growing body of evidence regarding its neglect as a social system capable of self-renewal under certain circumstances. This question and further exploration of the hypothesis absorbed our attention from 1966 into the 1970s.

TESTING THE WORKING IDEA

So far, this chapter has sought to describe both the substance of a working idea or hypothesis and the process through which it took shape and matured: the interplay between the theoretical-deductive and the empirical-inductive modes of thought and the identification of the idea's significance both in the practical business of school keeping and for educational research. By 1966, the idea was virtually a principle in my mind and was accompanied by the conviction Conant claims is necessary for subsequent testing. We were already looking behind classroom doors in sixty-seven schools, as described above. Back at UES, many visitors were asking for help in their own schools. It was common for a principal and several teachers from nearby school districts to visit and to seek our counsel. It seemed to me that to become simply a consulting resource would be limited usefulness and might well deplete our ability to cope successfully with never-ending challenges at home. Querying selected clusters of visitors led to the conclusion that they might be interested in some cooperative venture in school-to-school sharing. A planning grant from the Kettering Foundation then enabled me to put some thoughts together regarding the elements of a change strategy involving at its core a consortium of schools.

It is much easier in retrospect to trace the genesis of this strategy through the AATES, the Englewood Project, research and analysis leading to the nongraded concept, the University Elementary School, experiences with Conant, and other enterprises in the Schooling Decade. Little of this fell together neatly in my mind in the mid-1960s. I was too close to it all. But the hypothesis and the conviction were there, as unpublished memos, several to the staff of the Research Division of |I|D|E|A|, reveal.[37] They are reflected particularly in a report prepared for the California State Committee on Public Education during 1966–67.[38] There was not in 1966, either, any clear intent on my part to engage deliberately in empirically testing the working hypothesis. It was for me, rather, an hypothesis to be put to work through direct intervention in schools.

The Kettering Foundation provided that intervention opportunity and, subsequently and fortuitously, a chance to study the hypothesis about schools and change. The Foundation created |I|D|E|A| to be a force for effecting productive change in education. Early on, the two vice presidents responsible for its creation saw the need for some research-based activity focused on change and innovation. Arrangements for my involvement as director of the Los Angeles–based Research Division brought UCLA and the Kettering Foundation into some informal cooperative agreements and some sharing of a network of schools which had been brought into being, thanks to the aforementioned grant from the Kettering Foundation and moral support from the then-dean of UCLA's Graduate School of Education, Howard E. Wilson.[39] This network was named the League of Cooperating Schools.

The League itself was in large part a strategy comprising several essential elements of the hypothesis described earlier in embryonic and gradually emerging form over a period of at least ten years. The concept of the single school as both a focal point for and a primary agency in charge was central, as was that of the principal's key role. Both of these had been sketched in the 1955 paper referred to earlier. The concept of small group and total staff processes likewise was seen as important, although this was more developmental over time than precise at the beginning. The importance of this comes through particularly in descriptions of the Englewood Project and the UES staff processes.

The notion of a consortium was viewed initially as an opportunity to exchange ideas, for schools to learn from one another by trying different things and passing along the results of these experiences. The full power of this concept came to be realized only in subsequent years, as did the power of certain other elements both built in from the beginning—not necessarily with clear foresight—and developed during the maturation of the project. The sharpening of a research purpose and design also came later. The umbrella for the entire project, involving intervention and development of a change strategy together with research on this strategy and feedback of research findings into the strategy itself, became known as the Study of Educational Change and School Improvement (happily and conveniently—SECSI).

The next three chapters describe and analyze certain aspects of SECSI. An effort is made to avoid duplicating other reports on our work, while still providing some repetitive information in order to give cohesion to the points made here. The reader is urged to consult these other volumes to round out the picture as necessary. The attempt here, somewhat different from the other volumes, is to place SECSI within the context of a more general analysis of educational change, beginning in the 1950s and projecting into the late 1970s and 1980s.

NOTES

1 James B. Conant, *Two Modes of Thought*, Trident Press, New York, 1964. This little-known work was written on invitation for a series designed to ferret out the credo guiding significant, influential persons. Conant's career is of particular interest here since it combines high-level scholarly work (as a chemist) with the arena of practical affairs. Actually, Conant's life has embraced four careers: scholar, university president (Harvard), U.S. High Commissioner (Germany), and precollegiate educational critic and reformer.

2 Ibid., p. 31.

3 Ibid., p. 30.

4 John Dewey, *The Sources of a Science of Education*, Horace Liveright, New York, 1929, pp. 54–55.

5 Ibid., p. 26–27, 33.

6 Presidential address delivered to the American Educational Research Association, Feb. 8, 1968, and subsequently published. See John I. Goodlad, "Thought, Invention and Research in the Advancement of Education," *Educational Forum*, vol. 33, no. 1, pp. 7–18, November 1968.

7   W. W. Charters, Jr., and John E. Jones, "On the Risk of Appraising Non-Events in Program Evaluation," *Educational Researcher*, vol. 2, p. 5–7, November 1973.

8   The experiences of the Ford Foundation in this regard are reported in *A Foundation Goes to School: The Ford Foundation Comprehensive School Improvement Program*, The Ford Foundation, New York, 1972.

9   Joseph J. Schwab, "The Structure of the Natural Sciences," in G. W. Ford and Lawrence Pugno (eds.), *The Structure of Knowledge and the Curriculum*, Rand McNally, Chicago, 1964, pp. 31–39.

10   After attempting several alternative approaches to what follows, I concluded that the form of a personal odyssey best suited the purposes already stated. Afterward, I become once again the spectator of Chapter 2, whereas Chapter 3 is devoted to my role as an actor in many of the events already described more dispassionately in the former. The personal role included authorship of several books and many papers on educational change and innovation, active promotion of certain reforms, staff member with James B. Conant in his study of the education of American teachers, participant in and writer of a volume for the Project on Instruction of the National Education Association, participant in and critic of the curriculum reform movement, consultant to various foundations and federal bodies, service on two Presidential panels, participant in the 1965 White House Conference on Education, chairman of the committee leading to the creation of the National Laboratory on Early Childhood Education, as well as a leadership role in the several activities subsequently described in this chapter.

11   Conant, op. cit., p. 95.

12   For a description of the genesis and early structure of this unique organization, see John I. Goodlad and Floyd Jordan, "When School and College Cooperate," *Educational Leadership*, vol. 7, pp. 461–465, April 1950.

13   Seymour B. Sarason, *The Culture of the School and the Problem of Change*, Allyn and Bacon, Boston, 1971.

14   Prescott's early formulation of the substantive elements in coming to understand children appears in a book he wrote which was not clearly identified as authored by him: *Helping Teachers Understand Children*, American Council on Education, Commission on Teacher Education, Washington, D.C., 1945. The structure of his Child Study Program was laid out a dozen years later in chap. 13 of Daniel A. Prescott, *The Child in the Educative Process*, McGraw-Hill, New York, 1957.

15 Early years of the Prescott Child Study Program paralleled in time the ascent of what often has been referred to as the Group Dynamics Movement, a forerunner of modern sensitivity training, "T" groups, and the like. The former employed techniques of group leadership, management, and analysis developed to high degree in the latter movements. For a background discussion of terms and concepts, see Dorwin Cartwright and Alvin Zander (eds.), *Group Dynamics: Research and Theory*, 3d ed., Harper & Row, New York, 1968.

16 Jesse W. Lilienthal III and Caroline Tryon, "Developmental Tasks: II. Discussion of Specific Tasks and Implications," *Fostering Mental Health in Our Schools*, 1950 Yearbook, National Education Association, Association for Supervision and Curriculum Development, Washington, D.C., 1950.

17 Also, the late Virgil Herrick drew attention to the conceptual problem of moving from a relatively detailed, comprehensive framework for studying children to developing reasonably clear implications for the organized chaos of schooling. Categories for analysis simply do not fit; bridges are not easily built. The problems on which he was beginning to make some progress remain almost as little studied and unclarified as they were at the time of his death in 1963. See particularly chaps. 7 and 11 of Dan W. Anderson, James B. Macdonald, and Frank B. May, comps., *Strategies of Curriculum Development: The Works of Virgil E. Herrick*, Charles E. Merrill Books, Columbus, Ohio, 1965.

18 As an illustration of how bits of research coalesce into theories and how certain practices seemingly come to parallel relatively long-term theories, Getzels presents the example of four school buildings within walking distance of the University of Chicago. Clearly, he says, each of four quite different physical entities represents differences in intent prevailing at a given period of time. Hence, what happens over a decade or a generation appears markedly uniform but, in the perspective of a longer period, reflects changes in thought and perspective occurring over time. Such analyses are needed in seeking to throw greater light on elements of the change process, particularly the interplay between theory and practice. See J. W. Getzels, "Images on the Classroom and Visions of the Learners," *School Review*, vol. 82, no. 4, pp. 527–540, August 1974.

19 Philip W. Jackson and Egon Guba, "The Needed Structure of In-Service Teachers: An Occupational Analysis," *School Review*, vol. 65, pp. 176–192, June 1955.

20 Garth A. Sorenson, *Toward an Instructional Model for Counseling,*

University of California, Los Angeles, 1967 (Center for the Study of Evaluation Report no. 41).

21 Dewey, op. cit., p. 34.

22 Throughout much of the preparation for and the actual writing of this book, I was negotiating with most of the major philanthropic foundations of the United States, seeking funding for a large-scale analysis of schooling. This was a most revealing, exhausting experience. Many foundation officials expressed skepticism over our assertion that comprehensive data on the functioning of schools do not exist. There are, however, but scattered bits of information. Interestingly, many officials, in agreeing that comprehensive information does not exist, saw no need of it, maintaining that what is needed is action—now. Some, in writing and speaking, made eloquent statements regarding the need for holistic rather than piecemeal reform. But just how one proceeds to the holistic reform of our educational institutions without a reasonably comprehensive grasp of their holistic functioning lies beyond my comprehension! Fortunately, a sufficient number of foundation staffs were patient enough to bear with us and trusting enough to provide the necessary funds for a detailed study of some seventy-two schools in twelve states now in process. Recommendations and strategies for reconstructing the schools and for alternative modes of educating the young should be available in 1978 and 1979. Final reports will endeavor to set directions for precollegiate education for the concluding decades of this century.

23 Joyce envisions a nucleus of responsible parties in each school, a group which continuously examines the school's current operation in the light of the kind of setting it should seek to become. See Bruce R. Joyce, *Alternative Models of Elementary Education*, Blaisdell Publishing Company, Waltham, Mass., 1969.

24 John I. Goodlad, "The Individual School and Its Principal: Key Setting and Key Person in Educational Change," *Educational Leadership*, vol. 13, pp. 2–6, October 1955.

25 The William H. Vanderbilt family had established a residence on a nearby key and was beginning to develop ranching and real estate interests. They wanted to provide the best possible public school education for their elementary-school-age son and other children in the community. Consequently, they offered an annual subvention over a period of years for purposes of upgrading the Englewood School.

26 Elsewhere, I have described the trial-and-error, discuss-and-evaluate, staff processes of moving over several successive years to an

increasingly sophisticated set of guiding concepts and both struc-
tural and instructional practices to match. See John I. Goodlad, "In
Pursuit of Visions," *Elementary School Journal,* vol. 59 pp. 1–17,
October 1958.

27   His interest in this fascinating array of human problems led to a
doctoral dissertation: John M. Bahmer, "An Analysis of an Elementary School Faculty at Work," unpublished doctoral dissertation,
University of Chicago, 1960. No doubt, also, this powerful experience in working problems through with a total staff influenced
Bahner's efforts, years later, to create a program whereby school
staffs might get assistance for internal processes directed toward
meeting individual differences and developing instructional pro-
grams in creative ways. This is the |I|D|E|A| Change Program for
Individually Guided Education (IGE).

28   John I. Goodlad and Robert H. Anderson, *The Nongraded Elementary School,* Harcourt Brace Jovanovich, New York, 1959; rev. ed.
1963.

29   In 1958, on learning of the Englewood Project, a distinguished
sociologist at the University of Chicago expressed the view that the
innovations involved were easier to bring off in that setting than in
one where parents were highly educated and relatively sophisticated
in educational matters. While there is some truth to this statement,
my experience in both kinds of settings suggests that the problems
differ more in degree than in kind. The former group moved more
slowly and laboriously through the concepts and probably accepted
them more out of faith in the people responsible than out of
understanding. The latter group challenged continuously, watched
intently for conceptional loopholes, and became ardent supporters,
once convinced intellectually. It was clear that the prestige of the
University of California provided a stamp of approval. And trust in
the individuals involved was for them, too, an important—although
insufficient—factor.

30   The past constitutes a formidable presence in any effort to effect
change, particularly when that past was distinguished. Often, present
images of that past far outdistance any reasonable approximation of
what actually went on. This phenomenon continued for years,
plaguing the lives of new superintendents long after the distinguished era of the Winnetka schools under Superintendent Washburne, for example. See Carleton W. Washburne and Sidney B.
Marland, *Winnetka: The History and Significance of an Educational
Experiment,* Prentice-Hall, Englewood Cliffs, N.J., 1963.

31   The school emerging during the first half of the sixties is described

in John I. Goodlad, "Meeting Children where They Are," *Saturday Review*, Mar. 20, 1965, pp. 57–59, 72–74.

32 James B. Conant, *The Education of American Teachers*, McGraw-Hill, New York, 1963.

33 John I. Goodlad, *School Curriculum Reform in the United States*, Fund for the Advancement of Education, New York, 1964; and Goodlad, Renata von Stoephasius, and M. Frances Klein, *The Changing School Curriculum*, Fund for the Advancement of Education, New York, 1966.

34 John I. Goodlad, M. Frances Klein, and Associates, *Behind the Classroom Door*, Charles A. Jones, Worthington, Ohio, 1970; a rev. ed., 1974, entitled *Looking Behind the Classroom Door*, reflects some of the findings on educational change reported later in this volume and in other volumes of the series listed in note 35.

35 Reports on this work include, in addition to the present volume, the following: Carmen M. Culver and Gary J. Hoban (eds.), *The Power to Change: Issues for the Innovative Educator*, McGraw-Hill, New York, 1973; David A. Shiman, Carmen M. Culver, and Ann Lieberman (eds.), *Teachers on Individualization: The Way We Do It*, McGraw-Hill, New York, 1974; Richard C. Williams, Charles C. Wall, W. Michael Martin, and Arthur Berchin, *Effecting Organizational Renewal in Schools: A Social Systems Perspective*, McGraw-Hill, New York, 1974; Kenneth A. Tye and Jerrold M. Novotney, *Schools in Transition: The Practitioner as Change Agent*, McGraw-Hill, New York, 1975; Mary M. Bentzen and Associates, *Changing Schools: The Magic Feather Principle*, McGraw-Hill, New York, 1974.

36 John I. Goodlad, M. Frances Klein, Jerrold M. Novotney, and Associate, *Early Schooling in the United States*, McGraw-Hill, New York, 1973; Norma D. Feshbach, John I. Goodlad, and Avima Lombard, *Early Schooling in England and Israel*, McGraw-Hill, New York, 1973; and Ruth Bettelheim and Ruby Takanishi, *Early Schooling in Asia*, McGraw-Hill, New York, forthcoming.

37 The Archives of the Research Division of |I|D|E|A| include thousands of pages of primary source material, much of it in the form of letters, memos, mimeographed working documents, and the like, which reveal initial formulations and subsequent development of the change strategy which ultimately emerged.

38 John I. Goodlad and Associates, *Project III: Instruction*, State (California) Committee on Public Instruction, 1967. (Mimeographed.)

39 There was no formal agreement for cooperation between the two institutions. The linkage was to be provided primarily by my joint appointment worked out in an exchange of letters between the

Vice-Chancellor of UCLA and a vice president of the Kettering Foundation. For several years, the latter institution provided funds directly to UCLA for certain operating costs. Many UCLA graduate students, mostly in education but also in fields such as sociology, political science, economics, psychology, and business administration, were employed as research assistants. Many of these students, in turn, studied aspects of the work for their doctoral dissertations (see Appendix A).

CHAPTER 4

THE LEAGUE
OF COOPERATING SCHOOLS:
THE FIRST TWO YEARS

If a fraction of the money that is currently being spent to change educational practice were spent to find out how to succeed in making such change, a great deal would thereby be saved. Few things would be of greater significance for education today than for a group of behavioral scientists to work with a group of practitioners in an effort to change significant aspects of the educational system. ... Until we know far more than we know now, it is likely that we shall continue to waste many hours of time and countless millions of dollars in abortive efforts to modify educational practice.

—B. Othanel Smith ("The Anatomy of Change," *The Nature of Change*, National Association of Secondary School Principals, Washington, D.C., 1963, pp. 9–10)

Chapter 3 attempted to trace the genesis and maturation of a working hypothesis pertaining to the school as locus of and agent for improving educational practice. This chapter describes the initiation and development of a strategy designed both to implement and test this hypothesis. The real-life laboratory was a consortium of eighteen elementary schools in eighteen districts in southern California, the League of Cooperating Schools.

My initial formulation of this type hypothesis (1955) was that the single school with its principal, teachers, pupils, parents, and community links is the key unit for educational change. Subsequent thought and experience teased out three subhypotheses. First, the school is a social system with regularized ways of behaving by those who inhabit it: certain expected activities, patterns of rewards, and the like. Second, no matter what the approach to change, it must reckon ultimately with the functioning reality of this social system. Third, the school itself is an agent for change, potentially or actually.

Chapter 3 revealed that thought, experience, and surveys of educational practice not only strengthened the working hypothesis and these major components but also added and strengthened an array of corollary elements, such as the importance of the principal as inhibitor or promoter of change and of staff processes. A host of fascinating questions was raised about initiating change, limits to self-directed change, the role of external agents, the effects of school district rules and regulations, and relations to external administrative and supervisory personnel. While any change strategy need not necessarily encompass all these components in its design, there is no way of escaping them in its functioning; its success will be dependent in part on the ratio of assets to liabilities for coping with such realities.

The assets-to-liabilities credentials of the local school in the way it has operated as an agent for overcoming restraints in the surrounding district are not impressive. Guba's words give one pause, "Generally speaking, the bureaucratic structure of existing agencies will not allow for the factors of high risk-taking, sanctioned freedom to fail, and delayed gratification which will be required to attack meaningfully the conceptual, personnel, and organizational impediments to effective planned change in education."[1] The League, partly by design and partly fortuitously, was intended to secure leverage for change through combining inside and outside resources into a unique amalgam of old and new institutions.

THE LEAGUE: CONCEPTION AND BIRTH

The ideas governing the League of Cooperating Schools were not all neatly laid out at the beginning; those sketched so far were vastly expanded and enriched subsequently by the staff members in research and development who came to work with them. Other ideas were added. It was only after about two years of working with the strategy that we were in a position to sort out, strengthen, and study in some detail what appeared to be the most promising, powerful ideas.

Chapter 3 described the many requests for help which we received from visitors to the University Elementary School, requests which led to the notion that we might establish a family of schools which could work together on common problems of improvement. It will be recalled, also, that the Kettering Foundation had provided me with a grant in 1965 for purposes of sharpening some embryonic ideas about change and bringing them to a stage of readiness for implementation in practice. The League was a direct product of that grant, embodying at the outset many of the ideas developed to that time.

Twenty-five superintendents of districts in southern California were invited to a meeting to explore this idea in April 1965. If interested, each was to indicate by subsequent letter willingness to designate one school as a member of such a collaboration and suggest any necessary conditions of participating. Through correspondence and visits to school districts, a rather general agreement was approved by eighteen superintendents, sometimes following meetings with their boards (Appendix B is the document prepared to explain the League and propose conditions of participation). Then followed a fascinating set of written and personal communications for purposes of selecting the schools.

My colleagues and I had decided initially that there should be only one school from each district and that about a dozen schools could provide a sample of considerable diversity, both as to schools and as to comparative restraints in each district. We wanted the League to represent schools of mixed pupil population, size, socioeconomic status of parents, age and experience of teachers, and variety of problems. Final selection was left to the superintendents. After the first six or seven schools had been selected, however, it became increasingly necessary for us to negotiate to assure that each additional school would add to rather than detract from variability in the sample.

The process of selection at the district level was suggestive of considerable variability in restraints and in working relations between superintendents and local schools, strengthening in our minds the desirability of having only one school per district in order to create the possibility of there being as many different patterns as there were schools in the sample.

In one instance, for example, the superintendent invited me to explain the project in its embryonic form to his principals, with whom he met for coffee, rolls, and discussion at 7:30 most Monday mornings. Presumably, considerable discussion ensued after my departure; he called several days later to convey his decision. In another district, I was invited to meet with the superintendent and his immediate associates—no principals. They made the decision following my departure and announced it in a news release. Not only did we learn of the decision in the morning paper, but so did the principal and teachers of the selected school. One needs no great imagination to conjure up rather precisely the reactions of this school staff. Though this school ultimately became one of the most productive in the League, nearly two years passed before the school's staff members were over the hostility and resentment to the superintendent's action, a good deal of which washed over us. After selecting his school, another superintendent gave a pep talk in which he spoke glowingly of the opportunity to innovate and told the principal, "Change anything you want." Then he added, "But don't rock the boat."

We began, then, with a mixed set of expectations and restraints. As will be seen from Appendix B, district concessions were minimal: willingness to free the school from certain unspecified districtwide requirements, to release the principal one day a month for League business, to free a little staff time (no concession, really, since the California code already provides for a minimum day, releasing children by 2 P.M. to facilitate staff meetings), to provide a little secretarial help, and so on. We made no effort to involve superintendents closely with the project, although we hoped they would involve themselves. Each identified a liaison person—in a few instances, himself.

Likewise, we promised little other than to encourage school improvement and to encourage exchange of ideas and projects. There was to be no direct financial contribution, although we expressed willingness to help schools write grant proposals. Nor was there to be any consulting help in the usual "expert" sense, although we again expressed willingness to help schools find and use such persons at district expense. The one thing of considerable importance we did assure was to hang in there with the schools for a three-year period or longer, given continuing mutual interest (see Appendix C for the agreement renewing the League for an additional two years).

The quid pro quo was that we, on one hand, would lend unspecified support and encouragement to the schools in their efforts toward self-improvement and, on the other, that the schools would provide an open laboratory for our study—not yet defined—of the process of change. We promised to feed back to the schools any data they thought might be useful; the schools (through their superintendents) promised to make their accomplishments available to each other and to a broader array of interested persons and schools. The structure and conditions envisioned and, to a degree, established at the outset approximated Smith's notion of a group of behavioral scientists working with a group of practitioners in an effort to change significant aspects of the educational system, in this instance, the schools.[2] Admittedly, the behavioral scientists were made up almost exclusively of re-treaded practitioners.

The League, as finally constituted, consisted of eighteen schools scattered within an elongated ellipse bounded roughly by the Pacific Ocean on the west and the San Bernardino Mountains on the east, reaching from north of Santa Barbara south to San Diego. The schools were selected in an attempt to provide as much diversity as possible in general characteristics and in an administrative-organizational context. One district in the League enrolled 1,232 pupils, another 662,565. The pupil population of the smallest school was 250, the largest 1,300. One school was built in 1925, another was still in the planning stages. Almost 80 percent of the pupils in one school were of Mexican-American descent; in another, 27 percent were black, 13 percent Oriental, and 23 percent Mexican-American, Cuban, and Puerto Rican. One faculty was made up almost entirely of individuals with little or no previous experience and an average age in the early twenties; a second had eight new teachers out of thirteen; in a third, eight of twenty-three had been members of the original staff brought together in the 1950s.[3] Teachers across the United States might readily identify their own situation with at least one of these schools.

ESTABLISHING THE RESEARCH ORGANIZATION

During the time that negotiations for establishing the League were taking place and League schools were being selected, the |I|D|E|A| Research Division consisted of only an office manager and three part-time people, including myself. As the League began, we had to divide our attention between nourishing the new organization of schools and establishing a new organization of researchers. We had offices to equip, jobs to fill, procedures to establish. I found myself, for example, approving the purchase of supplies at one moment and struggling in the next with what was or what was not an appropriate involvement with the schools. Too many people had to be absorbed too quickly into a new organization lacking established routines; there were neither "old-timers" nor institutional regularities to socialize the newcomers. An old-timer in our shop was someone who had come aboard the previous week![4]

The newness and obvious challenges in our situation created great expectations. Most members of the staff saw in it a chance to escape what appeared to have been shackling in previous work settings.

Highly individualized expectations were not discouraged—in fact, they were reinforced, whenever any of us had time to reinforce anyone else. But these expectations ultimately had to be molded into some reasonably harmonious, goal-directed unity; whe had a job to do.[5] The process was painful for all of us, excruciatingly so for some. My senior associate and I remember very clearly establishing one institutional expectation by moving chairs from one room to another when several graduate assistant/spectators saw this as inappropriate work for one aspiring to a doctorate!

The year was an exceedingly difficult one for anyone who had become seriously involved in the League or touched by it in any significant way—and this meant all our staff. Certain exigencies of life came perilously close to destroying us and the project completely. The staff of the |I|D|E|A| Research Division had scarcely moved into offices in the fall before rapidly changing signals from the head office in Dayton raised serious doubts about there being any future for the League. And, in December 1966, I became so seriously ill as to be completely out of the picture for three months, except for occasional short sessions with two senior associates, and on a sharply abbreviated work schedule for an additional three. Although the staff rose to this challenge remarkably and gratifyingly, we simply had not been together long enough to hammer out a conceptual framework from which individual roles and activities might readily have evolved. It is of particular credit to the staff that our associates in the schools, as we learned later, saw us as knowing what we were about and as having a certain serenity in and from that knowledge. Sometimes, it would appear, what one doesn't know serves some situations well.[6]

Conceptualizing the League: First Attempts

The conceptualizations guiding the League were based on a series of ideas which had been percolating in my mind since 1955. Here are some of them paraphrased from what I set down several months after the formal creation of the League:

1 The key unit for educational change is the individual school, with its principal, teachers, students, parents, and community setting. The basic ingredients for learning and teaching are here. Anything from elsewhere must find its way into the school or it will be impotent.

2 The principal is the designated, responsible leader of this unit. Individual teachers control only a segment of the school's ball game;

what they do not control can make the difference. To develop new programs, it is necessary to convince principals of their value.

3 The "systems" of which the school and its principal are a part exercise enormous constraints, constraints which are essentially conservative and which serve to discourage change and innovation. The systems are not only the formal, political ones of state and local education organizations; they are also informal, exerting subtle pressure by way of implicit and explicit expectations for schooling and for the behavior of teachers and administrators.

4 If change is to occur with reasonable speed, then the existence or creation of a countercyclical or redirecting system of considerable salience may be critical.

5 The new directions posed by the countervailing system inevitably will call for new behaviors on the part of those for whom this system is salient.

6 Threat and insecurity for these individuals and for others in the traditionally oriented system are bound to result.

7 If the threat and insecurity are great—and they are almost bound to be substantial if the changes in behavior called for are significant— then the salience of the countercyclical system (in the form of significant rewards, for example) must be insistent, persistent, and sustained over continued crises. The countervailing system must not be regarded as a temperamental, waxing, and waning, short-term arrangement.

8 But even a countercyclical system in time becomes harmonious with what it sought to change. Therefore, such a system must have built into it either self-terminating or unique self-renewing facilities.

9 The provocation to change must be accompanied or followed by access to the new knowledge and skills that are called for on the part of those who are to effect change.

10 Any significant change calls for access to both conceptual and operating models of the changed condition and to opportunities to learn whatever new behaviors are called for.[7]

Our first task was to reformulate these ideas so that they could provide us with some guidelines in our interactions with the League. We had to establish a research design and techniques for monitoring the whole. Early in the fall, with guidance from our field coordinator, graduate students began to forge a link between our office and the field on a school-by-school basis. Ignoring for a moment the fact that the eighteen schools constituted no neat geographical distribution, one might envision a hub and spokes of a wheel without a rim (see Figure 4.1).

Although a light circle connecting the schools might be drawn to suggest intended relationships, our early efforts were designed to strengthen the spokes. Progress toward this end was highly variable. Schools, like people, differ from one another, often in subtle ways.

THE LEAGUE'S FIRST YEAR

The complete set of agreements was signed, finally, late in the 1965–66 school year. For the schools there was time remaining for little more than the dawning realization of being in something called the League of Cooperating Schools with an organization named |I|D|E|A| and some kind of undefined relationship with UCLA. Our first activity was to call a meeting of the principals just before the end of the term and to schedule another for late summer, after vacations had ended.

These meetings themselves make good case material for analysis. The first did little more than provide information and an opportunity for learning each other's names and school affiliations, information forgotten by the second meeting. The principals had never before met each other; a few of us had met a few of them. They knew not what to expect and, clearly, were frustrated by our inability or perceived unwillingness to provide specifics. They went away more puzzled than enlightened, some no doubt saying the meeting was a waste of time.

The second meeting, a two-day retreat at a conference center in late summer, undoubtedly was even more frustrating. There was virtually no agenda. Much of what had been said at the earlier meeting was repeated in one way or another. The general purpose, enunciated many times, was to develop a kind of problem census growing out of

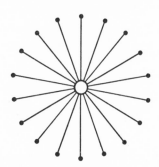

FIGURE 4.1

the principals' experiences with their particular schools. Little progress toward this purpose was made. Only two or three principals came close to defining a problem, real or imagined, but the problems identified had an artificial ring to them, as though formulated for an evening education class (and they were all experienced students in such classes) rather than representative of any gut-level concern. This was to be a continuing difficulty for at least two years. There were gripes about rules and regulations set by the state and school district as well as about teachers' limitations, especially in regard to change and innovation. Seldom did participants see themselves as part of the problem in any way. For the most part, principals saw themselves on one side and the teachers on the other; each had a job to do; there was little overlap or relationship between jobs, in their view.

There had been some expectation on our part that the work of the UCLA University Elementary School (UES) would provide both goals and models for change and, indeed, UES initially was the nineteenth school in the League, with its principal playing an active role. But one of the more vocal principals rejected this notion at the outset, saying that his school was going to innovate *de novo*. While others were less outgoing in this regard, clearly there was no great enthusiasm for what was seen as riding on the coattails of UES. UES was quietly dropped from the League after the first year.

One tangible accomplishment of this second meeting was the working out of a general agenda and operating structure for the coming year. The principals would meet together for approximately five hours on one Monday of each month and would hold at least one more two-day retreat during 1966–67. We were in the process of bringing aboard a dozen UCLA doctoral candidates—some attended this meeting—who would serve as resident fellows and research assistants. It was agreed that most of them would serve as liaison persons between our office and the schools, none to have more than two schools as his or her responsibility. Most were experienced educators but none was at the level of accomplishment and visibility normally looked for in the traditional concept of the consultant—and we endeavored to make clear that none was to perform in this role. Working through the principal, they would help the total staff find and develop an entry point for improvement and report back to us regarding progress, needs, and problems.

The principals left this second meeting visibly more frustrated and puzzled than they were on leaving the first. Two or three were angry, although firm evidence of this came out only later; they were playing the usual polite roles too carefully to reveal much of this so early in the game. Nearly all were perplexed and restive over the lack of a bill of particulars regarding our expectations, especially in regard to procedures with their own staffs. Further, there was disbelief—a measure of distrust—over our repeated insistence that what happened in the League was in large measure up to the participating schools. Ultimately, some were convinced, the missing agenda would appear and they would get down to doing what somebody else wanted; this almost always had been the case before. As one principal put it later, on film, "We sat around and waited for John Goodlad and his staff to tell us what they wanted done—just tell us and we'll do it. It didn't happen. Believe me, it didn't happen."[8]

Our anecdotal case materials reveal enormous differences in the way principals and teachers began—or did not begin—to work together. One observation in almost all the schools, however, was the absence of regular faculty meetings devoted seriously to substantive problems; some groups met rarely almost exclusively for announcements and for completing certain tasks required by the district office.[9] One simply cannot assume that ongoing staff processes devoted to the school's general welfare are built into the regularities of schooling in the United States.

Some principals literally were frightened at the thought of conducting a serious educational discussion with colleagues. When our field representatives sat in on staff meetings, as they frequently were invited to do, they sought to do so only as observers, but many principals sought to inveigle them into leadership roles, often with great skill turning over the reins in complete abdication. It was not unusual for a member of our staff, suddenly introduced, to be required to talk about the League, other schools, innovations—anything to take up the meeting time. For example, Adam S. encouraged our staff members to act in the role of principal at faculty meetings. He was terrified at the thought of trying to play that role himself. During that first year, a member of his staff said of him: "Adam is an administrator. He attends to little details but don't give him anything else to do."

This was not the only pattern, however. One principal, politely and carefully, tried to keep the League and its staff at arm's length. Another saw it as the vehicle for advancing innovations with which he personally had become intrigued. The principal in the school which had learned first of League membership from the newspaper struggled to find and attack school problems with an initially angry, hostile staff. All had different, rather fuzzy conceptions of what the League was and might become; almost all had difficulty conveying something tangible about it to their teachers. Few saw any need or possessed the skills for involving the teachers in developing their own programs. Most perceived teachers to be comfortable when decisions were made for them.

Meanwhile, principals met according to the schedule set forth at their second meeting. Here, they assiduously avoided reference to their own inadequacies as leaders—avoiding, in fact, almost any reference to the schools' internal processes other than to praise highly the association with our field personnel, frequently revealing the extent to which they were looking to them for help. They spoke a good deal of teachers' lack of readiness to innovate and of district restraints, reminding me nostalgically of my early 1950s association with the fourth-year child-study groups in the AATES.

Almost at the outset, they called for input regarding many of the much-touted innovations of the Schooling Decade. Although several of us were aware of the "postponement syndrome" with respect to real problems inherent in these requests, we went along, partly because this was in keeping with the stated spirit of our association and partly because this brought some time for dealing with our own problems of internal management and research development.

We met this demand in the usual ways: making presentations ourselves, bringing in "experts," and providing annotated bibliographies. One innovation was a microfiche system, providing at cost the necessary machine and accompanying software made up of hard-to-get journal articles and fugitive materials. And we began early to produce a periodic newsletter, *Changing Schools*. Though it was designed to exchange information, with little of League relevance yet going on in the schools it became more of a potpourri of what we, in the hub, thought might be of interest (and which was, of course, more interesting to us than to those for whom it was intended).[10] We shall have more to say later about *Changing Schools* and its gradual evolution toward the initial intent.

Such data as were available to us by the end of the first year could hardly give an impatient financial sponsor any great joy. We certainly had no new curricular packages or bright new innovations to exhibit from our efforts. And even on our different criteria for success, about which more will be said later, self-congratulation was not in order.

There is no doubt that, by the end of the first year, all the principals were inescapably entangled with the League—as one might be entangled with a long rope of kelp or with an enticing romance, depending on highly personal individual circumstances. But the same cannot be said for teachers and schools. Some were scarcely touched; our data reveal teachers reporting that "the League means nothing to me" or that "the League has done nothing for us." Some were busily investigating what might be done to enliven their schools and teaching, to the point of at least looking at innovations elsewhere. To our knowledge, one staff, or elements of it, was running ahead of its principal, who had been jokingly but nonetheless pointedly told he wasn't needed.

As one member of our staff insightfully pointed out, it is helpful to have a summer break in academic life. It provides a transition for employees who are going on to other things, either voluntarily or involuntarily. More important, it provides a kind of ending and, of course, a new beginning. And so we moved somewhat gratefully from what had been a most trying year into what undoubtedly would be better.

THE SECOND YEAR

Our staff used the summer and early September of the second year for some restructuring. Worried about what appeared to us to be overdependence by the schools on our staff associates, we decided to revise the nature of the field relationship. The precise form of this revision was influenced by a somewhat lower budget than originally projected and by the fact that our graduate assistants were feeling the pinch of getting on with their dissertations, on one side, and involving themselves with the schools, on the other. Further, the need to get on with the research side of the joint enterprise was pressing; we simply had to direct more of our resources there. Consequently, most of our staff associates became research assistants. We added a full-time professional to join with our field coordinator and just two or three staff associates to constitute a small, mostly on-call, field staff. It was made clear, however, that this staff would endeavor to get themselves invited to schools, if only to keep up-to-date with what was going on.

This was neither fully unanimous nor a completely happy decision on the part of our staff. What ultimately became a chasm between the more research-oriented and more field-oriented members appeared as a fissure. At the extremes, one argument was that the most useful intervention we could engage in was to provide school staffs with research data relevant to their situations; another faction argued that the schools needed our help and unless we got out there and gave it, the school people would not take kindly to our research interests. There seemed to be merit on both sides. We were not withdrawing support but we would have to do some explaining in regard to a changed role for the field staff.

Early in the fall of the second year, we launched what turned out to be a four-month period of conceptualizing what the Study of Educational Change and School Improvement (SECSI) was all about and of relating specific activities and staff roles to the meaning of this formative conceptualization.[11]

First, we looked at the concept of the League itself. Although the structure of the League deliberately provided different schools, principals, staffs, and restraints, and behind the structure lay the notions of the single school collaborating with other schools of similar interests, little had been done to firm up and capitalize on this structure. In an intensive, day-long talk-and-chalk session, we spoke to the need to emphasize the rim of the wheel, not at the expense of the spokes but in addition to them. Thus, the diagram of the League now looked like the one in Figure 4.2. We envisioned the day, in fact, with the connecting rim grown very strong, when the hub and the spokes might disappear. I shall have a good deal to say about this later, especially about the role of the hub. The intent here, of course, was to capitalize on the budding interests of some teachers in visiting other schools and talking with other teachers. We came to call this the peer-group socialization process, ultimately a very powerful part of the emerging strategy for change.[12]

FIGURE 4.2

But our commitment was not just to developing a strategy in the context of educational practice. We were to study it simultaneously, using inquiry to revise it in progress and, ultimately, to formulate some summative judgments about strengths, weaknesses, and potential usefulness. The hurly-burly of the preceding year had inhibited this inquiry so that we had only contextual information on the schools and their personnel, some anecdotal data, and various other kinds of descriptive material. We could not go on trying to study everything in such a complex array of environments.

This proved to be the most fascinating, vexing, difficult, satisfying, frustrating part of the four-month dialogue, taking place a full day each week in total staff sessions and for hours on other days in subgroups. Meanwhile, of course, our somewhat redesigned relationship with the schools had to be sustained and the school-to-school bonds strengthened, but our recurring internal theme had to do with what we were willing to call evidence of growth or success.

We had great difficulty, like the rest of American education, in divorcing ourselves sufficiently from criteria of pupil achievement. To deliver the *coup de grace* in negating educational innovations, one asks, "And did the students learn more?" It is a safe, pointed academic question—and to a degree appropriate. After all, we are, ultimately, concerned with what happens to students in any educational experiment or reform. However, it is a potentially destructive question, too, and has been used as such.

In its most destructive form, it is used not only to squelch embryonic reforms but also to attack the value of educational research. One of the things we know about research into comparative pedagogical techniques, for example, is that study after study concludes "no significant differences." This is especially true in studies comparing two rather narrow methodologies, such as in the teaching of reading. Much of the problem here, however, is that reading and reading disabilities are much more complex phenomena than can be accommodated by such a simple research paradigm. When such problems are encompassed by more carefully conceived, comprehensive theories of instruction, the results come out differently.[13]

Using pupil achievement as a criterion for judging the worth of innovations presents several other problems, as pointed out in Chapter 3. First, there is the danger of studying nonevents. To date, in measuring schoolwide innovations such as team teaching or nongrading, we have paid little attention to the problem of determining if and in what form the change has been established. Second, some reforms can be argued initially on the basis of other conditions that become possible or can be created along with the innovation. For example, although I would not attempt to defend team teaching on grounds of improved pupil achievement, I would be prepared to make a substantial argument based on what it does to facilitate ready involvement of student teachers in real-life teaching experiences. There is no evidence to suggest decline in student achievement in securing this opportunity. Similarly, I am prepared to argue a good many other reforms on the grounds that they are pleasing to teachers: aesthetic surroundings, a comfortable meeting place, accessible files of instructional materials, and so on. While I believe happy teachers with good morale likewise are good for their pupils, I am not at all confident that the direct benefits of any one of these is likely to show up in improved pupil achievement at the .01 or even .05 level of statistical significance in controlled studies. But this does not say that we should not or, thank heavens, do not make such changes. Also, in making such changes, I might be more interested in using affective rather than cognitive measures of pupil effects.

Schools are not factories using any means at their disposal to turn out young people who can read, write, and spell. They are social work places—places of joy, places of sorrow, places of fun, places of boredom—where people of various ages live together five or six hours a day, 180 days a year. If they are failing, as many people think they are, they are not failing because teachers should have eighty semester hours rather than fifty in English literature and related subjects or because teachers use the wrong one of several possible methods of teaching reading. They are failing because they are malfunctioning social systems, more preoccupied with maintaining their daily routines and regularities than with creating a setting where human beings will live and learn together productively and harmoniously.

And so we came, more and more, to talk about criteria for determining progress as being something to do with the health of the school itself, more than the apparent healthfulness of the school for pupils as revealed in achievement scores. Until the school is in a healthy condition, it is unlikely that its residents will show signs of returns in the form of their own improved health. But isn't the health of a school determined by looking at the health of its students? We were back to the pupil outcomes criteria again.

Slowly, however, we returned to the working hypothesis and its subconcepts from which the League had been fashioned in the first place. The school is a key unit, not just for change but *of* change. It must become a more effective place—and that means the people in it must make it so; nobody is going to do it for them. But what kind of school is a more effective place? We teetered once again at the edge of that half-truth: the effective school is one in which the children perform well (which, of course, eliminates at least half of the schools in the United States from consideration, since half always are below average on achievement test scores. We could use criterion-referenced tests, however, and I shall return to our use of some later).

One possibility was to define a model toward which each of our very different schools would strive. We played at the edges of this one, too. After all, we did have, among us, some strong beliefs about what schools should be like. I, among others, had written more than one paper on the topic, and most reformers are trying to put across a model of some kind. And, the preceding year, we had emphasized the individualization of learning and certain practices believed to be appropriate, largely at the request of principals and teachers. Why not make our preferences clear and explicit?

This recurring theme faded more quickly than that of pupil effects. By now, we simply were too much aware of the varying conditions, assets, and liabilities of the eighteen schools to see much hope for developing even several guiding models. Increasingly, it became apparent that our interests were more in the human drama of school life: how the principals were struggling with growing awareness of the need to provide some leadership, whether and how teachers were becoming more meaningfully involved in schoolwide and programmatic decisions, what kinds of school-to-school communications were being established, and so on. Were the schools trying to change themselves? What structures and processes were being established for this purpose? What problems were being encountered? What skills seemed to be needed?

By February 1968, we had reached reasonable consensus on several important matters. We concluded that our prime interest was in the school's developing ability to become, for want of a better term, self-renewing: sensitive to its own needs for productive survival and capable of utilizing resources effectively to that end. We recognized, for some of the reasons put forth in Chapter 1, that schools must change. The central question for us was whether schools could develop a propensity for change and an ability to effect constructive change.

We saw as central in this a staff process of engaging in dialogue about school issues and problems, selecting certain specifics and making decisions regarding actions to be taken, and then taking these actions. These concepts subsequently were refined and defined; the idea of evaluation was added; and attention to the schools' DDAE (dialogue, decision making, action, and evaluation) became central to our own DDAE.

The major implication of this for intervention was that we were not promoting any innovations, a puzzling situation for visitors and critics to understand. This did not mean, however, that we were promoting nothing. We were not prepared to turn ourselves into eunuchs with respect to ideas, and though we were promoting a process, it was not a content-free process. Subsequently, teachers and principals, with our help, constructed a rigorous set of criteria for good DDAE, including those of examining the assumptions underlying specific innovations and reviewing whatever research literature was available.

Our decision here was tested early. One school was pursuing vigorously a plan for interclass achievement grouping. Several of the SECSI staff, knowing my research and views on the subject, asked me what I was going to do about it. I replied, "Nothing." But might not the emergence of such old-hat practices in what increasingly was being seen as a ground-breaking venture be embarrassing to me and bad for the project? My response was that the school staff should employ the criteria and that, if they did so thoroughly, they probably would change their minds. They did both.

A group of teachers in another school plunged quickly into an ill-fated team-teaching project.[14] Since no work had as yet been done on the DDAE criteria, they failed to do any of the planning and study to which these criteria would have directed them. They learned the hard way, later providing some good input regarding both the importance of such criteria and who should determine them.

The step forward in regard to our research was the sharper focus for observation, instrumentation, and data collection. Although the concept of "dependent variable" from experimental research is somewhat inadequate and even misleading here, we began to view DDAE[15] as such, with manipulable conditions designed to enhance it as independent variables. We saw the possibilities of shifting part of our research approach from a field study to a limited, admittedly primitive, field experiment.[16]

We agreed, also, that the data about DDAE and other matters which we might gather could be exceedingly helpful to principals and teachers and that providing them might, indeed, be an important part of our intervention role. The possibility of using ongoing research to refine the change strategy as it developed had been envisioned from the beginning, as had been the desirability of giving our colleagues in the schools such information simply as a matter of courtesy and information. But the use of research as an integral part of an intervention had not been envisioned.

It must not be assumed that the general consensus reported here was complete.[17] Differing values had been brought more sharply to the fore than at any time previously. They were to appear again later in many settings and almost explosively halfway through the third year. The usefulness of research as an intervention tool aroused some skepticism but was put aside as an issue at the time, only to rear its head later.

Educators are not accustomed to following a rigorous set of intellectual or conceptual guidelines even while engaging in activities presumably guided by them. Criteria, goals, and guidelines are seen as appropriate elements of the rhetoric accompanying educational activity. They rarely are sufficiently precise or clear, however, to reveal which behaviors are appropriate and which inappropriate. And so educators become accustomed to the slippage from lip to cup, not necessarily because they want it this way but because this simply is the way it is.

And so, even if our conclusions did at least suggest appropriate as opposed to inappropriate staff behavior, a good many of the staff probably saw them as not sufficiently prescriptive to redirect their lives if that redirection was considerably countervailing to present, established, satisfying behavior. There seemed to them little point in prolonging what had been an exhausting period of dialogue when one could go about one's business as before, regardless of how the sought-for consensus came out. "Let's satisfy Goodlad's propensity for conceptual frameworks and get on with the show out there in the schools where the action is."

There were those, too, who took the conclusions most seriously, to the point of being willing to put their jobs on the line if subsequent actions failed to reflect them. There is no way of determining just how widespread either view was, just as there was no way of determining at the time the extent to which the general consensus was all of a piece or fractionated. Differing value positions subsequently found expression in relation to the intervention strategy.

Four major focal points for research activity reflected virtually unanimous and, I think, genuine agreement. First, as indicated above, were the internal processes of the individual schools, with special attention to DDAE. Second were the sets of relationships among the units making up the League, including our office, though at the time we had uppermost in our minds the peer schools rather than the hub. The significance of the latter only dawned fully upon us much later. Third was the potential ripple effect—that is, the extent and the processes of League school influence on other parts of the educational system. Fourth was our own internal operation in which persons primarily oriented to research and persons primarily oriented to intervention in the field were endeavoring to agree upon and fulfill common ends.

All but a small portion of our effort and funds were expended on the first two categories; they were closest to our charge and easiest to justify budgetarily. The third we recognized as intriguing and we do have some data, but we simply lacked the resources to tackle this elusive area in any systematic way. The fourth was of considerable personal interest. The drama of human beings of professional experience and preparation trying to work out their personal needs within the framework of a mission-oriented institution is fascinating.[18] There necessarily are accommodations, adjustments, adaptations, and compromises to be made. Making these advance the mission while still retaining personal integrity and some individual autonomy poses a never-ending series of difficult decisions. It is a humbling experience in which everyone ultimately is revealed to have clay feet and each person probably comes to examine himself or herself at last.

The need for an ongoing study of all of this surfaced several times at our meetings. There was no clear enthusiasm for it; presumably many people saw it as threatening. I finally decided to commission such a study early in the third year.[19] At a minimum, I thought it would provide information which would be useful to me in modifying our organization as we went along—a feedback mechanism similar to the one provided by feeding back our research data to the schools.

While these decisions were being worked out, the shift in our intervention role ostensibly was taking place. There no longer were liaison persons identified with individual schools. Rather, there was a small staff of resource persons responding to needs and specific requests while gathering information about the schools. Presumably, too, we were committed to advancing the utilization of peer schools and personnel as a source of ideas and assistance. In sociological terms, our intent was to strengthen school-to-school linkages so as to create a new social system of eighteen schools. From the beginning, as previously noted, some of us had seen such a social system emphasizing constructive change as essentially countervailing to the more conservative district system of which each school was a part.

MEANWHILE, BACK AT THE LEAGUE

Most of the principals, it seems, had ended the first year of their association with the League with various feelings of dissatisfaction and guilt, particularly over the failure of their staffs to do what they perceived as expected by us—that is, to define a problem area and method of attack or, better, come up Topsy-like with a full-blown innovation. It is difficult to say how we contributed to the formulation of this exceedingly common expectation; certainly, we had done little to disabuse anyone of it. Some of my own initial formulations, pre-League, had envisioned a family of schools, each of which developed some exemplar practice to become the currency in a medium of exchange.

In October 1967, the principals held their first meeting of the year, a two-day retreat. Only those few who had something going from the previous year had done anything resembling "League business" since the opening of the school year. Most were looking, ever hopeful, to the upcoming meeting when at long last we would tell them what it was all about and then, together, we would all get on with it. We had been withholding quite long enough—too long in fact. We would not, could not, hold out any longer. But we did.

The meeting opened with two presentations, pretty much as requested by the principals (who by now had constituted a small steering committee with our field coordinator). These proved to be the last of such input sessions for a long time to come. The first speaker, much respected and viewed with some awe by the principals, told them that it was about time they got on with something substantive in their schools. As the second, I told them that it was by now reasonable to assume the existence of some ongoing staff process in each school by means of which substantive business might be conducted.

Both speeches were seen as very threatening. Partly, no doubt, out of genuine perception and partly, perhaps, to keep blame and responsibility safely elsewhere, the two speeches were juxtaposed in subsequent discussion, particularly the coffee-cup variety, as mutually contradictory and as evidence of considerable vacillation and uncertainty on the part of the |I|D|E|A| staff. A possible crack in our image of confidence and assurance was appearing. The first speaker exhorted the need for projects. The second, it was perceived, was for process. Both were viewed as hard-line and even punitive.

Responsibilities connected with the opening of the fall term forced me to go back to UCLA later that day. This removed at least the physical locus of and for discontent. Apparently, it also removed certain restraints. As one principal put it later, "Papa Bear went home and all the other bears misbehaved."

For more than a year, the principals had been looking, apparently, for some recognizable clues for what was expected of them—that is, expected by others. They were accustomed, one might presume, to doing what others, especially those in positions of higher authority, expected or asked of them. They simply were unable to respond to contrary external expectations, to listen and respond to their own problems and needs. They looked in vain for "John Goodlad and his staff to tell us what to do." In this expectation, they were not unlike the teachers who, in turn, wanted principals, consultants, somebody to tell them what to do. But, after a year, no familiar clues were forthcoming. They were in a new kind of ballgame. Nothing much would happen unless they initiated and fostered it.

There had been glimmers of such a realization before but, somehow, they had been put aside. Now, there was a full dawning during and after those two speeches in Santa Barbara. The message got through and it was unnerving. By nightfall, the tension of self-confrontation was high. The cocktail hour was jokingly dubbed "tension-reduction." But an hour was not sufficient. Rather grim, boisterous revelry picked up after dinner and continued well into the night.

The amount of detail here in recounting this meeting may appear to be out of proportion. But subsequent information and events emphasize its significance as one of several major watersheds in developing the League of Cooperating Schools. At that meeting, most of the principals sensed and several confronted the realization that "We have met the enemy and he is us." News of what happened that boisterous evening of defiant protest began to reach me even before the meeting adjourned. It was a long time before the principals could speak about it openly but, later, they came to do so increasingly freely. Since that meeting, the various events of vengeful, self-punishing celebration have been told and retold by the principals, no doubt with some (but not much) embellishment. Most of what appeared at first to be embellishment actually was the gleeful recalling of temporarily forgotten details. That night became a benchmark toward brotherhood, a time when former strangers began to look differently at one another. And especially at themselves.

They were "in it" and they were in it together. There was nobody else left to blame. There was no safe place of retreat. And John Goodlad would not (could not) bail them out. One's life space suddenly had closed in very close to the elbows.

While this was a significant—and, ultimately, very positive—development in the life of the League, it also was a potentially dangerous one. Suddenly being revealed to one's self and, to considerable degree, to others can be catastrophic.

If ever there was a time for us to move, it was now. And, if ever there was a realization of how potentially fatal that first year had been, it was then. We simply were behind schedule in creating the kind of structure and support mechanisms to sustain an enterprise of this kind through a crisis which, other research shows, is relatively predictable as to ultimate occurrence, if less so regarding its seriousness and specific timing.

Fortunately, there is, among other things, a certain therapeutic quality in happenings such as this. A great deal of growing self-doubt and uneasiness had been kept under academic cloth for a year. Principals just don't "blow their cool"—it's not appropriate for one in whose care the lives of several hundred children are placed each day. Above all else, principals are required to keep the ship on an even keel with a steady hand on the helm. Some people are surprised to learn that principals "drink at conventions." Perhaps we should be thankful few drink on the job!

During the first year, we had become increasingly aware of the inability of most of the principals to take the lead in conducting serious staff meetings and especially developing a structure for conducting school business in a systematic, reasonably democratic way. However, the full extent and seriousness of this inability had not entered sufficiently into our consciousness. Because of the tentativeness and, on occasion, tension surrounding formation of the League, we had opted for a rather relaxed, get-acquainted approach to principals' meetings, with emphasis on nonthreatening input of ideas. Nothing in what the principals brought to these meetings suggested either their fears or feelings of inadequacy regarding the development of these staff processes. We failed to recognize what we should have known: leadership of this kind is not really expected of principals; they are not selected for purposes of providing it; and they have had little, if any, preparation for it.

One major agenda item, then, became one of finding a way to help the principals confront the problem and develop techniques for dealing with it. The trauma of the October meeting helped, although the events themselves subsequently were ignored until the principals themselves began not only to recall them but also to interpret them.

Another set of events helped, too. The potentialities of the League were getting through to clusters of teachers in several schools: from *Changing Schools*, visits of our staff, bibliographies, references on microfiche, and so on. Some already were being guided by their principal to visit other League schools; others were asking for this opportunity. Some were demanding that principals quit "playing their League experiences so close to their chests"; teachers wanted in on it, too.

Our data suggest that this second year was a good one. We had hammered out many of the unclarified concepts in the initial design, added some new ones, and—of great importance—had an opportunity to internalize their meaning. It was a sustained effort, one restoring a good deal of pride and confidence in a research staff that had skidded downhill the previous year after a heady, overly optimistic beginning. During this second year, too, the principals inevitably became aware of and, in fact, party to our own internal soul-searching. Clearly, it was encouraging to them to discover that we, too, had our problems of working together, that we were not a staff united at the outset and subsequently. The way in which we were trying to work out our agreements and disagreements was, on one hand, encouraging and, on the other, indicated that we were not suggesting anything for the school staffs which we did not have to do ourselves. The principals obviously felt a kinship with us, replacing the awe and then disillusionment of the previous year caused in part by our not having "the answers." A true partnership was emerging.

During the summer of 1968, several principals participated in the |I|D|E|A| Fellows Program.[20] Because of badly snarled air traffic, some of the speakers were unable to arrive on schedule or at all. The director was forced to improvise, making last-minute program adjustments. The League principals stepped into the breach again and again, surprising themselves and earning the admiration of the director and their colleagues. Needless to say, this experience did a great deal for their feelings of self-worth and potency. Later, they spoke frequently of the personal growth experienced.

Things also were going well in many of the schools. There had been a variety of teachers' meetings, including a "League day" involving nearly everyone in sessions designed to assure maximum interaction. Several principals were beginning to exercise considerable leadership, especially in creating a decision-making structure; and teachers in a few schools were carrying along nice but ineffective principals on their own wave of enthusiasm. True, as other reports reveal, two or three schools and some teachers still appeared not to have been touched by the League.

Toward the end of this second year, we also picked up evidence regarding League teachers appearing as resource persons at teacher institute days in neighboring school districts—rarely their own. More and more, too, we found League teachers and principals identifying themselves as being associated with the League, describing their experiences to colleagues from other schools with pride and enthusiasm, though earlier they sometimes had been viewed with curious amusement and their schools labeled "funny farms." These and other signs suggested that the embryonic social system of the League was beginning to form and take hold.

PERSPECTIVE

One might well ask at this point whether the two turbulent years had been worth it, especially since one could not point to very much of a tangible sort for which the League clearly was causal. A good many people had grappled with difficult problems and confronted themselves in nonflattering ways.[21] Might it not have been better to leave things alone?

The question leads to sleepless nights. Principals and teachers would not have been in the project on their own. Is it proper to intervene in their lives as described here? One could argue defensively that nobody was stopping them from dropping out. There were no material rewards for staying in the League and no punitive sanctions for dropping out. But, after all, once in the League, it was no casual matter to drop out. There might be difficult explanations to make.

One could argue that the open partnership for change represented by the League is to be preferred to manipulation toward specific reforms or innovations by external agents. One can argue, also, that school principals and teachers are not free spirits with respect to their educational responsibilities. The schools are not performing adequately and must go about their business more effectively. Unless school people get at the job themselves, with whatever help they can get, they will be told what to do whether they like it or not. Nevertheless, change agents must be exceedingly careful about motivating and employing the time and energy of others for ends that are not their own.

An aspect of our work must be kept clearly in mind. These first two years and those following would have been infinitely easier and less strained had we not been trying to accomplish so much simultaneously: develop a strategy for which there was no precedent; bring together not just behavioral scientists and practitioners but several different orientations within these broad categories; not merely to feed back research data for decision making but to inquire reasonably systematically into an exceedingly complex enterprise; to get jobs done with part-time student help while furthering their doctoral studies;[22] and (not mentioned in this narrative) to conduct simultaneously major surveys of early childhood schooling in Asia, England, Israel, and the United States.[23] Obviously, with this work done, utilization of the League concept in the improvement of educational practice would be infinitely less complicated and considerably less fraught with the kinds of tensions described in the next chapter. Nonetheless, the kind of relationship recommended in the quote from Smith with which this chapter begins is not one to be entered into lightly. It must be remembered that the two groups—behavioral scientists and practitioners—have different goals. Any collaborative relationship must further the ends and foster the satisfaction of both.

NOTES

1 Egon Guba, in a letter to the writer, Sept. 2, 1966.

2 B. Othanel Smith, "The Anatomy of Change," *The Nature of Change*, National Association of Secondary School Principals, Washington, D.C., 1963, p. 10.

3 For other details regarding the League of Cooperating Schools and its creation, see John I. Goodlad, "The League of Cooperating Schools," *California Journal for Instructional Improvement*, vol. 9, no. 4, pp. 213–218, December 1966.

4 The kind of balance required between established regularities and territory open to restructuring or creating from the beginning is a fascinating one. Many of us in education have fantasized at one time or another what it might be like to create a completely new institution, and some of us have had that opportunity. The sheer magnitude of beginning everything at once almost guarantees that most of the decisions will be made along familiar patterns. Consequently, given certain favorable conditions, it may be easier to make an existing institution self-renewing than to create an exemplary one from the beginning out of raw materials, so to speak.

5 Toward the end of the first year, I became dean of the Graduate School of Education at UCLA and then continued in my dual capacity throughout the length of the project. It became necessary to play two essentially contradicting roles: at UCLA, the facilitator trying to create opportunities for the Graduate School and to open doors for the faculty, encouraging individuals to "do their thing"; at |I|D|E|A|, the necessarily gentle taskmaster, constantly repeating the nature of our broad goals and our responsibility to the funding agency. Since some of the staff and all the graduate assistants also moved in and out of and across these two environments, confusion was assured. Some were very critical of any effort to direct their daily activities toward institutional goals; several were openly critical of what they perceived to be my overtolerance of behavior seemingly not productive of goal attainment.

Lazarsfeld has had some interesting things to say about accelerating advancement in the behavioral sciences through the creation of institutes more goal- and task-oriented than is customary in university life. The difficulties of redirecting academics so as to harmonize their life-styles to the demands of such institutes must not be underestimated. See Paul F. Lazarsfeld and Sam D. Sieber, *Organizing Educational Research: An Exploration*, Prentice-Hall, Englewood Cliffs, N.J., 1964.

6 The answer to the question of what the staff of an organization should know about factors *potentially* but not yet affecting them is not as neat as any commitment to "openness" might suggest. The issue of whether or not or when to reveal certain information poses a formidable dilemma for leadership. Perhaps everything of any potential significance should be revealed when it is first learned— and, no doubt, many readers would challenge me for even suggesting that other alternatives exist. In regard to the two sets of traumas mentioned here, however, I chose to withhold what might not happen. My illness was known, of course, but the fact that recovery for a time was in question was not. There was no way of obscuring

the fact that there were tensions in the parent |I|D|E|A| organization itself—it, too, was experiencing severe "coming out" problems. But not until much later did even my closest associates know that I received during the period of illness a letter ordering me to dissolve the League of Cooperating Schools because, during my absence, some policy decisions had been made regarding the discrete functions of |I|D|E|A|'s three divisions; maintenance of the League simply did not fit new policy. In my judgment, given the magnitude of our own problems at the time, I considered it better both for individuals and for our part of the institution that the staff remain ignorant of this information at least until, as I esimated, policy would change again (which it did). But the issue remains a troublesome one.

7 These were brought together for purposes of delivering a speech early in 1967 and subsequently appeared in the paper from which they have been extracted here. See John I. Goodlad, "Educational Change: A Strategy for Study and Action," *The National Elementary Principal*, vol. 48, no. 3, pp. 6–13, January 1969.

8 In addition to keeping extensive written reports, we recorded some of what happened on documentary film. Approximately 60,000 feet of film were edited into films running about three hours, to provide a visual summary. Entitled "The League," this material is available from |I|D|E|A|, P.O. Box 628, Far Hills Branch, Dayton, Ohio 45419.

9 It will be recalled from *Behind the Classroom Door* (reported in Chapter 3) that the general absence of such processes characterized all but four of the sixty-seven schools studied.

10 In spite of the fact that |I|D|E|A| staffers were mostly retreaded practitioners, their orientations toward life and interests deviated significantly from those of the practitioners in the schools, as revealed by the Omnibus Personality Inventory. Perhaps these differences reflect an early bent toward scholarly work; perhaps doctoral studies contributed to them; perhaps socialization in different kinds of institutions was a contributing factor. At any rate, such differences must be taken into account in any collaborative relationship between behavioral scientists and practitioners of the kind suggested by Smith.

11 A great deal of what is described here appears rather clearly in our documentary films, described in note 8.

12 Mary M. Bentzen, "A Peer-Group Strategy for Intervention in Schools," Institute for Development of Educational Activities, Inc., Los Angeles, California, 1970. (Mimeographed.)

13 For an interesting analysis of the role of theory in educational

research, see Patrick Suppes, "The Place of Theory in Educational Research," *Educational Research*, vol. 3, no. 6, pp. 3-10, June 1974.

14   See, "The Corona Affair" in the League films described above, note 8.

15   Although the E (evaluation) was originally considered a step in A (action) and DDA became DDAE only later in the project, for the sake of consistency, I refer to DDAE throughout this volume.

16   There is no way for me to express adequately my appreciation of Mary M. Bentzen's input regarding this crucial stage of our work. She moved into a nearly full-time role sometime after the project's beginning, with a fresh doctorate in the sociology of education and long-term interests in our problems. A continuing dialogue about the critical dependent variables in schooling, and Louise L. Tyler and Donald A. Myers playing key and at times devil's advocate roles, was of enormous usefulness in sharpening the issues.

17   The consensus model of decision making is an interesting one, but its appropriateness for various situations requires further study. Some individuals simply are unable, it would seem, to make a decision until all the data are in or all the implications are seen. But the data are never *all* in; and the implications never are fully clear. At some point, decisions must be made—wherever possible with the option of turning back still open. Those persons with the dispositions suggested above make excellent consultants in this process because they weigh so many influencing factors. But to wait for them to say, "Let's go," could mean waiting forever.

18   The work of Getzels and Guba on the interplay of a psychological element represented by the central concept of personal disposition, a sociological element represented by the central concept of role expectation, and an anthropological element represented by the central concept of cultural value is seminal with respect to this relationship. The theoretical model involved proved exceedingly useful in our work. See Richard C. Williams, Charles C. Wall, W. Michael Martin, and Arthur Berchin (with a foreword by J. W. Getzels), *Effecting Organizational Renewal in Schools: A Social Systems Perspective*, McGraw-Hill, New York, 1974.

19   Louise L. Tyler conducted this work, commencing formally in the fall of our third year. Since she had been with us almost from the beginning as a general consultant, she was in a good position to reconstruct some of the dynamics of the preceding two years. Starting with the third year, she was able not only to gather a cumulative body of written observations but also to conduct interviews and employ a number of scaled instruments, particularly to get at

attitudes and interests. It is anticipated that some of her findings and observations ultimately will be published in various forms.

20 These summer institutes for educational administrators have been conducted by |I|D|E|A| almost since the inception of the organization, normally enrolling approximately 100 at each of four sites for an intensive week of presentations and discussions pertaining to highly relevant problems and issues.

21 During the second year, one of my associates suggested a negative impact of our project on some personal lives, as evidenced by the number of divorces occurring. We did not gather such data. We do not know whether more divorces were actually occurring or, as appeared to be the case, whether we simply got to know more people (over 700 were directly involved) and, consequently, more such information. Also, regarding the impact on personal lives, we have some evidence to the contrary, but generalizations might well be left unformulated.

22 One aspect of this is particularly challenging and intriguing. Many researchers have pointed out the need for Ph.D. recipients to have had experience with some ongoing research project, quite beyond the scope of their own dissertations, before joining the faculty of a university. How feasible this is prior to postdoctoral status remains an open question, even if the opportunities are available. A research institute or program is necessarily task-oriented; its director must see to it that these tasks are accomplished. On the other hand, one of the most important aspects of the dissertation is selecting and defining a problem; the candidate should have considerable freedom in pursuing the topic. It is exceedingly difficult to satisfy simultaneously these two somewhat contradictory criteria.

During that first year, we had not progressed far enough with research for our staff associates to begin to see the prospects of selecting a dissertation topic from this work. During the second year, when the need for a dissertation topic usually begins to press, they began to look elsewhere. Some returned later, following discovery that advances in our research were opening up possibilities for small studies (see Appendix A). Ultimately, we moved to the position that employment with |I|D|E|A| as a research assistant was one thing and completion of a dissertation quite another. We would worry about getting the job done; the sponsor could worry about the dissertation. As director and a professor, I was faced more sharply, however, with the problem of keeping the two separate or, blending them when compatibility appeared promising.

23 Reported in Norma Feshbach, John I. Goodlad, and Avima Lombard, *Early Schooling in England and Israel*, McGraw-Hill, New York, 1973;

and John I. Goodlad, M. Frances Klein, Jerrold M. Novotney, and Associates, *Early Schooling in the United States*, McGraw-Hill, 1973.

CHAPTER 5
THE LEAGUE MATURES

Literally, every step we take in life is determined by a series of interlocking concepts and conceptual schemes. Every goal we formulate for our actions, every decision we make, be it trivial or momentous, involves assumptions about the universe and about human beings.

—James B. Conant (*Modern Science and Modern Man*, Doubleday, New York, 1952, p. 80)

By the fall of 1968, the end of the first two years of our Study of Educational Change and School Improvement, the major components of the League strategy were at least in some state of functioning. More important, there was a growing conceptualization on our part as to how these components had to function if individual schools were to reflect not simply the working hypothesis, but indeed, the *principle* of their key role in educational change.

It is doubtful, however, that this conceptualization was widely shared throughout the League, in spite of the considerable rhetoric regarding the combined power of individual school effort and peer school sharing. Further, as the third year progressed, it became sharply and painfully apparent that members of our own staff were operating on differing assumptions, whatever the verbal consensus we thought we had reached as a result of our internal dialogue during the second year.

The task now was to refine this conceptualization and strengthen each functioning component. There were three: the individual school, relationships among schools (the peer school network), and the hub (our offices). Although we sought to move forward simultaneously with all three, the last was seen as a poor third cousin whose importance would decline as the other two matured.

INDIVIDUAL SCHOOLS AND PEER SCHOOLS

It will be recalled from Chapter 4 that we made considerable progress during 1967–68 in focusing on total school staff and small group processes of conducting the school's affairs. We came to call this process DDAE—dialogue, decision making, action, and evaluation. Consequently, the appropriate involvement for us was to be at the level of the total staff or with small, working teams of teachers, not with the pedagogical problems and needs of individual teachers. Further, we would continue to work through the principal, normally responding to invitations from him or her but, in any case, calling in advance or at least stopping by the principal's office in responding to or visiting with groups of teachers.

Our small field staff was called upon, then, to play an exceedingly difficult dual role. From the schools' perspective, these individuals were resource personnel to be drawn upon in advancing staff processes, although the limits as to how they might be used were not yet clear—and, in fact, were not precisely defined for some time. We had agreed, internally, that this field staff would endeavor to clarify to school personnel the restraints on their services, in part using specific requests to develop inclusion/exclusion criteria. For our research needs, the field personnel were to gather information on the functioning of the staffs and provide periodic written reports.

Meanwhile, the slightly larger research staff continued to define the nature of what we would study, prepared questionnaires and other instruments, and gathered various kinds of data on schools and their personnel. By now, this part of the staff was divided into two parts, one concentrating on schools and League structure and the other on developing procedures by means of which schools might evaluate themselves.[1]

Adhered to closely, the model of intervention in and study of educational practices which we envisioned, admittedly at an embryonic stage, represented a rather marked departure from convention. The conventional paradigm for both improvement and research, expressed experimentally, is focused on instructional interventions such as new teaching methods and materials with the expectation that these will enhance pupil outcomes. Figure 5.1 portrays this conceptualization, D.V. standing for dependent variables and I.V. for independent variables.[2]

The assumptions underlying this model guided much innovation

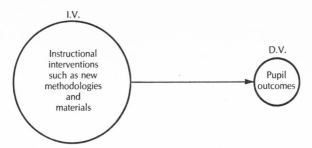

FIGURE 5.1 CONVENTIONAL MODEL FOR EFFECTING AND STUDYING ENDS-MEANS RELATIONSHIPS WHEN THE FOCUS IS ON INSTRUCTION AND PUPIL OUTCOMES

and reform during the Schooling Decade, as we have seen. To date, single manipulations such as class size, teaching method, or pupil grouping have not produced significant changes in pupil outcomes. Techniques for studying the effects of multiple manipulations are now available, but operating models in schools are virtually nonexistent; hence, definitive studies are thwarted. It is reasonable, however, to anticipate early breakthrough here.

As traced in Chapter 3, my long-term concern has been, of course with the difficulty of installing and sustaining instructional reforms, even if we could be assured of their potential effectiveness. The explanatory thesis for this difficulty, held here as a working hypothesis, is that the regularities of the school sustain certain practices, through expectations, approval, and reward. Teachers, as individuals, usually are not able to run successfully against these regularities or to create the schoolwide structures and processes necessary to sustain new practices.[3] This suggests the need to focus on the entire culture of the school, not simply on instruction, although the latter would not be neglected in this approach, instructional regularities being one of several elements in a school's culture.

This kind of thinking leads to a modified version of Figure 5.1. We now see everything constituting the culture of the school—its operational curriculum, written and unwritten rules, verbal and nonverbal communication, physical properties, pedagogical regularities, principal's leadership behavior and so on—influencing what pupils learn, for good or ill (Figure 5.2). Consequently, if one could come to grips successfully with changing school cultures in significant ways, one could then begin to formulate some explanatory hypotheses regarding any

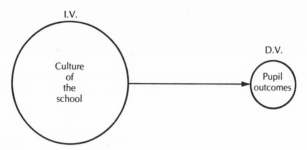

FIGURE 5.2 A PARADIGM FOR EFFECTING AND STUDYING EDUCATIONAL IMPROVEMENT AND PRACTICE, WITH PUPIL OUTCOMES AS THE CRITERION MEASURE AND THE ENTIRE SCHOOL ENVISIONED AS SUBJECT TO MODIFICATON

observed differences in pupil outcomes. The task is a formidable one but appears to point in some promising directions.[4]

Even if we wish to place considerable weight on the teacher as one major factor—as most people will wish to do—at least the model suggests that teacher behavior may relate significantly to other factors in the culture and that, consequently, sole emphasis on teachers in reform efforts is likely to fall short. Further, the paradigm suggests that holding only individual teachers accountable for pupil performance is inadequate and even misleading. By conceptually removing the individual teacher from the rest of the school's culture, we get a clearer picture of the proposition that often factors besides teachers determine what pupils learn in the environment of the school (Figure 5.3).

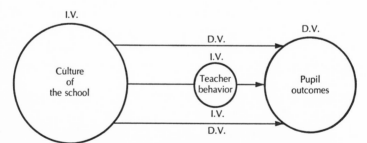

FIGURE 5.3   A PARADIGM FOR STUDYING AND IMPROVING EDUCATIONAL PRACTICE WITH THE TEACHER CONCEPTUALLY REMOVED FROM THE SCHOOL CULTURE, THE CULTURE PLAYING UPON THE TEACHER AND PUPILS AND INFLUENCING THE TEACHER'S IMPACT ON PUPILS

Figure 5.3 suggests that changing certain elements in the school's culture, such as replacing the principal, could have a marked impact on the teacher. Thus, in an experimental design, the school's culture is the independent variable and the teacher is dependent, just as the pupils also are dependent on the school's culture. But Figure 5.3 also includes the conventional model of the teacher as independent variable acting upon pupil outcomes. The important aspect of Figure 5.3 is clear depiction of actual or potential teacher ties to the school as a source of expectations, restraints, support, guidance, and the like.[5]

This brings us to the most significant aspect of emphasis on the individual school as a total entity, the proposition that entire schools can and should be regarded as malleable and capable of changing, and that, as schools change in their cultural characteristics, so do the people in them. The converse proposition also follows: as the individuals in them act upon or neglect the cultural elements of schools, schools become places that support and mold or inhibit certain kinds of behavior.

Following this line of reasoning, it becomes possible to think about and devise various conditions which might or might not be conducive to those in schools reconstructing their own environments. For example, varying degrees of centralization or decentralization might be encouraging or inhibiting. A threat to abolish the school and send the children elsewhere might lead to some interesting changes. Or the charge to clarify goals in preparation for an external evaluation fifteen months later might draw a response. Unfortunately, the usual response is a ceremonial rain dance replete with announcements, public programs, classroom demonstrations, and self-congratulatory rhetoric.

Part of our thesis with the League was that there had to be an internal sense of need, a desire to change old regularities or act according to neglected values. The League was created both to provide the necessary stimulus and to enable us to observe processes of initiating and developing changes. But the major mechanism for encouraging and supporting change was to be the peer-school network. In our design, then, League affiliation was to be an influence on the school's culture, one which we hoped would become increasingly powerful. Figure 5.4 suggests the model, again within the experimental paradigm employed above.

Our intense staff discussions of the second year should be recalled once again. We decided, not without considerable debate and disagreement, to focus our attention on the development and study of

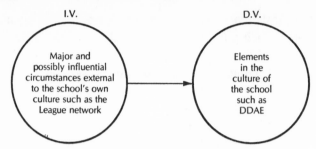

FIGURE 5.4   A PARADIGM FOR IMPROVING AND STUDYING
EDUCATIONAL PRACTICE, WITH CHANGES IN THE ENTIRE CULTURE
OF A SCHOOL THE FOCUS OF ATTENTION

DDAE, plagued continuously for both practical and philosophical reasons by our difficulty and, at times, reluctance to back away from using pupil effects as the criterion. Intuitively, we believed that DDAE would be slow in developing, posing as doubtful the possibility that pupil effects from it would show up during the term of our project. DDAE is a process; it could be used to achieve various goals. Consequently, summative evaluation of pupil outcomes should be delayed until the process of DDAE produces activity pertaining, say, to the improvement of mathematics instruction. We did conclude, however, that certain outcomes in the affective realm bore a face validity relationship to DDAE itself, whatever the content, and so we developed and used several instruments to measure them.[6] Figure 5.5 suggests the paradigm involved in this line of thinking. The school's culture is seen as dependent on influences from the larger culture of which it is or

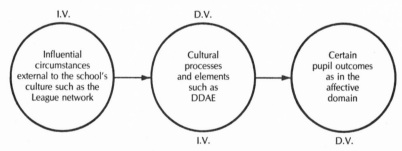

FIGURE 5.5   A MODIFICATION OF THE CONVENTIONAL PARADIGM
REGARDING ENDS-MEANS RELATIONS, WITH PUPIL OUTCOMES
AS THE END BUT THE TOTAL CULTURE OF THE SCHOOL, ITSELF
SUBJECT TO CHANGE, AS THE MEANS TO IMPROVEMENT

could be a part but also as an independent variable influencing pupil outcomes.

There is a temptation at this point to embark on extensive discussion of fundamentally different philosophic alternatives available for viewing these models and, consequently, for research and evaluation. A brief word must suffice here. Most traditional thinking about schools, teaching, and learning leads naturally to a linear paradigm of ends, means, and possible effects. Thus, if we pluck the teacher out of the school's culture in Figure 5.5, we get a model showing various contextual, external factors influencing the culture of the school, this culture influencing both the teacher and pupils but the teacher remaining as a factor of special importance in the total pattern of influence on pupil outcomes (Figure 5.6). Such a paradigm at least has the virtue of placing the ends-means-effects relationship in its proper complexity, moving us well beyond the popular but overly simplistic model of Figure 5.1.

But the model of Figure 5.6 is overwhelming in its implications for both research and intervention. It is difficult enough to show relationships between teacher and pupil behavior—and the findings usually are inconclusive—but at least the problem is manageable. Consequently, the literature is replete with reports of studies and experiments characterized, in Schwab's terms, by short-term syntax. Several such studies, representing solid methodologies, can get one a promotion in the university setting! To go beyond, following the model of Figure 5.3, let alone Figure 5.6, presents formidable problems of design and execution. And then, when one goes beyond Figure 5.6 into a still

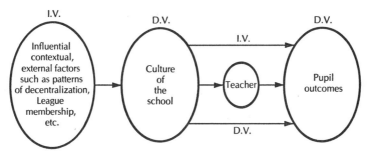

FIGURE 5.6 A PARADIGM FOR STUDYING ENDS-MEANS-EFFECTS RELATIONSHIPS AND FOR IMPROVING SCHOOLING AND LEARNING WITH THE TEACHER EXTRACTED FROM THE SCHOOL AS A WHOLE BUT INFLUENCED BY IT

more accurately representative model, all the influences external to the school which bear directly on the student come into the picture. No wonder the educational researcher becomes myopic! The implications are virtually terrifying. Nonetheless, this is the territory needing to be explored, a territory which currently may be ploughed most productively from a cross-national comparative perspective. The work will tend to attract researchers committed primarily to the empirical-inductive mode of thought.

There is a quite different way to view the ends-means-effects relationship, however, as represented by Figure 5.4. Here, the culture of the school includes everything common to cultures everywhere: physical conditions and resources, adults, young people. They interact in a "we" relationship, fashioning an ecosystem for living and learning. The central concerns for change are guided by questions like "What kind of relationships?" and "What kind of environment?" and the answers involve fundamental assumptions about the universe and human beings. The work involved is particularly attractive to those of a theoretical-deductive mode of thought.

Much could be said here about the fascinating frontiers for educational science and educational practice emerging from these two seemingly contradictory but necessarily complementary perspectives. The first leads to large-scale documentation of existing practices and relationships and, ultimately, complex experiments with sophisticated, multifactor analyses of pupil behaviors and performances. The second leads to a resurgence of interest in value questions as they pertain to educational settings and practices and to innovative ventures in educational alternatives.[7] An example of the latter involves a fusion of the two circles in Figure 5.4 so that the school and the society of which it is a part are fused—in essence, society is deschooled.

Our concern in SECSI was, of course, not with deschooling but with reconstructing the culture of the school. It is fair to say, I think, that most of us shared a general conceptual orientation to this task, leaning more toward the second than the first of the two modes of thought cited above. Consequently, although shedding preoccupation with pupil outcomes, at least for the duration of the project, had not been readily accomplished (and we did proceed with measures in the affective domain), concentrating on the culture of the school presented few problems of conceptual disagreement. And although the range and depth of our value position never were made fully explicit, we shared substantive, interlocking concepts about education and a common desire to develop intervention strategies and procedures reflecting them. Even those who ultimately came to disagree with and to disassociate themselves from our approach shared these central values, I believe. They simply differed in how best to reflect them in action.

IMPLEMENTING THE NEW CONCEPTUALIZATION

We sought to wean schools, principals, and teachers from their dependency on |I|D|E|A|. Adapting the picture of the League as a wheel with spokes and a hub, we sought to diminish the school-to-|I|D|E|A| links and strengthen the school-to-school links. But, of course, this did not result in a neat pattern of bonds between neighboring schools. Figure 5.7 shows the crisscrossing of relationships and seeks to conceptualize the intended pattern while revealing the hodgepodge of reality.

As Culver, Lieberman, and Shiman put it, we had begun the League in the fall of 1966 with the implicit assumption that we were the "haves" and the schools were the "have nots."[8] In general, this assumption was more than acceptable to the schools; they could be relatively passive receivers of whatever we had to offer. But the principals, at least, soon became aware that more was expected of them and, it will be recalled, confronted this realization traumatically in the fall of the second year.

Early in this second year, we knew enough from our first-year body of data to realize that general input, whether from our staff or from outside consultants, simply did not meet the varied interests and needs of the eighteen schools. We also realized that some principals were not adequate conduits of information, ideas, enthusiasm, and support from our joint meetings to faculty meetings in individual

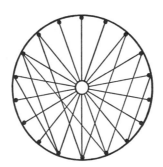

FIGURE 5.7

schools. During this second year, therefore, we encouraged principals to bring teacher representatives to these monthly meetings. Also, an all-day, all-League conference provided teachers with an opportunity for close personal identification with the League, an opportunity which they seized with surprising, gratifying enthusiasm. They particularly enjoyed the opportunity provided to discuss specific common problems with peers from peer schools. Undoubtedly, this stimulated some cross-school dialogue, paving the way for subsequent interschool visitation and for "area" meetings involving teachers from several schools in neighboring districts. Some came to the realization, for the first time, that they were part of something not previously encountered, something larger than their daily routines and associations. This is probably an important element in change, one to which I shall return later.

The very structure of the League grew out of initial awareness of the need to provide school membership in a new social system which would be supportive of activities not necessarily endorsed by the school district of which each school also was a part. But we had done relatively little during the first two years to make this social system functional. We were too busy with other things, many of them unanticipated. And, probably more important, we had not ourselves internalized the importance and potential of this structure. Consequently, we were ambivalent regarding our own interventions, talking passionately about countervailing social systems but experiencing great difficulty in shedding familiar roles of consultation. But the third—and especially the fourth—year saw this important part of the League strategy take hold and mature.

What had to happen is well-stated by Culver, Lieberman, and Shiman:

> The overarching change strategy which ultimately emerged from our efforts was rooted in the creation of a social system whose members— the principals and teachers of the eighteen League schools—were encouraged to view each other as peers. . . . Central to the success of this strategy was that membership in the new peer group be viewed by group members themselves as important and desirable. Without feelings of identification with the new group, its individual members would be apt to continue to hew to the change-inhibiting norms of their own districts. To accept the risks of disapproval and criticism from schools within their own districts, then, League members needed to perceive the League itself as highly valuable.[9]

They then go on to describe three tactics which were used to increase the importance of belonging to the League: the generation of opportunities for League members to serve as resources for each other and non-League groups; the development of decision-making ability in the League itself; and the development of effective interschool communication. These called for changed perceptions and behaviors on the part of all involved, those in the schools and those on our |I|D|E|A| staff.

The principals had developed a good deal of League identification during the second year but, for several and perhaps most, it was still a personal kind of thing. The idea of total school identification and their responsibility for bringing this about was still somewhat beyond the boundaries of personal comfort and identification (beyond what Fritz Perls would have called their "ego boundaries"[10]). For four or five principals, the summer experience with the |I|D|E|A| Fellows Program had provided an acceleration in perception of personal leadership potential which paid off handsomely during the third year. Increased self-confidence led to greater risk taking and, therefore, greater willingness to support teacher activities which would not have been encouraged before. The growing involvement of teachers in League activities incurred new problems and potential risks for principals.

Maturation of the League social system called for much greater use of its own resources. Clearly, the growing expertise of a teacher in school X to use an array of instructional resources should be employed in school Y. School Y's year of experience in studying nongrading should be available to school Z now just contemplating such a plan. More and more, our office became a clearinghouse, referring teachers' questions to peers rather than attempting to provide answers or resource personnel ourselves. But some of the logistics inevitably fell to principals. They had decisions to make for which there were no precedents and no established guidelines. Should three teachers be excused during the regular school day to visit classes elsewhere? If so, how? And how might teacher A react, who closed her classroom door behind her, kept her teaching to herself, and thought the League was a lot of nonsense, anyway?

And what about that carload of teachers somewhere out on the freeway? How responsible were they? Suppose some parents saw them? And what crazy ideas might they come back with? This thought probably was the most threatening of all; the greatest potential risks lay in the possibility that the teachers might actually want to do some of the things they saw! Also, their physical absence from the school "during working hours" moved teachers out of the principal's span of control. Just as schools without walls for students can be threatening to teachers who derive security from their traditional front-and-center status in the classroom, teachers outside of school walls could be very threatening to principals who derive authority from being the "presence" in the office down the hall.

Sanctioning teacher visits to other schools presupposed a readiness to make use of this effort in some way, at least at the level of allowing or, indeed, encouraging sharing reactions with colleagues. This, in turn, presupposed some structure for facilitating communication. As we have seen, schools generally are marked by the absence of such structure; its creation in each school was an early goal of the League. To take the first step is to create the necessity of others, each making some demand or requiring an adjustment or new skill.

The power of the principal peer group went gratifyingly to work here. The content of their monthly meetings clearly reflected the growing interschool activities of teachers and the accompanying problems created for principals. Probably, more than anything else, it was the apparent willingness of a peer principal to accept and grapple with these new demands that gave courage to one beginning to falter in the face of that first step. And it was their monthly discussions that began to bring principals back again—but this time with the urgency of confronting the issues involved—into questions of the nature of worthwhile innovations and, ultimately, the nature of a good school.

Of course, visitation was only one of many evidences of interschool communication and involvement, much of which was still channeled through our office. What teachers sought from one another tended to be quite specific. From various sources, including our early input into the League, they had developed an awareness of extant innovations. They knew the language, but now they wanted very specific answers to very specific questions: When do you get together to plan in team teaching? What do you do with the nonreaders while you are working with another group? How do you get parallel reading materials when you need them? Teachers appear to look more readily to one another, given the opportunity, than to "university types" for answers to questions like these. Confronted by "experts," they usually don't even ask the question, for fear of appearing stupid.

As time progressed, of course, the differences among schools and teachers in regard to need and interest became increasingly apparent.

By the fourth year, the direction and substance of conferences and workshops fell to the Teachers Activities Group (TAG) which insightfully sorted out and sought to provide for several levels of readiness: teachers new to League schools; those who wanted peer group interaction on specific problems and interests (the largest group); and those who were now rather sophisticated in innovative practice but who were seeking deeper understanding and new ideas. TAG also moved into the role of setting standards for interschool visitation so that this time-consuming activity might be maximally productive. TAG's work paid off handsomly during the League Fortnight in the fifth year, when each school played host for an entire day during this two-week period of intensive visitation.

The change in format, substance, and authorship of *Changing Schools,* the League newsletter, provides interesting documentation of a steadily maturing conceptualization of the League and of the changing dominance in certain kinds of activities over the five years. Although there were expectations that League activities more and more would find their way into the newsletter, early issues conveyed an impression of the traditional linear approach to educational improvement, with principals and teachers as the target and somebody else manufacturing the ammunition. There were articles on what, presumably, was going on elsewhere, no more or less relevant to League schools than to schools generally; statements regarding the League and its importance; bibliographies and information on |I|D|E|A|. Toward the end of the second year, attention was given to the principal's key role in change and to the League principals specifically.

But it was not until the third year that teachers and their activities appeared, with some of the articles actually written by them. During that year, a League reporter for each school was chosen to provide information regarding school and League activities, which was then used as a basis for identifying potential articles. From that point on, changes of many kinds began to appear: to assure distribution of *Changing Schools* to each teacher; to gain the widest possible body of school information; to assure widespread teacher and principal involvement; to assure meaningfulness for all in the schools. Even the format changed—from a rather "finished" journal appearance to a more informal style, masthead, and organization of material.

One new feature has been well described elsewhere and is now being picked up in other school settings: a section of want ads called "LCS Classified."[11] This column drew upon the varied body of information now coming from the schools to draw attention to help available or wanted. Names, addresses, and telephone numbers encouraged interaction.

Our data suggest that the newsletter did contribute to the goal of the peer group awareness and League identification, which, in turn, was seen as a means to strengthen change processes in individual schools. Interestingly, readership was highest in those schools which had the most advanced processes of dialogue, decision making, action, and evaluation. This observation returns us to the major reason for fostering the League network in the first place—the development of readiness for and power to change in the schools constituting its membership.

By the third year, some of the principals were becoming very interested in the quality side of change and innovation and, as already noted, were raising questions not only about "good" innovations and schools but also about knowing how well a school is doing. They wanted some kind of tool to take them beyond personal impressions in seeking to assess the functioning of their schools—not, it soon became apparent, to gain a status picture with respect to relevance of curriculum, adequacy of instruction, and the like but, rather, to determine the vitality of processes through which curricular and instructional improvements might occur. They discussed everyday school activities and from this extracted evaluation questions designed to get at the adequacy of each activity. Then, they consulted with teachers back in their schools, adding and refining questions until they had fleshed out six major categories of activities and roles: dialogue, decision making, action, meetings, principal, teachers. All the DDAE components were included, since evaluation was present as part of the action category. The questions were put together and the instrument called "CRITERIA."[12]

Both the process and the substance of this three-party effort involving principals, teachers, and members of our staff represent a quantum leap from input from us, passivity in the schools, and "confronting the enemy and he is us." Essentially, principals and teachers were recognizing as important and developing criteria to appraise the very self-renewing processes which the |I|D|E|A| staff finally had accepted as critical during our marathon staff discussions of the second year. To protest that they simply picked up what we clearly wanted, that we finally had seduced them, is to convey a possible half-truth. But it is also to miss part of the central point.

We were, indeed, testing a working hypothesis about the school's role in and as an agent for change. This fact never was hidden. It was clearly there in the first meeting with superintendents, the letter of agreement, meetings with principals and teachers, early issues of *Changing Schools*, early articles on the League. Our strategy and deliberate changes in that strategy were designed to keep this hypothesis up front. Here, we were little different from other would-be reformers and certainly no less honest. In contrast to many, however, we were not trying to install anything. And, in contrast to much of the reforming discussed in Chapter 2, we were beginning to succeed in our goal, visibly and gratifyingly, during the third year. The fact that the principals—and, with them, the teachers—were devoting time and serious effort to accomplishing their own goals is an indication that the League strategy was working. School personnel now saw that there could be better ways for schools to function, wanted their schools to function better, and found the League mechanism useful in getting a difficult, challenging job done. The League was a partnership. It is difficult to say, once the strategy began to work, who influenced whom the most or, if you please, who was seducer and who was seduced!

It would be unfortunate, however, to leave the reader with the impression that, after two rather turbulent, difficult years, the water suddenly flattened out ahead of us, leaving only smooth sailing for the remaining three. There was not unanimity in our staff regarding precisely how to use our resources most effectively for school improvement, however much we may have agreed on the unique potential of the League. Further, there was not universal acceptance in the schools of our decision to back away from direct service to teachers in order to cultivate the use of peer resources and develop the power of the League social system. It is not surprising that a certain mutuality of viewpoint and a drawing together occurred between those |I|D|E|A| staff members and school personnel who envisioned an alternative relationship between the hub and the schools, one somewhat closer to the consultative model.

One of the intriguing puzzles is whether, under certain conditions, the two sets of views and approaches might live and, in fact, work together productively in a comprehensive approach to educational change—and, indeed, I include this possibility in a later chapter. But it must be remembered that there had been, from the start, a quid pro quo relationship in the League agreement and overall strategy. We had a research commitment to fulfill—a commitment necessarily extending beyond the confines of eighteen schools and our staff. I was forced, ultimately, to decide that this commitment and a two-path intervention strategy were incompatible.

There was no need to go beyond the nature of initial agreements and commitments in seeking to justify or explain this decision. But had it not been made on these grounds, a decision to go with one rather than both of these paths, whatever the possibility of their being followed side-by-side under certain circumstances, probably was inevitable. Most staff members by then had too much at stake; most believed strongly in one path or the other and felt that his or her commitment represented a basic principle; few were neutral. Several believed a crossroads was just ahead and that a collision was inevitable. One was very direct in saying that the crossroads already had been reached and that my decision was overdue.

THE HUB

Although the League agreement covered a rather long period of time (five years), considering the brevity of most projects, we had always in mind the fact of ultimate termination. We wanted there to be no sudden letdown. Consequently, there were frequent deliberate reminders of what each partner might gain out of a successful relationship. We had no money to give to anyone. Conceptually at least, there was a balance of potential return: that satisfaction of doing a better, more rewarding job on the part of teachers and principals and of gaining insight into problems and processes of change on the part of the |I|D|E|A| staff.

Early on, then, our rhetoric stressed the potentiality of human resources already in the schools. In speeches and articles, I stressed the futility of a small university faculty in education, for example, serving the ongoing needs of teachers as a prime function. Within two or three hours of driving time from UCLA, I pointed out, there are more than 150 independent school districts which quickly would swallow up any and all such resources made available. The resources of the Research Division of |I|D|E|A| were puny by comparison. To use them in a consulting capacity would be the height of folly and futility.

Nonetheless, a consulting role for the "expert" is the customary model. The schools looked for this, and we had trouble envisioning the specifics of an alternative, even while uneasy about direct consulting. Further, the embryonic League required care and feeding during those first two years especially. The line between expert advice on specific practices and supporting or encouraging certain self-renewing processes in a school is a fuzzy one, especially when there are not extant models for reference and guidance. That line was not clear in our minds; it certainly was not clear among school personnel.

Although the principals were coming to some realization of what we were about early in the second year, it must be remembered that by the beginning of the third year what they were gaining from their League association was for some of them a semiprivate matter. Our case records show them to have been at widely varying points on any continuum of leadership, in regard to both perceived responsibility and skills.[13] Some principals were viewed by their teacher-colleagues as ineffectual: unable to lead the staff to any decision, arbitrary in cutting off discussion and making decisions, preoccupied with administrative details, or inept at curricular and instructional matters. Not surprisingly, teachers sometimes looked to our staff for leadership not otherwise provided. And not surprisingly, members of our staff sometimes stepped into the breach—frequently even encouraged to do so by an insecure or threatened principal.

It becomes apparent, then, in retrospect, that our series of decisions to cultivate DDAE processes, to provide a clearinghouse rather than a stable of consultants, and simultaneously to maximize the peer role and minimize our role clashed with some other realities and expectancies, however neat and sound the rationale may have appeared. The situation was compounded by our decision to minimize direct school-to-|I|D|E|A| ties, leaving more responsibility to initiate contact with us to the schools. It was further compounded by the difficult dual role expected of our field staff: to provide some of the support needed for DDAE in the schools and peer school interaction to mature and to gather observational data to supplement data gathered by the research staff. Although we were almost all, to a degree, practitioners with subsequent research training, the field staff had a stronger initial orientation to direct service to teachers, a view naturally strengthened by the press of close association.

By early fall of that third year, members of the field staff were expressing considerable concern about our role and image in the field. Even the member most committed to the potential power of high quality DDAE and the League network had some misgivings about whether or not this strategy would take over in time to satisfy the apparent desire for immediate "expert" help. Increasingly, evidence was coming to me as to how unevenly the time of our field staff was being distributed as a result of our decision to leave the schools to initiate most of the school-to-|I|D|E|A| communication. There was a natural tendency of our field staff members to go where they were most wanted, where they thought there was something worth developing. Sometimes, these were places where teachers appeared ready to move and principals, partly on the basis of teachers' perceptions, appeared unlikely or unwilling to lead. In many ways, the emerging situation provided an ideal one for exercising the consultative role: a ready client perceiving a helpful organization and a resource person cognizant of need and wanting to help. To turn one's back on it would be to appear uncaring. Rhetoric on what "we really were trying to do" would sound empty.

The films on the League portray some of this and document the two differing orientations of the staff coming to a head by midyear. In one memorable scene, the chairman of our small field staff makes an eloquent plea for all of us to get out there to help those schools. If not, he says, the League most assuredly will go under and irreparable harm will have been wrought. My role, clearly visible on the film, was to get as much of the information as possible before the staff so as to pose as sharply as possible the dilemma confronting us.

Staff dialogue was a way of life with us: total group on a regular meeting schedule; small groups (one on research, one on evaluation, and one on field relations) on a more irregular, impromptu schedule; and various pairs and teams working on specific tasks. Total staff dialogue became difficult during concluding months of the third year. It was clear to me and, I think, to most of the staff that we could not turn back the clock in regard to our commitment to intervention. Whether or not some kind of compromise would be made and, if so, how much of a compromise was not at all clear to the staff, however. They looked to me and at me very carefully, watching for clues as to my thinking. They sought me out, usually individually but sometimes in pairs, to tell me what they thought was happening or should happen. They gave me advice, solicited and unsolicited. There was far more talk than came to me and, of course, strongly expressed viewpoints I never heard.[14]

In spite of the fact that there could be no turning back and that "all going out there to help those schools" could not be a viable alternative, it was seriously sustained in the dialogue, nonetheless. This was not artificial sustenance designed merely to placate those holding opposing views. Assuming the genuineness of the perspective and the real nature of the fear, clearly there were circumstances to be taken into account in fostering the League strategy. We were confronted not with a truly open decision as to major alternative strategies available—the decision had been made with the very creation of the League and reinforced ever since—but with a crisis arising within the context of our present strategy.

The perception that the League might fall apart and the schools go under without our direct help was in part generated by efforts, intensified early in the third year, to expand direct teacher involvement instead of waiting for principals to effect that involvement through exercise of leadership. This had almost universal support from the principals. Those who had come the farthest in confidence and development of leadership ability welcomed increased opportunity to use the full range of resources thus opened up. Those who were most insecure saw a way to minimize their own inadequacies while appearing to keep up with peers within the socializing fabric of the League. But it meant for all a widening in the boundaries of their span of control. For some, it was exchanging one set of insecurities for another. As we saw earlier, this problem tended to work itself out during the year, primarily because of the growing effectiveness of peer-group interchange.

Ironically, this very working created its own backlash. Much of human history reveals gratifyingly what happens when opportunities to learn are enhanced, whether through learning to read the Bible for oneself or by extending the opportunity to read to books not officially prescribed or sanctioned. But opportunities create a kind of insatiability and new kinds of problems. At the beginning of the third year, the League strategy was just beginning to take hold. Success to date, although limited, had created certain expectations and awarenesses and some accompanying dissatisfaction. For example, our data show that those schools making the most visible progress in DDAE expressed high dissatisfaction with their own internal processes. Awareness of need heightened a feeling of inadequacy, even though commendable progress already had been made.

Opening up the League network so as to emphasize peer interaction thus created its own demand, a demand which could not yet be fully satisfied by peers because the logistics for doing so were still in a formative stage. But our field staff was known and, furthermore, was made up of "experts." So what if there were some restraints on their use? Rules made under one set of circumstances could be changed in the face of new ones. So what if there were some idealistic rhetoric about the real strength of the League residing in member schools? This strength would be used, but it was not enough. So what if principals were to exercise leadership on behalf of the staff? Clearly, some were not doing so nor were likely to do so soon. (Our data on teachers' perceptions of these matters are spotty but are sufficient to suggest that some held such views.) The important consideration from the perspective of some teachers was that they were ready to learn new ways, to do new things, to move. Now was the time for |I|D|E|A| to come to the aid of its constituents: "Tell us what to do."[15] To meet this rising tide of readiness and opportunity was tempting for the organization and for at least some members of the staff. And it presented us with the most critical decision confronted by the |I|D|E|A| staff throughout the Study of Educational Change and School Improvement.

It is in some ways easier and in others more difficult to reconstruct in retrospect the decision-making processes of those concluding months of the third year. There were varying interpretations of my efforts, some revealed in the films, to draw out the nature, extent, and seriousness of these teacher expectations for us to consult. Even those senior staff members most likely to see the reason for this were uneasy about the possibility of ultimately deciding to endorse and legitimate both paths. This, I was told by several, could lead only to resignations. Others pushing the "get out there and help" path informed me that any other decision would make their continuation on the staff improbable.

It is difficult, probably impossible, to trace the threads which gradually were pulled together into a reasonably comprehensive understanding of what was happening and an accompanying decision as to what the continuing role of the hub should be. Intuitively perhaps, there was a dawning realization that the original League strategy, strengthened by many small and large decisions, was working and that the data interpreted to be evidence of pending doom could be otherwise interpreted. If, indeed, the League was responsible for the surging tide of teacher readiness, why change paths now? Instead of reversing ourselves by engaging as a matter of policy in the called-for consultation, why not ride even more positively and firmly down the path already taken? This was the decision arrived at as the third year moved into its concluding months.

It did not represent consensus; that would have been too much to expect. Perhaps it is an oversimplification, possibly even incorrect, to say that most members of the staff knew, down deep, how things would work out soon after the necessity for an ultimate decision surfaced at midyear—and, if so, that knowing probably was based in part, but only in part, on an awareness of my own orientation. My views on direct consultation as an intervention strategy were well known; my point of view regarding the importance of people "becoming," in large measure through their own efforts and the feelings of potency likely to accompany each little success, were by then rather well documented. It was both the intervening period of time until it was made and the potential consequences of the sensed decision that troubled our staff deeply—not only because of the possible repercussions in our group but also, probably more important, the implications for and perceptions of those in the schools.

It was another watershed, one of perhaps even greater significance than the trauma of self-confrontation experienced by the principals—and, consequently, by us—some eighteen months before. It is to the credit of those who stood to lose most by the decision that they accepted it with considerable grace. But it was a decision some staff members could not really live with. For them to back away during subsequent months from giving direct help to those who would have continued to seek it would have been exceedingly difficult, if not impossible. One who had been preparing for a teacher education post decided that now was the time to make the move. For another, on a two-year leave, return to the previous post was mandatory anyway. One, personally identifying with the League strategy but troubled by our ability to survive the crisis, accepted the decision with relief—and, in fact, contributed significantly to the direction in which it was made.[16]

Interestingly, the deliberately prolonged period of decision making (which, of course, unfortunately meant prolongation of the period of pain and tension) brought forward evidence to increase confidence in the decision. Clearly, the League strategy was beginning to work, as other volumes in this series substantiate. Agenda for principals' meetings, planned by the principals with some input from us, were designed to confront them with the problems of their schools and to develop the necessary knowledge and skills. Teachers leaving the building to confer with peers now presented little threat. And teachers were beginning to gain stimulation and help from peers in other schools far beyond what had been anticipated just months before. Some at least understood our reasons for downplaying the |I|D|E|A| staff role, even though the tension between wanting to become self-directing and wanting "expert" help remained high. It began to look to some of us on the |I|D|E|A| staff more and more as though the problems surfacing in somewhat alarming proportions the previous fall were symptoms of the same self-confrontation experienced by the principals a year earlier. Subsequent months, with an accompanying growth in the peer-group socialization process, presumably had eased the tension.

But it was clear during the third year's concluding summer months, which always offered a certain rebirth, that the period immediately following our exhausting period of introspection would not be an easy one, an observation confirmed as the fall began. Some principals and teachers perceived that those no longer on the staff (some of whom were better known in the schools than some continuing members) had been punished for differing views—especially for being in disagreement with Goodlad (I received two or three complaining letters, the most vitriolic and least flattering from an anonymous source. I had expected more). Some thought we had let them down, especially since the persons perceived to be most able to help them no longer were available. Scattered criticism of this kind still showed up in our summative evaluations nearly two years later.

Two or three principals and probably a much larger number of teachers were deeply shaken. They had come to see me as supportive of individuals, even when I disagreed with them. Now, it appeared to them, I had revealed my true self in the breach. One angrily confronted me with how he felt and why, an act that no doubt was very difficult for him. Another expressed his displeasure and discomfort nonverbally. There is no way of responding or defending oneself against such accusations; indeed, they created considerable self-doubts. Many times I relived events of the preceding months to see if and how they might have been guided otherwise.

Far more serious was the charge of a few that the |I|D|E|A| staff (which mostly meant Goodlad) were prepared to sacrifice teachers—and, therefore, children—in the name and cause of research and, indeed, had already done so. The "dismissals" of those "who really care about us" was evidence. So was our decision to consolidate our field and research staffs into a single whole (we were so closely involved with the schools by now that even relatively small internal changes in our organization were quickly known in at least some schools). Our subsequent announcement to the effect that we wanted to provide better channels of communication back to the schools regarding data of potential use to them was fuel for this fire, even though such feedback had been part of the original agreement.

Since the study of change was, indeed, our announced and central purpose, our expected return from a collaborative enterprise, this commitment could only be acknowledged and reiterated. In view of the track record of many of the staff members as able practitioners in various kinds of schools, however, the charge of sacrificing teachers and children was felt keenly. It is to their credit that they simply went quietly about their business, convinced that time would provide the negating evidence. Summative evaluation toward the end of the fifth year revealed considerable understanding of our desire to study change and of the quid pro quo nature of the relationship.

There was another, quite different response to our apparent intensification, in the fall of the fourth year, of those hub activities designed to support DDAE in the schools and the League network. An active leadership role on the part of principals increasingly was part of their self-perception and generally desired by teachers. But some of our direct help on teachers' pedagogical problems had tended, more and more, to bypass principals. For the most part, principals resented this and were glad to see its termination in reality rather than only in rhetoric and, thus, compatibility between cup and lip on our part. Further, they were growing in their ability to take pride in teachers' accomplishments, learning to bask in the reflected glory of teachers serving as resource persons in other places, both League schools and elsewhere. The maturing League framework now served their needs and interests.

Also, it appeared, the uneven nature of our direct field contacts had tended to give us a somewhat distorted picture of developments in the schools. Perhaps, unwittingly, we were overutilizing certain teacher resources in League activities and, by so doing, drawing attention to some schools and some individuals at the expense of others. A few principals and their staffs had seen us as playing favorites and had been becoming increasingly resentful. Principals who once had been willing to turn over their leadership responsibilities to almost anyone were now jealous of them and did not enjoy being bypassed.

here were those, then, who rejoiced at what appeared to be lessened ambiguity on our part and greater trust in our own beliefs and in our colleagues in the schools. Confidence, so long as it appears to be accompanied by competence, breeds confidence.

Perhaps some crises appear less formidable in retrospect, but postmortem reflection suggests that the bulk of the schools, principals, and teachers was relatively untouched by our internal trauma. Presumably, it had not been visible to them to the degree we feared. By the end of the third year, the League had become an integral part of daily existence for |I|D|E|A| staff members. Many viewed it as the most meaningful professional experience of their lives; they learned something every day. Visitors—our materials center was in use by teachers almost daily—were impressed by the enthusiasm and dedication of the staff. Apparently, whatever their misgivings about the direction ultimately to emerge from a prolonged decision-making period in those concluding months of the third year, staff members went about their business very much as usual. I guess it is no great stretch of the plausible to say that the League was working for us as well as for those in the schools.

OBSERVATIONS ON PROCESS AND PRODUCT

During the fourth and fifth years, the three major elements of the League took on definitive shape. All schools worked at the improvement of internal staff processes but, of course, spread out widely on both effectiveness and conscious concern for them. (Barry's study revealed one school that had made little progress suddenly spurting and making the most progress during the two years immediately following conclusion of the project.[17]) Schools differed widely, also, in their ability to use the peer resources available in the League and to reciprocate by making resources readily available to other schools. The hub considerably refined its role as a clearinghouse and research center. But because its mortality had been ordained from the start, we remained somewhat myopic in regard to its potential as a vital element in the consortium.

I have more to say about all of these elements and particularly relationships among them in subsequent chapters. However, the reader's best source for details as to procedures, successes, failures, outcomes and the like is *Changing Schools: The Magic Feather Principle,*[18] which gives considerable attention to a cluster of factors suggesting varying degrees of dynamism or, as Barry phrases it, propensity toward change in the schools.

As Bentzen and her associates point out, we were interested in how well DDAE might stand up as an indicator of conditions which, taken as a cluster, would suggest a school's responsible receptivity to change. A summary DDAE score was obtained for forty-nine schools— eighteen League schools and thirty-one schools not in the League. The schools were then ranked and divided into thirds, which were classified as high, middle, and low on the DDAE criterion. Low and high groups were then compared to produce descriptions of differing sets of school conditions.

In the high DDAE schools there were more cooperative teaching arrangements, more friendship networks among teachers, and more task-oriented communication networks among teachers. Teachers had more influence in decision making, especially in areas affecting schools as total units. The quality of principal leadership was higher and principal influence depended more on competence. The principals in high DDAE schools were more apt to see teacher influence in schools as a desirable condition. These schools ranked higher on indices of school climate. By contrast, there were more self-contained classrooms in low DDAE schools. Teacher influence was more narrowly limited to areas affecting only a few people rather than the school as a whole and the principal was more apt to see teacher influence on schoolwide decisions as undesirable. The principal's influence was more likely to depend on status and power to reward. (No causal relationships among these factors are to be deduced.)

DDAE involved a good many properties of school faculty groups working together. For example, the salience of dialogue was no doubt improved by the habit of going to appropriate references for purposes of bringing to bear relevant research and views on the subject. But this and other behaviors might be clustered under the rubric of professionalism. When this is done, we find high DDAE, high teacher professionalism, high teacher sense of power or potency (being able to participate in schoolwide decisions), and high teacher morale to be associated. Clearly, the categories are not discrete; they overlap at points. Nonetheless, taken together, they helped us observe and describe a school's propensity for change, a school's readiness for and ability to work toward self-improvement. These characteristics, found together at a relatively high level of development, suggest enormous potential for and probable significant ongoing growth and self-renewal.

There is not, then, some single powerful factor associated with or operating to explain openness to innovation and change. This conclusion parallels closely conclusions from research into student learning. There is a whole array of contributing factors, not just one critical variable.

Exceedingly important, our work suggests, is the functioning of these factors in faculty subgroups. There has been a growing tendency toward larger elementary schools, with resulting problems of communicating and conducting staff business arising from sheer size. Frequently, as some of our other work suggests,[19] there is not even a good place to meet. Consequently, it becomes necessary to work together in subgroups. Also, Bahner's study of the Englewood School[20] suggests the necessity of small-group work between meetings to assure productive total staff meetings even in a small school. Perhaps more important, while cohesiveness and communication among all members are essential to give a school its spirit and shape its program, the details of instruction are more easily and naturally worked out by teams of teachers whose daily work has much in common.

Our experience suggests that a school with high DDAE, teacher morale, teacher power, and teacher professionalism can survive considerable trauma, including the loss of its principal. Our observations over the five years of the study suggest that a school is even better fortified against disruption from external forces when these factors are present to high degree in faculty subgroups. In fact, there is room for experimentation with schools run by such subgroups, perhaps with an elected chairman of each serving as a steering committee and with one of its members serving for a time in a rotating principalship.[21]

However, this might be a useful way to find principals rather than to do away with them since such a process and structure might well prepare principals for leadership. Barry's study, referred to earlier, shows that although high DDAE, high professionalism, and high morale help to sustain a school in time of stress, the principal has something to do with their development and unless he or she is able to exercise leadership toward their development, the presence of these factors ultimately will fall off. The principal's role in a school disposed toward change is important—he can block or he can facilitate it. Lieberman, adopting categories employed by Gordon in studying teachers' classroom leadership styles,[22] was able to develop composite pictures of principals' leadership styles embracing three components: their orientation toward setting tasks, their use of authority, and their expressive, supporting behavior. Her conclusion is similar to that of others who have explored the composite impact of several such factors: "... the principal can provide a powerful leadership role in changing the school culture by attending to the various means of organizing the school to look outside its walls, to work toward shared decision making, and to provide consistently for the support and needs of the school faculty."[23]

In a study of the University Elementary School conducted just before the League was launched, McClure took a look at aspects of the relationship between staff processes and products in the form of curriculum plans. Although the DDAE criteria were not then available, he looked at very similar aspects of process. He was able to differentiate among three faculty subgroups, ranking them superior, fair, and low on process. Interestingly, the products of their work together were rated by a panel of curriculum experts as excellent, fair, and poor, respectively.[24]

We cannot be as precisely definitive regarding a relationship between process and product in the League schools. However, toward the end of the fourth year, I attempted a rough sorting. Even at that late date, two schools had scarcely made a beginning. There was evidence in both of some of that familiar combination of eagerness and frustration which seems almost invariably to signal a readiness to take off. But neither revealed any signs of the next stage—of teachers getting started on something exciting to them. In neither of these schools was there evidence at the time of a small core of the most interested teachers organized into a working subgroup from which there might have been a ripple effect ultimately reaching other teachers. The principals either were encouraging only selected individuals or were ineffective in reaching the staff as a whole. Teacher morale, teacher feelings of power or potency, teacher professionalism, and DDAE were low, and classroom and school programs were flat and routine, lacking peaks of excellence.

These two schools suggest the importance of factors which fell outside of the League structure and what it sought deliberately to cultivate. Neither enjoyed much enthusiasm for the League from its board of education. Interestingly, both schools were located in semi-rural communities marked by transience, somewhat bland—even dull and uninteresting—physical surrounding, and absence of cultural resources. There was little for teachers to do but go to school and then go home—a situation not unlike the Englewood School described in

Chapter 3. Each school had three different principals during the League project. Clearly, there are elements in the larger social system of which the school is a part as well as in its own internal resources which have much to do with how fast and far a school will move toward becoming a dynamic entity. I shall return to this later.

At the other extreme were two schools operating with a smoothness and demonstrating programs at a level one might have hoped for but rarely saw in that now nearly extinct species, the university-based laboratory school. How they came to get that way and the nature of their functioning deserve book-length analysis, but space permits only a few observations here. Both were blessed with modern plants—one with open structure and the other constructed in pods, with considerable ease of access from room to room within each pod. Both were relatively close, physically and collaboratively, to the homes of their students. Parents moved in and out of the two schools freely and comfortably, many serving as aides, though in neither instance was there an elaborate parent-teacher or school-community structure. There were joint discussions of school policies and activities, but most of the support for the schools seemed to be generated by parents who participated in the daily program. Parents spoke for the schools to other parents—and to critics from neighboring schools.

Although both were in districts changing superintendents once during the League's existence, both enjoyed the support for at least three years of superintendents who took an active interest in the League. They did not have to contend with top-level displeasure.

Neither was an urban school; both were in housing tracts populated by lower middle to middle socioeconomic groups; both were in fast-growing districts. Although not in the first ring of suburban communities with ready access to urban resources, both communities had access to at least modest cultural resources.

Teacher morale, sense of power, and professionalism were high and both schools ranked high on DDAE, with small-group DDAE being particularly well developed. Although outwardly markedly different in personality and leadership style, both principals were relatively low in their use of authority, rather task-oriented, and characterized by highly visible support of their teachers and pride in their schools. They stood out in League principals' meetings, both assuming considerable leadership but each for different kinds of responsibilities. In their schools, they seemed very much at the heart of things, spending more time in classrooms, in the staff lounge informally with teachers, and on the playgrounds than in their offices. Both took active roles in school-community relations, especially in work with parent volunteers. Although one was much more formal than the other in interpersonal relations, both seemed to have rather comfortable, relaxed relations with teachers, pupils, and parents.

Both schools at the time of my visits were virtually nongraded and team taught. Several teachers and clusters of children ranging several years in age worked together in a smoothly functioning flow of activity in which it often was difficult to isolate separate subjects, particularly at the primary level (K–3). Although the teachers planned together before and after the school day, what might be called "planning and deciding on the run" was particularly impressive. As one teacher moved toward the door with children heading for recess on the playground, the others moved together for a standing-walking consultation on how things were going and whether ongoing activity should be redirected in some way. Clearly, in both schools, a diagnostic process was almost continuous, with provision being made for those children who needed more time or more specialized help— and for this the volunteer-aide role became particularly visible.

Standing back somewhat detached from the whole, I was able to see the structural elements of an integrated, sequential curriculum design which somehow managed to blossom in the form of children making choices among a rich array of alternatives—choices which seemed to offer promise that curricular intent would be fulfilled. There was a delightful, virtually aesthetic, rhythm to it all, with ends and means as one, with children, teachers, and activities somehow blended into a harmonious whole. Although some things happened spontaneously and although it all looked as easy as the professional outfielder catching a long fly ball, one knew that a lot of work had gone on, that these relatively young teachers knew what they were about, that professionals were at work. One could easily recall some of what Dewey said about the nature of the educational experience; or Whitehead's cycle of romance, vigor, and application in learning; or what Bruner had to say about the spiral curriculum.

A visitor from the outside would have had difficulty isolating an innovation, but most of those being widely advocated were there: considerable use of audiovisual aids, especially by two or three children at a time and on their own; some of the new curricular materials; modified, flexible classroom space; multiage or nongraded groups and classes; use of parent volunteers in the instructional program; team

planning, teaching, and evaluating. They blended together, each modified and adapted through faculty DDAE but especially through small-
group decision-making processes. In neither school had there been a
formal or even informal agreement with some outside group to
employ a given innovation. The teachers selected from all that they
were exposed to in the League and in any other professional associations.

Three schools, according to my ranking, would fall only slightly
behind these two. Placing them in some order of excellence would
not be possible; they differed in their kinds of accomplishment, each
being stronger in regard to some features than the two schools described above. Two of the three had experienced rather difficult problems: lack of central-office support in one and turnover in the principalship (three principals in five years) in the other.

My reasons for placing these in a slightly lower category are two
in number. Although marked by some outstanding features, the programs did not mesh with quite the same smoothness. Nongrading
and team teaching, for example, were a little more mechanical and
seemed to lack a little of the friction-reducing grease produced by
teachers able to guess each other's next moves. Also, they seemed
not quite to have the necessary deep insight into what they were doing. Although articulate about and attached to new ideas, they had
not always internalized their meaning in practice. Their programs
throughout were slightly more traditional and conservative.

The remaining eleven schools suggest classification into two more
categories. Eight of them by the end of the first four years were reasonably satisfying places to visit; each had something of interest from
which a visitor could learn. One could sense that they were on the
way to better things. They differed from the top five schools in consistency of commitment and program, being marked by valleys as well
as peaks. On the whole, they were less able to explain or give clear
reasons for what they were about. While one could feel good about
having his or her child with almost any cluster of teachers in the other
five, in these eight one would want to be able to pick and choose.
Rather consistently, they were markedly below the others in their
small-group DDAE processes.

The other three schools in the eleven were still at the talk stage.
The general morale and quality of adult life seemed satisfactory, and
faculty meetings suggested readiness—even eagerness—to change and
good interpersonal relationships. Individual teachers here and there

were undertaking new things, frequently stimulated by what they had seen in another League school. But schoolwide or even small-group programmatic results were not yet in evidence. The processes had begun; the products were yet to come.

It is possible that given these groups, a more diagnostic approach to interschool visitation might have paid dividends. For example, schools in the lowest category might have been exposed to schools just a little ahead of them as well as those at a high level of development. The latter would provide new visions, the former an antidote to the probable resulting discouragement. As a matter of fact, we did set up some such deliberate intervisitation arrangements during the fifth year, with promising results.

One concluding observation suggests that we cannot rely on the local school alone, without supporting and connecting mechanisms for self-renewal. Almost universally among League schools, the most satisfying programmatic accomplishments occurred at the primary or lower elementary level. Our other studies have suggested that the school program tends to rigidify as one moves upward through the grades, with textbooks and workbooks becoming almost universally guiding fare in the upper elementary years. Lower elementary and particularly kindergarten teachers apparently feel less constrained, less expected to cover a fixed, prescribed curriculum.

Even in what I have described as the most fully developed League schools, able, dedicated, hard-working upper elementary teachers seemed unable to compensate for what might be called the formal or prescribed curriculum. It simply seemed more difficult for them to provide markedly fresh or different experiences from what the children already had been through. I left even good schools, by conventional standards, with a vague uneasiness about the upper elementary years, a feeling that there will have to be much more radical departures from tradition if the learning potential of preadolescents is to be adequately tapped. These may very well be the forgotten years in schooling, the years in which being turned off later is assured. The breakthrough needed will require both an infusion of ideas—perhaps through a League hub—and support not only from peer schools but also from the larger system of which each school is a part. Superintendents who pay attention primarily to budgets and public relations will not suffice for the difficult problems of changing those regularities of schooling over which teachers have or perceive themselves as having only limited control.

NOTES

1   There was some early collaboration between the |I|D|E|A| Research Division and UCLA's then new Center for the Study of Evaluation on problems of evaluation. For example, the latter worked with League schools in developing and testing certain instruments. The |I|D|E|A| evaluative emphasis turned toward staff processes, ultimately resulting in *The Problem Solving School Program* available from |I|D|E|A|, 5335 Far Hills Avenue, Dayton, Ohio. The R&D Center at UCLA became an increasingly effective force in the development of procedures and materials for the improvement of evaluative technology.

2   Carroll has developed a useful, comprehensive model for examining the full range of factors at the instructional level likely to influence pupil outcomes. See John B. Carroll, "A Model of School Learning," *Teachers College Record*, vol. 64, pp. 723–733, 1963.

3   Lloyd's study is revealing here. She compared two experimental groups of teachers who had received special training in new instructional procedures with a control group lacking such training. She was able to elicit the criterion performance in the experimental groups at a high level of statistical significance. But there was no difference in pupil achievement. This is a common finding in such studies. But Lloyd, on the basis of further study and rather intimate knowledge of the two experimental groups, went on to hypothesize about the failure of the teachers schools to encourage or sustain the new, countervailing methodologies. In effect, the teachers knew but apparently did not practice them—and so, the absence of pupil gains could not necessarily reflect on the methodologies themselves but rather on these being, once again, nonevents. See Dorothy M. Lloyd, "The Effect of a Staff Development Program on Teacher Performance Behavior and Student Achievement," unpublished doctoral dissertation, University of California, Los Angeles, 1974.

4   Some beginnings have been made in analyses of data from studies conducted by the International Association for the Evaluation of Educational Achievement, in which explanations for differences in pupil performance in various countries are being sought in contextual differences. A major problem, of course, is the lack of adequate descriptive data on schools. And, of course, as with the Coleman Report, there is no way of ferreting out differences in the climate or culture of schools. The more one gets into such matters, the more one realizes our neglect of schools as total entities in explaining pupil performance.

5   At this point, the reader is urged to turn to Chapter 3 in another

volume in this series, *The Power to Change.* Here, Lieberman not only summarizes Gordon's seminal research on teachers' classroom leadership styles but also employs his model to study principals' styles and their possible relationship to certain ways teachers behave in the classroom. See Ann Lieberman, "The Power of the Principal: Research Findings," in Carmen M. Culver and Gary J. Hoban (eds.), *The Power to Change: Issues for the Innovative Educator,* McGraw-Hill, New York, 1973, pp. 35–47. While research in general into such relationships has not to date been definitive, part of the problem again lies with the lack of adequately discrete comparison situations. This is a promising direction for further inquiry and experimentation.

6 These affective realms included Attitude toward School, Attitude toward Learning, Self-Concept, Attitude toward Technology, and Peer Relations. Each of the scales developed to measure them is presented as a paper-and-pencil questionnaire utilizing multiple choice items, and each is available in two forms. For most of the instruments, the score is the mean rating, on a five-point scale, of the student's response to approximately twenty questions. One scale, Peer Relations, has differentially weighted items. Sample sets of the |I'D|E'A| *Affective Instrument Package* are available from the Institute for Development of Educational Activities, 5335 Far Hills Avenue, Dayton, Ohio 45429.

7 See, for example, John I. Goodlad (et al.), *The Conventional and the Alternative in Education,* McCutchan Publishing Corporation, Berkeley, Calif., 1975.

8 Carmen M. Culver, Ann Lieberman, and David A. Shiman, "Working Together: The Peer Group Strategy," in Culver and Hoban, op. cit., p. 76.

9 Ibid., p. 75.

10 See Frederick S. Perls, R. F. Hefferline, and Paul Goodman, *Gestalt Therapy: Excitement and Growth in Human Personality,* Dell, New York, 1965.

11 See Culver, Lieberman, and Shiman, op. cit.

12 The CRITERIA instrument may be found in Appendix C of Mary M. Bentzen and Associates, *Changing Schools: The Magic Feather Principle,* McGraw-Hill, New York, 1974. Development of the instrument and its use are described in detail in Bette Overman, "Criteria for a Good School," in Culver and Hoban, op. cit.

13 See Lieberman, op. cit.

14 Various members of the staff might tell this part, especially, of the League story differently. The data gathered by Louise L. Tyler,

referred to earlier, reveal that some did, indeed, at the time and immediately following. And their perceptions may be different today. The perceptions revealed here are, of course, mine, as best as I am able to sort them out.

15   Culver, Lieberman, and Shiman, op. cit., recount the maturation of what had been a "show us, tell us" syndrome. During the fourth year, a group of teachers sought to share their fears, failures, and successes in written form. They discussed the tension between the desire to become self-directed and to lean on "experts." Suddenly, one said, "You know, we should call our monograph, 'Tell us what to do, but don't tell *me* what to do'!" That became the title. (An |I|D|E|A| monograph, Institute for Development of Educational Activities, Inc., 1971.)

16   The problem of staffing what the late Ole Sand referred to as deviant organizations—those not characterized by permanency as are universities—comes to the fore again. Necessarily, our staff was appointed on a year-to-year basis. This practice in itself creates some insecurity and, as a project draws to a close, considerable distraction, as staff members begin to look around for other opportunities. And, certainly, the continuity of a research and development organization not attached to a university is threatened. On the other hand, location in the university and employment only of university personnel, while assuring continuity and security, sometimes endangers the task- and mission-orientation of such institutes because of the tradition that university personnel follow their own hunches. Clearly, some kind of balance between security, stability, and mission-orientation and a certain freedom to follow one's creative drives is called for. It is an important problem for funding agencies and the institutions they support.

17   Elizabeth F. Barry, "The Relationship between Propensity toward Self-Directed Change in School Faculties and Selected Factors in the School's Subculture," unpublished doctoral dissertation, University of California, Los Angeles, 1974.

18   Bentzen and Associates, op. cit.

19   John I. Goodlad, M. Frances Klein, and Associates, *Looking Behind the Classroom Door*, rev. ed., Charles A. Jones, Worthington, Ohio, 1974.

20   John M. Bahner, "An Analysis of an Elementary School Faculty at Work," unpublished doctoral dissertation, University of Chicago, Chicago, Ill. 1960.

21   Gary J. Hoban, "The School without a Principal," in Culver and Hoban, op. cit.

22 C. Wayne Gordon and Leta McKinney Adler, *Dimensions of Teacher Leadership in Classroom Social Systems*, University of California, Los Angeles, 1963.

23 Lieberman, op. cit., p. 47.

24 Robert M. McClure, "Procedures, Processes and Products in Curriculum Development," unpublished doctoral dissertation, University of California, Los Angeles, 1965.

CHAPTER 6

REFLECTIONS ON THE HYPOTHESIS AT WORK

What we need ... is playfulness. Playfulness is the deliberate, temporary relaxation of rules in order to explore the possibility of alternative rules. ... In effect, we annouce—in advance—our rejection of the usual objections to behavior that does not fit the standard model of intelligence.

> —James G. March ("Model Bias in Social Action," *Review of Educational Research*, vol. 42, no. 4, p. 417, Fall 1972)

The Study of Educational Change and School Improvement (SECSI) led to no neat conclusions about how to improve American education. My initial statement of the hypothesis (1955) surmised that certain conditions were necessary for the school itself to become an effective agent of and for change. SECSI was an attempt not only to postulate some of these conditions but also to explore their potential usefulness in what might be rather loosely defined as a field experiment. Consequently, we developed and to some degree tested in the process of development major elements of a structure within which the improvement of schooling might proceed and be nourished. These are built into the more comprehensive strategy proposed in Chapter 7. Also, some of them are included in the |I|D|E|A| change program for Individually Guided Education, now embraced by hundreds of schools across the country with participating clusters of schools built into league-type networks.

What SECSI does provide, then, by way of product is a considerable body of experience on what happens when the school itself is taken as the locus of and a force for change and certain peer and nonpeer resources are built into a structure intended to provide support. Examples of collaborative, relatively long-term, data-based enterprises of this kind in American education are, indeed, few. Consequently, it is incumbent on those of us who were involved to endeavor to sort out the problems likely to be encountered and the things that appeared to work or not work and why and to reflect on implications for others who might wish to make their own paths, employing the central hypothesis. This is what this chapter is about.

Although the schools were picked to provide considerable diversity, a sample of only eighteen schools presents its own cautions. However, a great deal of what has been written about educational change is based on single case studies or smaller samples with a far less comprehensive inclusion of interacting elements. Some is based on no direct experience at all; a great deal involves extrapolation and deduction emanating from other segments of society, particularly business and industry. Furthermore, there is a paucity of experiments and reports involving such close relationships of practitioners and researchers sustained for so long. Consequently, the match between our observations and those contained in extant literature or the absence of any fit takes on considerable significance.

Once more, the reader is reminded that these are my observations from the point of view of principal investigator with overall responsibility for the project, tempered and conditioned by examining our various kinds of data, certain archival material, and, of course, the several volumes written by my colleagues. What follows is less a summary of conclusions than reflections on our experiences placed against the backdrop of the problems discussed in earlier chapters. I look, first, at what the hypothesis came to mean to us and what its utilization as a working principle for educational intervention carried us into. Then, I probe into what seemed to be happening to the institutions and people involved, with some attention to cycles of change. The chapter concludes with some reflections on the League as an infrastructure designed to support the kinds of change processes implied by the hypothesis.

THE HYPOTHESIS TAKES ON MEANING

It should come as no surprise that the most difficult part of testing in action the hypothesis regarding the school as the key unit for educational change is the necessarily close involvement with people. No doubt, this is why Robert M. Hutchins' University of Utopia was to have no students! One is not dealing simply with a concept and an accompanying plan for educational improvement but with the particular people making up the school or schools. Consequently, there is no way of escaping one's basic assumptions about the nature of man nor one's prejudices regarding certain types of people and, indeed, certain individuals. It is much easier to be idealistic in the face of a concept than in the face of a reality involving the idiosyncrasies of people.

To sum up the required perspective and accompanying behavior with the word "trust" is too easy, although trust came to play an important part in the League. One of our documentary film segments is called "A Matter of Trust" and reveals how important it is for a community to trust its school, the superintendent to trust the principal, the principal to trust teachers, and teachers to trust students. But this can be a too-available simplification. Complex issues are obscured: Where does trust come from? What are the limits to its usefulness as a concept? Many students of the change process are openly distrustful of the concept of trust as a mover and shaker in the change process, while recognizing the importance of its ultimate emergence.

Employing the working hypothesis necessitates confronting a fundamental belief for which trust may be one of several conventions. It is a belief in the necessity for humankind to shape its institutions and destiny and that it indeed does so for better or for worse. There is a further belief that, given open choice, human beings want a voice and a reasonably free hand in creating their environments and that the process of doing so brings personal growth and satisfaction—and autonomy within the restraints of what has been created. It is clear that human beings create institutions and things to serve their interests. Individuals are then shaped by their institutions and things, becoming slaves to them unless or until refashioning and renewal occur.

The evolution of labor unions and their demands is a case in point. Unions came into being to protect the workers from exploitation by management, and their demands were focused on shorter hours, better wages, earlier retirement, job security, and physical safety for the workers. Certain regularities were established in the process. However, as unions became more and more powerful, their focus shifted from protection of workers to protection of their own members, thus ensuring their survival as institutions. Therefore, part of what they achieved, especially in the realm of protecting classified jobs for specialized workers, resulted in increased piece work and routinization on the assembly line, which restricted the satisfaction to be achieved in work. Union power did not necessarily achieve person power—a feeling of worth, dignity, and potency. And the very regularities established through negotiations tended to backfire, becoming more powerful than established custom and fashion in blocking change.

Since it has become increasingly recognized that people want satisfying work as well as good salaries, labor and management in many places have begun to look for ways of changing regularities in order to reduce the tedium involved in the assembly line and other routine work. Examples are found in the shift from the worker in the assembly line to a team of workers building a whole car in the production of Volvo and Saab automobiles. Similarly, changes in the hierarchical and decision-making structure of ships are revolutionizing the Norwegian shipping industry as each member of the crew performs any and all roles, including participating in decisions traditionally reserved for the captain.[1] Thus, mechanisms are being created to give the workers more control in shaping their own environment. But, like all changes, these could be seen as highly threatening to established regularities and, therefore, could not simply be mandated. Rather, they were instituted as experiments. These were not experiments in the sense of comparing groups under different sets of controls, but, in a way, experiments in human freedom and responsibility, agreed to by labor and management, in which it was expected that those involved would find, or grope, their way to solutions affecting their welfare. There was research, there were projected alternatives to be tested, and there was feedback from research to aid in formative evaluation. Perhaps, in many areas of human activity, it will be increasingly necessary for precedent-breaking reforms to arise within the context of social experiments thus perceived and conducted.

SECSI was, in this sense, an experiment in human freedom, not with predetermined controls but with an agreement for dissimilar organisms to work together, to experiment, in order to satisfy differing interests. Given the prevailing, linear model of change, SECSI was countervailing, essentially conforming to Schwab's definition of fluid or long-term inquiry (see Chapter 3). Nobody, presumably, was going to do anything to anybody else. There was not a common set of objectives; in fact, there were no objectives at all in the sense of persons being expected to acquire or improve certain precise behaviors. Trust was not part of the agreement, although it soon began to play a formidable role. There were no oaths of commitment to this or that concept or innovation but only a loose expectation of improving certain school practices, gathering certain data, and testing an hypothesis.[2]

Ironically, although schools supposedly are "people places" and could be exemplary models-in-miniature of the educative society, little attention has been given to the role the people in them should play in their continuing reconstruction. In focusing on this role, SECSI was countervailing, especially at a time when teacher professionalism and teacher power increasingly were being defined in organizational and collective terms. Teachers came late to unionization; the labor-management model they adopted was the very one already being subjected to inquiry, research, and experimentation by the most advanced segments of business and industry. It is the irony of ironies, even though understandable and to a degree predictable, that the education profession, which might have been expected to think first of basic human values in its negotiations, simply fell into the conventional pattern of salaries, pensions, and other material benefits, important as these are. The tendency to separate administrators and teachers in the bargaining process and to equate classroom teaching and work expectations may be creating the very conditions and accompanying blocks to change which can now be tackled only in the framework of "experiments."

SECSI was countervailing, too, in regard to its conceptualized approach to research. Chapter 5 reveals the tortuous path we followed in defining what we were about here, partly because of our own difficulty in breaking with convention. While recognizing the ultimate importance of pupil outcomes as a criterion and, therefore, the locus of relevant data, we relegated these to secondary status in recognition of the belief that it is futile to look for pupil gain until the conditions thought to be potentially influential are established.

In fact, we deemed this point to be so important that we strained to keep the creation of conditions in the school front and center at all times. The notion of pupil gains on standardized achievement tests and teachers' presumed role in them is so dominant in American schooling that it tends to obviate all else. The goals built into these tests are still traditional ones; there is not yet a standardized test in general use reflecting the more recently emerging goals. But perhaps more important, since in our hypothesis the culture of the school was central, we finally decided to ɔ nothing even by way of implication to pay homage to other gods such as pupil achievement scores in the conduct of this particular project.

Countervailing, also, in the SECSI approach to research was the notion of feeding back data for purposes of enabling the school people involved to strengthen or redirect their efforts as appropriate. This is not at all a novel idea in those experiments conducted in business and industry mentioned earlier. But it is unadulterated heresy in some educational and especially psychological research quarters where "pure" experimentation is worshipped. Fortunately, more and more, educational researchers are coming to recognize the importance of testing intermediate theories using a variety of methods and then revising the theory in the light of feedback and analysis, ultimately searching for larger theories for understanding otherwise messy educational phenomena.

Embedded in this last sentence is an assumption about the purposes of educational research. Ultimately, it must serve to improve educational practice; its ongoing conduct must not harm practice. It is useful and valid when it either derives conclusions about the nature of aspects of the educational enterprise or when it aids the decision-making process. Consequently, for researchers to be in close, collaborative association with practitioners enhances the possibility that what they do will be relevant and that what they learn will find its way more quickly into practice. We learned a good deal about the hazards and difficulties involved, but the benefits gained nonetheless outweighed them. And, of course, we carried the added burden of excessive ambiguity about a relationship not adequately communicated to the schools in the first place, partly because it was an experiment involving only dimly perceived variables. Many of the conventions in research were suspended.

One of our strong conclusions pertains to the importance of research and hypotheses testing as necessary ingredients of educational change. Education as a profession and as an enterprise suffers dearly because of their near-absence. Schools and school systems simply do not have an attitude of inquiry about what they do, let alone any mechanisms for data-based action. This is in large part why they have fallen victims to outmoded practices from industry as well as of gimmicks touted by their own would-be reformers and innovators. For example, a good deal of what goes on in schools in the name of planning (program planning and budgeting systems and program evaluation review technique—PERTing) and some approaches to teacher accountability simply do not account for enough of the variables involved. The input-output product model derived from the military and from industry not only fits schools poorly; many kinds of businesses and industries increasingly are recognizing its limitations. Further, it may not be merely ill-fitting; it may be quite wrong, leading us to think of schools and education in ways that are dangerously misleading. Perhaps growing realization of the difficulties in applying and refining the input-output model of schooling will lead us to ultimate disenchantment with it and accelerated progress toward alternative conceptions. The presence of a well-staffed and reasonably independent research unit becomes indispensable in any genuine search for new conceptions and ways of educating.

Even more countervailing was the SECSI intervention strategy. It was here that our ability to understand the meaning of the hypothesis and to test it with real people in real schools underwent the most severe testing. The strategy itself is not that complex; in fact, it is deceptively simple. After I carefully describe the League to various audiences, people frequently ask, "Yes, but what did you do?" This is part of the trouble. It often is much easier "to do" than to let others do for themselves or, even more difficult, *help* others do for themselves. This last is essentially what the hypothesis and the League strategy called for, as we saw in Chapter 5.

Both school personnel and our staff were unprepared for the roles demanded of us. So long as our mutual relationship was defined within the framework of "we," the experts, and "they" or "you," the receivers, there were no crises of self-confrontation. We have seen the extent to which this orientation prevailed during the first year—our continued input of ideas, the format and substance of the newsletter, the building of hub-to-school relationship—even while our rhetoric proclaimed otherwise. The staff associates were caught in the ambiguity. Presumably, they were not to act as "expert" consultants and yet they were confronted quite consistently with this expectation in the schools. Lacking clearly defined alternatives, it was exceedingly difficult to back away gracefully from these expectations.

This foreign character of the articulated relationship showed up immediately in the principals' discomfort with relatively unstructured agenda and their expectation that, ultimately, "John Goodlad and his staff will tell us what to do." When this did not occur, tension increased to their self-confrontation early in the second year, described in Chapter 4. The realization that they were to provide leadership and, later, growing awareness that leadership meant not telling what to do but engaging in a continuing dialogue with teachers and involving them in the decision-making process presented challenges for which the principals were variously ill-prepared.

No doubt, there were many individual cases of teachers' self-confrontation early in the game, but the collective one which affected an unknown but probably quite large number of teachers was delayed until the beginning of the third year, partly because of perceived ambiguity on our part and of having principals to blame for personal shortcomings. The teachers' self-confrontation led to a serious crisis in the hub and demanded that we, too, confront ourselves. Much more was at stake, I realize now more clearly than I did then, than whether or not to redirect the strategy in order to "save the project, the schools, and our reputations."

This brings me back to Conant's point to the effect that one must have faith in the working hypothesis, must believe in it as a principle. Though most of the staff did so by the end of the second year, some saw it wavering in the face of the "people realities." Clearly, some principals were not giving the expected leadership. Some literally had been given up on by a few members of our staff who found working directly with teachers to be easier and more satisfying. Consequently, although the hypothesis was "all right," it just did not take account of some people. Therefore, some staff members believed, we had to follow an alternative route, at least for a while. Although the analogy is far from perfect, in a way this is like saying that democracy is a good thing for some people. There is, of course, some truth here in that people differ in their readiness to participate. Some people need more and longer support for their own becoming and should have access to it on a highly individualized basis.[3]

What we saw as inappropriate in our playing the expert role involved several considerations. First, we did not possess in any extensive amount the kind of expertise most teachers were looking for. That could be found in rich variety among peers in League schools. Second, some principals require more and larger opportunities for their own becoming as leaders and should have them. To give up on the principals was to withdraw the needed support. Since we were going to be out of the picture, it was more important that our limited resources be used for support than for "expert" consulting. Third, our purpose was for everyone to be better off at the end of the five years. This meant that principals and teachers had to be free of us by then. We should not get into entanglements from which disengagements would be difficult and, indeed, more painful than withholding now in the face of demand.

This is a common problem in the expert-client relationship and, too frequently, the teacher-student one. Helping others is seductive; personal needs on both sides are fed by the relationship. Growth on the part of the client can be threatening to the helping partner who intuitively sees himself surpassed rather than the client freed. And so, in subtle ways, he may block the client's growth under the guise of helping—thus, ironically, blocking his own growth and restricting his freedom. Soon, he is heavy laden with the chains of an ever-dependent client. One can carry the chains of only a few but can help to set many free.

The hard lesson, then, was that we had to believe in more than the hypothesis. We had to believe, as well, in the people for whom it presumably applied—all of them.

Preceding paragraphs must not be interpreted to mean that all individuals now serving as principals and teachers under even the most ideal conditions of support will achieve deep personal satisfaction and experience a full sense of worth as teachers or principals. But who is to make predictions and the implied decisions? Had we been in a position to make them, I suppose we would have voted out the principal who seemed unable to take off after three years of support and encouragement. But, in the fourth, his growth was more noticeable. By the end of the fifth year, he still would have been ranked at or near the bottom on the principals' and our criteria of leadership. But, subsequently, he continued to grow more rapidly than anyone else, as best we are able to determine.[4]

Most gratifying was that our data suggest that so many were able to look at themselves candidly and self-appraisingly after several years in the League. For one principal, confrontation with the perception of the leader he wanted to be was too much. He opted out with dignity, coming back from time to time to join former colleagues at their meetings. Understanding the hypothesis, then, meant accepting the concept of freedom to fail. This is one of the most indigestible lumps for American education. Success is so much touted that there is neither room nor freedom to fail. Unsuccessful projects which might usefully fill Ole Sand's mythical *Journal of Educational Autopsy* are quietly buried. There are not enough alternative paths for careers in education and so it is dangerous to rock the boat. But, worse, there is little possibility for failure to be perceived as the wholesome self-confrontation, the success, it may well be.

One of the strengths and weaknesses of the hub was its lack of power in regard to creating career alternatives and providing some of the specialized help a permanent hub probably should make available. The strength, of course, came from our being perceived as relatively powerless in regard to employment futures of school personnel. We could and did help them advance their formal preparation and secure jobs suited to changing interest and competence. But we did not influence their present job security. The weakness, however, came from our inability to open doors to persons whose self-confrontation suggested the desirability of a career change. We were ill-equipped for opening up a sufficient number of alternative possibilities to take care of the rising tide of personal expectations. This did not mean that teachers no longer wanted to teach; quite the contrary seemed to occur. It is just that, once one accepts in principle the notion of people wanting greater control over their own destinies and helps create supporting mechanisms for this to occur, it is exceedingly helpful to have some keys for rooms where additional opportunities might be found.

INSTITUTIONS AND PEOPLE

Our hypothesis regarding the individual school was countervailing with respect to at least three conventions of school keeping and improvement. First, both intervention strategies and research almost invariably focus on the teacher as the key element, presumably because of the assumed linear relationship between teacher and pupil. While not denying the importance of this, our hypothesis focuses on the school's culture, which establishes certain teacher restraints and within which the behavior of both teachers and pupils is modified. Now, a rather large array of factors not otherwise seen as important come into play in a larger exploratory model of schooling, teaching, and learning: community expectations (which were encompassed only peripherally in our work), school district policies and restraints, school policies and procedures, peer group socialization processes, and the like. Normally, these matters are discussed and treated under rubrics such as administration, supervision, policy planning, and so on, but they are not brought into juxtaposition with learning processes. We think that this broader perspective opens up promising new avenues for all aspects of educational activity to be regarded as influencing learning.

Second, when the focus shifts from teachers and pupils, it usually passes by individual schools and moves to the district as a whole. The central office acquires functions and staff that have to do with the management and, indeed, survival of the entire district. Studies show that vast amounts of time and energy (and a considerable budget) go into the care and feeding of the board,[5] preparing state and federal grant proposals, assisting with bond levies, and simply managing the sometimes gigantic transportation, restaurant, construction, and athletic businesses and all the personnel problems accompanying them.[6] Improvement is thought of in district terms, whether it be the purchase and distribution of instructional materials or the improvement of reading. Too often, then, supervision is thought of in these terms, with the supervisors housed in, responsible for, and committed to district-wide policies and practices rather than local school growth and development.

Third, the principal traditionally is regarded as relatively impotent, primarily because of the first two conventions. His or her role is ill-defined, at best, but since the appointment is made "downtown," the principal is perceived to be an arm of the central administration. There is a lot of talk about leadership, but little is expected. Interestingly, a district consisting of a single high school, with the superintendent in charge of running the school, has had some of the most notable innovations in American secondary education, an observation giving some support to our hypothesis. Principals are not necessarily weak, although they are picked frequently for fitting rather than challenging the system and even more frequently seem to be enfeebled by it. Betting on their leadership potentiality is less an act of faith than an indication of intending to do something about their place of work and an expectation that differing processes of selection subsequently will occur.

As noted earlier in this volume, the interlocking character of these existing elements supports and, indeed, may be a major explanation for the basically conservative character of the schooling enterprise and the problem of getting through to it for reform and renewal. What a teacher can do alone is sharply limited. Indeed, in time the teacher's role is seen in its entirety by almost everyone as a teacher and a class behind the classroom door, going about their business in line with the nature of the unwritten teacher-pupil agreements. Teaching becomes not a profession at all but a job to be negotiated at the level of the best possible pay for the fewest hours, and this creates many of the work attitudes and conditions increasingly found by business and industry to be counterproductive. Teachers in constant danger of being underpaid in the competitive marketplace or of being held accountable look not to the central office—and certainly not to the principal—for support and guidance but seek a certain collective strength, accompanied by personal anonymity, in the union or at least in a "professional" organization with some negotiating clout.

For the school to assume a more central dynamic role in this rather self-defeating set of interlocking functions and expectations is potentially disruptive. Central resources might have to be diverted for goodness-only-knows what kinds of demands coming up from the local school. Principals might not be quite so supportive of head office directives. And, perhaps worst of all, ultimately there might be embarrassing queries from segments of the community and the need for tough decisions regarding parent demands and staff expectations regarding degrees of freedom. We witnessed all these occurrences during our years with the League.

Fortunately, these caveats regarding the power of the hypothesis at work were not at all well formulated, and certainly were not articulated, when the League was discussed and begun. From the district point of view, the idea apparently appeared rather harmless and even fit with some extant rhetoric regarding the importance of school district decentralization and shared decision making. There is no evidence to suggest that the superintendents of League districts saw the proposal as boat-rocking, although it did fit in well with the plans and strategies for change of at least two of the most energetically innovative ones. It is difficult to draw any conclusions from the several who decided not to pursue League membership but it is clear that several preferred not to do for a single school what would not be done simultaneously for all the others.

There were some other things going for the League, mentioned earlier. Many superintendents did have their backs to the wall; they were looking for some ways of gaining favorable attention. A hookup with UCLA and the new but intriguing organization, |I|D|E|A|, suggested some possible serendipity.[7] From the teacher viewpoint, there was enough knowledge of current innovations to motivate some interest in the proposed relationship.

It would appear, then, that the rather loosely conceived structure to which we were giving birth by testing the hypothesis had several essential ingredients and characteristics of a self-starting mechanism for a fundamentally conservative enterprise. First, the League had an array of experimental-type elements: the selection of only one school from each district, an agreement to "try some things," a time limit, the right to withdraw. Second, even if it was not expected to accomplish much—and there is evidence to suggest that only a very few superintendents held anything for it but the most modest expectations —there were potential public relations benefits: associations with

UCLA and the feeling that, even though the Kettering Foundation was granting no funds, association with a philanthropic foundation could only be positive.

Third, and perhaps most important, only a small part of the iceberg actually appeared: that is, the consortium of schools and some relatively "harmless" university-type research. What was on the surface, at least, presented little or no apparent threat. We know that, when an organism is alerted to almost any kind of interest coming from without, whatever the intent of that interest, it usually is sufficiently threatened to invoke such defensive mechanisms as are available, thus becoming more impervious to penetration. This is one of the major hypotheses explicated earlier to account for the failure of reforms of the Schooling Decade to get behind school and classroom doors (Chapter 2). The League apparently generated at the outset few such mechanisms of self-protection. Consequently, it was able to exist long enough to have some credence before the total nature of its character contributed significantly to the cycle of tension and crises recounted earlier and to constructive change.

The change agent who comes knocking on the door, if he bothers to knock at all, must not be carrying baggage which suggests to his prospective host that he plans to move in. It is better if he instead plans to move into the condominium next door and is merely paying a friendly call to discuss how to be a good neighbor. Under such circumstances, he may even be welcomed. Then, further, if it is revealed that a large down payment has been made, that the new neighbor is in a different but reciprocal line of work (he owns a pulp mill and the long-time resident owns a newspaper) and appears to know some things that might be useful, it may prove both significant and profitable to get acquainted. The analogy is not too far removed from what the League seemed to offer. The quid pro quo simply was not too specific, a condition necessary to mutual exploration by dissimilar organisms. Perhaps it was not very motivating but it was intriguing.

Having both an acceptable calling card and some goods to deliver is a rather neat combination. Benign innovations are not threatening but they are benign in their effects, too. Research shows the most acceptable innovations to be those demanding little or nothing in the way of changed teacher behavior—innovations, therefore, which do little or nothing. But innovations with anticipated clout frequently carry with them formidable baggage: computers, as with most modular scheduling plans; the necessity of planning and sharing with colleagues, as with team teaching; new ways of planning and even conducting the instructional program, as with many approaches to accountability; or collaborating with an outside agency, as with guaranteed performance contracts. All the defense mechanisms are activated. Sometimes, in order to do business at all, the change agent must bargain away certain key elements in the plan until all those with potential clout ultimately are declawed.

The League, apparently, possessed some of the qualities needed to get into the house; in fact, it was already in! But it was not going to share bed and board and might even have some benefits to share. Further, it was going to be around for a while and could not be fully ignored. Some SECSI baggage soon loomed into view but it was housed next door and appeared not to bring with it unfamiliar problems.

But could the League have clout? Was its somewhat benign appearance only indicative of its benign potential? Here is where both the network and the hub came into play.

In sharp contrast to most approaches to educational change, *SECSI established an infrastructure instead of promoting a specific innovative practice.* The importance of this observation cannot be overstressed. Historical study of human action and conduct again and again reveals the underlying principle here to be of profound significance in what we have chosen to call human progress. The harnessing of steam pressure to power an engine and, subsequently, move wheels was a great invention. But the invention was not of much use until the infrastructure of a network of railway tracks through the American wilderness came into existence. It was the structure that was significant in human terms. A new civilization was spawned along the sides of the steel tracks.

We seem to have missed the principle and its power in much educational reform by concentrating on the innovation to be established rather than the human activity and a supporting infrastructure to be fostered. Even after several years of League experience, we still tended to look for a list of specifics whenever asked, "With what innovations are the schools involved: individualized instruction, team teaching, nongrading, or what?" At the end of five years, there were those among us who still did not fully realize that the *League was the innovation.*

Suddenly, there it was—established. All the major elements it ever had were there from the beginning. Of course, these had to be refined and made to work, as we have seen. But they were made to work as people needed them and called on them to work. When the ideas were wanted, either as guide or crutch, they were available from the hub which, in turn, got them from wherever it could and provided the necessary resources for whoever would take the trouble to use them. When principals discovered they needed new skills, their own peer-group structure and the hub were there for the using. Likewise, when teachers needed to know how to proceed with ideas that appealed, the infrastructure was there to use in gaining access to others with similar interests. There was no need to fear trying the new and unknown so far as support and approval were concerned. That was what the League was for—to support the search for better ways to conduct school. Even failure was supported. Clearly, given the general character of schooling as we know it, what was innovative was the creation of an infrastructure to make these things possible which could itself change in order to meet new demands and which could manage the crises inevitably arising from the fact of self-confrontation.

One of our books, *Changing Schools: The Magic Feather Principle,* is dedicated to "... the principals and teachers of the League of Cooperating Schools in commemoration of the new world we made together."⁴ This sounds grandiose. But there is a core of fact here, especially if "the new world" is then taken as a collective symbol for the new environments those in the schools began to fashion for themselves. Nonetheless, there was a single environment, too, made up of all these and more, that is described best simply as "the League."

What still puzzles us most pertains to the essential long-term ingredients of the innovation. The League, like the railroads, was the innovation. Unlike the railroads, it was designed at the outset to be dispensable, to be thrown away when the schools were sufficiently self-renewing to need it no longer. My conclusion at this point, however, is that an innovative infrastructure designed to support continuing renewal is essential. Only in rare instances, if ever, will individual schools become and remain self-renewing when not part of some supporting mechanism. The problem is that human beings, too often, have a way of focusing on what is of instrumental rather than fundamental value. As Hannah Arendt once put it, "Man sees wood in every tree." Consequently, we must be careful not to come to worship the creature that was created at the expense of assuring that it continue to do an effective job. Failure to reexamine the function of railroads provides a case in point.

We were so concerned about coming to worship false gods that, at the outset, we planned for the League's demise as a formal entity. Instead, it would have been more important to focus on how it might have continued to evolve over a longer period of time since, clearly, something like it still was needed at the time the project officially came to an end. Perhaps the best way to envision what a supportive infrastructure of some type must do is to anticipate the cycles of change through which those to be supported by it are likely to go. Our experience provided some useful insights here.

The R,D&D model deliberately accounts in advance for as much as possible of what, presumably, is to happen. Proceeding as it does from and with the rational bias, purposes are formulated, activities are created to achieve the purposes, and the degree of success is determined by evaluating the attainment of purposes. Built-in is a self-fulfilling prediction as to how the change cycle will proceed; the bias provides the criteria for evaluating change. The direction for improvement is to improve rationality—i.e., make the process more efficient.

In Chapter 1, however, I pointed out that severe difficulties occur at the point where R,D&D encountered "the system" and observed that failure to take its characteristics into account has seriously blunted R,D&D as a *change* strategy. The process may even appear to be working when it is not, largely because the form but not the substance is readily made visible: the materials are on the classroom shelf, or the criterion behavior can be elicited, on demand, from the teachers. However, the teachers may be using the materials intended for individualized instruction in rote, total-group fashion and may not be exercising the specified performances most of the time. Teachers frequently become quite adept at such avoidance behavior. Their own self-motivated efforts to change, on the other hand, may proceed quite differently but be more powerful and lasting.

The cycle of change we observed in the League schools does not conform to the self-fulfilling prophecy embedded in the rational bias. Initial faculty meetings were directed rather safely to ideas; some groups talk a lot and rarely do anything. But the very presence of the League created a certain tension for action that was difficult to ignore. Then, frequently in small, informal clusters, teachers began to talk about the possibility of some kind of change; a period of "unfreezing" occurred. Meanwhile, faculty DDAE was increasing in salience. Next, some activity ensued and was accompanied by varying degrees of excitement. This was followed by doubt and questioning: of what they were doing, of themselves, of one another. Some kind of program began to take shape. It was accompanied by dissatisfaction and the asking of more questions. There was a renewed interest in ideas, but far greater specificity as to their utilization. This interest placed a strong demand on the hub for references, materials, summaries of research, and so on. Later, there was great interest in finding out what others were doing and for passing ideas along to others."

Membership in the League provided initial support and stimulation. The hub, at the outset, provided ideas and helped to legitimate new things to try. The process of DDAE brought faculty groups into communication and stirred activity. Peers in League schools provided a still broader reference group, a sounding board and specific assistance. The League as a whole provided a protective umbrella, a feeling of belonging, and that important ingredient of serving a cause greater than one's self.

Such an infrastructure does not rule out R,D&D. In fact, it makes the latter more important and its products more in demand. The rational bias is not abandoned. It simply is placed in juxtaposition with an alternative proposition: activities need not and, indeed, do not always follow purpose; purposes often follow activities; and in some human activities, there may be no purpose at all.

SYMBIOSIS, SYNERGY, AND SERENDIPITY

It is interesting to reflect on what appears to be a human tendency to want stability in all things. This is particularly the case, I think, in most aspects of the educational enterprise. And even when a stable state is not present, it is often faked. Children and teachers are not to show their anger, frustration, or irritation. The good school has a happy faculty that does not cause the system or the community any trouble.

To seek stability probably is good; to achieve it probably is not. To fake it is, at best, not productive and, at worst, fatally destructive.

What is required for constructive change is, I believe, a productive tension between an organism wanting a better condition for itself (an inner-orientation toward change) and an organism whose self-interests are served by assisting in the process (an outer-orientation toward change). The self-interests of the two parties, although different, have something to give to and gain from each other. This is what the League offered.

It is essential to remember that the collaboration between behavioral scientists and practitioners suggested by Smith (Chapter 4) implies a symbiotic* relationship—that is, one involving two essentially dissimilar organisms. Teachers, principals, and students constitute parts of one organism. Researchers, developers, evaluators, interventionists —whatever we were in the hub—constitute another. Their goals are different, however potentially complementary they may be. Likewise, the food on which they feed for nourishment, satisfaction, and even pleasure is different. Any reasonably comprehensive theory of strategy of change must take this into account.

If this symbiotic relationship is to be healthy in an ecological sense—and I think it is fair to say that the League was intended to be a new, even if only temporary ecosystem—then certain demanding expectations and restraints are placed upon both of the organisms and their constituent elements. Particularly, each must come to perceive its distinctive role, as well as its symbiotic one, the activities and skills demanded by it, and the rewards and satisfactions reasonably to be expected. The organism will be unhealthy unless personal needs are to considerable degree satisfied within the environmental context. This last concept is, of course, close to the theoretical model developed by Getzels with the collaboration of Guba, explored in part of our work and reported in *Effecting Organizational Renewal in Schools*.[10] However, the League brought together two organisms, each of which had to work out its own psychological, sociological, and anthropological tensions and demands (through DDAE) within an expanded environmental context (the League).

An intriguing thesis here is that, for healthy ecological interdependence to occur, each organism not only must come to know itself in the sense of awareness of role, skills, potential rewards, and disposition toward satisfactions but also must develop a sensitive awareness, a knowing, regarding what is right and appropriate for the other. Know thyself—yes; but know thy fellow, too.

This narrative and our other reports reveal that this is much easier said than done. Nonetheless, the analysis helps to explain some of what

* According to the *Encyclopaedia Britannica, symbiosis* denotes simply the living together or partnership of dissimilar organisms. However, three major types of symbiosis are identified. In *commensalism*, the host organism is unmodified, but the guest may make extensive adaptations which can lead to dependence. *Mutualism* implies relationships of equal benefit to both sides, while *parasitism* refers to relationships where the host may be injured to the guest's benefit. While all three types of symbiosis were evident at various times in the League, the term is used here to indicate a mutualistic relationship.

happened in the League and, more important, to prepare others trying to improve something by means of a symbiotic relationship. Within this conceptual framework, the self-confrontation experienced by principals, the tension of wanting to do for themselves but also wanting to depend on expert help experienced by teachers, and the relentlessly spreading fissure between two differently oriented groups of staff members in the hub all become to a degree understandable, explainable, and predictable. In fact, unless a good deal of this sort of thing occurs, the supposed change taking place probably is a fake.

Given such anticipation of problems, tensions, and even pain, why bother? Presumably, one enters into a symbiotic relationship because a synergism is anticipated—that is, a total effect that will be greater than the sum of the effects when each organism works independently of the other. The League was created in part out of the observation that organisms supposed to work together—i.e., schools apparently in need of renewal and reformers designing for their renewal—were passing each other like ships in the night. Our earlier studies and those of others revealed that there was no dearth either of schools needing reform or of promising innovations. But the former were not reaching out for or were incapable of incorporating the reforms and the latter were unable to get through school and classroom doors.

My colleagues and I are saying, then, that there cannot be significant change, certainly not a rebirth or a new beginning, through immaculate, painless conception. Unwillingness to confront the inevitable turbulence of serious interaction by two dissimilar organisms means that very little synergy will occur. There will be millions of dollars spent on developing "teacher proof" materials or innovative cosmetics but the fundamental changes now required of faltering schools simply will not take place. We will pretend that a happy state of homeostasis already exists or that any change is impossible.

Surely thoughtful analysis of the Schooling Decade lends credence to this conclusion—or hypothesis, if you wish. Nonetheless, acting upon it is something else again, given our propensity for the clean, homogenized approaches to educational reform which seldom causes anyone to confront self. It is our fond hope, of course, that our detailed narrative reports on one symbiotic experiment and the synergy accompanying it, experienced and potential, will turn increasing attention to the more difficult, hazardous, but ultimately productive and satisfying symbiotic approach.

The League started with a rather common, general expectation that the participating schools would produce and ultimately demonstrate innovations. One ambitious principal went so far at the outset as to reject the University Elementary School with its established reputation for innovation because its reforms were old hat; he and his faculty would break new ground. The general and this principal's specific expectation changed rather quickly. By the beginning of the second year, the principals were experiencing crises over being unable to get going even on "old hat" innovations. By the beginning of the third year, the process, not the innovation, was paramount—DDAE, peer group interaction, supporting and facilitating by the hub. From then on, there was little ambiguity regarding the desirability of developing all these processes. But what was happening to the people in the process was emerging as the overarching value.

It is clear that we in the |I|D|E|A| office learned a lot. There is little doubt that we began with the common we/they model of educational improvement. *We* had some goodies to offer; *they* wanted to receive them. At the same time, however, it is clear that *we* had some uncommon views regarding *their* becoming. We did not really want to do unto others; *we* wanted *them* to become. We would be a vehicle for this becoming and then would drive off into the sunset, leaving behind a state of happy homeostasis.

We had not fully bargained for the power of this becoming and what it would do to us. So long as we remained in the somewhat missionary, giving role, there was little or no need to confront ourselves. The expert role is an attractive, tempting one. Our self-confrontation occurred traumatically in the third year and was worked out in the dialogues and introspection described earlier.

During these painful months, we came to know a little about ourselves and what was true or untrue to ourselves, and we began to act with a confidence we had not known before. Perhaps this is why we were able to restrain ourselves in the face of some criticisms that were hard to take, particularly the one regarding our readiness to sacrifice teachers and students to research. As we came to know ourselves, our partners in the symbiosis could see us better, too, and thus know what we could not give to the relationship. During the fourth and fifth years, the processes we had come to value were working. But these processes did not require new skills and abilities only for *them;* they required them from *us* also. There was no way of hiding anyone behind the expert label, although we now had to become expert in new things.

The important point is that we did not become expert in the teachers' and principals' roles or they in ours. It became more and more recognized, I think, perhaps intuitively, that a symbiosis likely to produce synergy depends not only on mutuality but also on difference, not similarity, in roles, skills, abilities, and satisfactions. *Unless true distinctiveness exists and is recognized, by definition there can be no symbiosis.*

For too long, we tried (or pretended) and were expected to be better at what principals and teachers had to do. And so we delayed each other's becoming. There simply is no way for those outside of schools to be the kind of experts those inside the schools want them to be. Failing to realize this on the part of either organism inhibits the process of understanding self and impedes symbiosis.

Part way through the League's history, a member of the central staff of one of the school districts reminded us of the modern fable of Dumbo, the baby circus elephant with the huge ears. Bentzen and her associates exploit the fable in the title of their book in this series, *Changing Schools: The Magic Feather Principle,* and give this version of it:

> ...because Dumbo was afraid to try much of anything on his own, the mouse first had to convince him to use his ears as wings. So the mouse gave Dumbo a feather, a magic feather, he said, that would enable Dumbo to fly. Dumbo trusted his friend and so believed in the feather. With the feather he began to fly and win great praise from all who watched him. One day, to his horror, Dumbo dropped the feather in mid-flight. As he fell, he heard his friend call out "You don't need the feather! You can fly." Dumbo tried and he flew. At last he believed in himself.[11]

Subsequently, we joked about the fable but, in it, we saw what the League was doing for *them.* We referred to the magic feather principle from then on and watched it at work.

Serendipity means a gift for finding valuable or agreeable things not sought for. During the concluding two years of the League, we became increasingly aware of this quality in the League as demonstrated by *their* "becoming," that is, by the growing sense of worth and pride on the part of principals and teachers who began to perceive their roles more clearly and perform them with increasing confidence and ability.

It was only toward the end and in retrospect that we began to see the full power of the League: we in the hub learned to fly, too. It is easy to set forth self-understanding as desirable for others. Frequently, we even set it as a goal for ourselves. But, more often than not, it comes to us serendipitously as the by-product of a healthy symbiosis with a dissimilar organism that continuously tests our mettle. Without tension, there will be little change.

NOTES

1 F. E. Emery and Einar Thorsrud, in cooperation with Eric Trist, *Form and Content in Industrial Democracy: Some Experiences in Norway and Other European Countries,* Tavistock Publishers, London, 1969.

2 Realization of the countervailing nature of what we were about resulted, rightly or wrongly, in my insisting with the staff on a low profile for SECSI. We did not encourage visits to schools on the part of the curious, although some schools soon began to have visitors, because the name of the game in the late 1960s was innovation. We were not innovating in the conventional sense. I did not encourage publications or papers at the annual meetings of the American Educational Research Association, for example, until late in the game. We were not using standard, approved research designs or methodologies. I wanted the experiment to be left to run its course—not subjected to being pulled up or stopped short for conventional kinds of evaluation. That could come later; actually, it came early as well as late. Part of the problem, as noted earlier, was that funding of SECSI was at times in serious jeopardy. I feared that even a normal range of favorable and unfavorable review could undermine that shaky base. Summative review in the project's final year provided a solid base for the large-scale inquiry to follow (A Study of Schooling in the United States, 1972–1978).

3 There is, of course, a vast literature on what is involved in developing personal autonomy. See, for example, Carl R. Rogers, *Freedom to Learn,* Charles E. Merrill, Columbus, Ohio, 1969.

4 Elizabeth F. Barry, "The Relationship between Propensity toward Self-Directed Change in School Faculties and Selected Factors in the School's Subculture," unpublished doctoral dissertation, University of California, Los Angeles, 1974.

5 Tye's study of the Los Angeles Unified School District in 1968, for example, revealed that most of the top administrators attended literally dozens and dozens of various kinds of board meetings during the full year of activity which he monitored. See Kenneth A. Tye, "A Conceptual Framework for Political Analysis: Public Demands

and School Board Decisions," unpublished doctoral dissertation, University of California, Los Angeles, 1968.

6 An analysis of the San Francisco school district in the early 1970s revealed there to be more employees involved in these kinds of functions, including security and custodial, than in teaching.

7 More than passing interest in the League for this reason is suggested by the care taken to provide news releases in virtually all school districts. Interestingly, within a relatively short time, we were receiving inquiries from parents already in the area but especially from those expecting to move from other areas (even from abroad) into southern California regarding the names and addresses of League schools. One League school suddenly experienced a marked influx of applications and, indeed, some "smuggled pupils" from neighboring school districts.

8 Mary M. Bentzen and Associates, *Changing Schools: The Magic Feather Principle*, McGraw-Hill, New York, 1974.

9 This cycle is discussed in greater detail by Ann Lieberman and David A. Shiman, "The Stages of Change in Elementary School Settings," in Carmen M. Culver and Gary J. Hoban (eds.), *The Power to Change: Issues for the Innovative Educator*, McGraw-Hill, New York, 1973.

10 Richard W. Williams, Charles C. Wall, W. Michael Martin, and Arthur Berchin, *Effecting Organizational Renewal in Schools: A Social Systems Perspective*, McGraw-Hill, New York, 1974.

11 Bentzen and Associates, op. cit., p. 1.

CHAPTER 7

TOWARD A RESPONSIVE MODEL OF EDUCATIONAL IMPROVEMENT IN SCHOOL SETTINGS

In terms of human evolution, there are two ways of looking at the process, and both of them, to a degree, are represented among scientists today. There is one view which is inclined to say that the only way in which life alters or changes is when change is forced upon it. . . .

But there is another point of view, which is that in life itself there is a centrifugal dynamism of sorts, not just in man but in all living creatures. It does not wait upon its environment, instead it intrudes farther and farther into it, experimenting on its own.

—Loren C. Eiseley ("Alternatives to Technology," in Aaron W. Warner et al. (eds.) *The Environment of Change*, Columbia, New York, 1969, p. 166)

The preceding four chapters describe the formulation in my mind of an initial hypothesis regarding the improvement of schooling; the transformation of this hypothesis into a principle through a series of experiences and studies extending over more than a decade; the application and testing of this principle in a consortium of eighteen schools; and some reflections on the dynamics of the change process in and among schools and on this complex collaboration between researchers and practitioners. The hypothesis originally emerged from my observations pertaining to the propensity for change efforts to come from outside, to focus on teachers or groups of teachers or the school system as a whole, and to neglect schools as total entities. Subsequent observations strengthened these tentative conclusions and added the propositions that the school has a distinctive culture, that this culture is ignored or poorly understood by change agents coming from a different milieu, and that there rarely is "a critical mass of responsible persons" within this culture seriously engaged in its continuing renewal. The hypothesis, tested as a principle, is that the single school, with its principal, teachers, and pupils as primary participants, is a key unit for educational change which, *under certain conditions,* can become a responsive, dynamic entity in a process of renewal.

Many who have observed the educational system as a whole are doubtful that it can be revitalized. Rogers does not sound very optimistic when he asks: "Can the educational system as a whole, the most traditional, conservative, rigid, bureaucratic institution of our time . . . come to grips with the real problems of modern life? Or will it continue to be shackled by the tremendous social pressures for conformity and retrogression, added to its own traditionalism?"[1]

Some already have answered that question in the negative and proposed that society must be deschooled. Broudy answers the question differently: ". . . a public school system . . . is mandatory in a modern society. . . . Our loyalty to democracy has to be translated into democratic behavior suitable to a technologically mature society."[2]

Large, bureaucratized systems are a relatively new phenomenon in our society and so, until very recently, efforts to revitalize them took second place to efforts to sustain them. Harmony in the system was seen as preferable to tension, and so, frequently, the smooth functioning and interplay of subsystems was interpreted as health rather than merely survival and resistance to change. Griffiths points out:

> As a system operates, the sub-systems develop methods of interacting in which conflict is at a minimum. Each of the sub-systems has a function to perform and each does so in such a manner as to allow it to maintain a high degree of harmony with the others. Each says to the other in effect, "If you don't rock the boat, I won't". . . . Sub-systems resist conflict, and in the same manner resist change.[3]

Interest in how to rejuvenate large organizations has grown rapidly among behavioral scientists, who have developed theories, technology, and research directed toward the improvement of total systems —a different task from developing individual managers. For a time, the concentration was on an almost inevitably linear process described earlier as R,D&D and an assortment of rationally biased offshoots from it. Even in research activities seeking to find new paths, some managers still insist on converting everything to management by objectives and competency-based training. This may be moderately satisfactory for certain rather consistent and somewhat routine tasks and those who are to manage them, but they are quite inadequate for the creation of dynamic work places and the new kinds of settings vital societies require.[4] For the latter, there must be a "collaborative process of managing the culture of the organization—not something that is done *to* somebody, but a transactional process of people working together to improve their mutual effectiveness in attaining their mutual objectives."[5] Some theorists on the frontiers of thinking about organizational renewal suggest that initial agreement on objectives may have to be one of the traditional rules to be suspended.[6]

Many who despair of making the system effective or of coming to grips with it in some meaningful way turn their attention to the individual as the unit for and locus of change. While the problems of a bureaucratized technological society are a new phenomenon, there is a rich tradition, including a literary one, focusing on change and the individual. It imbues schooling, teacher education institutions, and most approaches to educational improvement.

Some of those who say, "It all depends on the teacher," and who concentrate solely on this individual as a strategy for change seem almost to ignore the existence of the system. There is great faith in the autonomy of the person. Unfortunately, as I maintained earlier, the power of the individual teacher is sharply constrained by the system. Most teachers simply conform to it, although a significant proportion would do otherwise if some reasonable alternative and chance for its success were available. Holt is optimistic about "ordinary people" being able to shape their lives and the society around them, but he is mute on how the school culture can be reconstructed and on the necessary support systems.[7]

My own view, implied in the principle, is that the single school falls nicely between the depersonalized, complex, amorphous school system and the somewhat intimidated, impotent, individual teacher. The schoolhouse is a physical entity (even when schooling is treated as a concept rather than a place, which I favor, there can still be a place called school); it is occupied by real people—not just "they"—who can be seen and talked with, face to face; it has an identity characterized by roles and people who occupy them, activities, ways of behaving, perceptions, and even elements of a special language. It satisfies at least some of the components of a culture, shaped in part by those who occupy it and, to a degree, shaping them. The concepts underlying the thesis are much like those in modern humanistic psychology. Applied to institutions and people simultaneously, they suggest a humanistic social psychology.

Most schools are, to a considerable extent, manageable. One can see one's self doing something about changing a school. Reconstruction is not completely out of sight or reach for those who spend part of their lives there. *Under certain conditions,* schools can be changed, perhaps even becoming quite dynamic, responsive to their needs and problems and to resources available for dealing with them.

Now that this hypothesis has been implemented and observed in practice, as previously described, it becomes important to reflect on self-renewal in schools as an attainable, sustainable condition. My present persuasion is that a single school, for all its convenience as a place to begin creating a more satisfying setting, simply lacks some of the ingredients it needs to be a fully self-renewing culture. What it offers is vital but not sufficient. Other elements are essential.

There are value grounds, too, for viewing the school as only a unit in a much larger enterprise. Even our so-called integrated schools almost invariably are much more homogeneous than our culture as a whole. We are a nation of minorities seeking some cohesion as a political democracy. Schools have a vital role to play which is certain to be inadequate if they are viewed as self-contained islands. I have more to say later about both the logistical and the ideological aspects of schools as self-renewing cultures.

It should become clear, then, that I am not advocating complete dismantling of our public educational system in favor of thousands of independent, tax-supported, alternative schools, perhaps loosely linked to one another in leagues or families. Consequently, I am proposing neither abolition nor diminution in the role of superintendents and some other central office personnel. But I am proposing a quite different conception of their role and, as a result, an array of different priorities and ways of behaving than commonly characterize their operations today. Also, I believe I am holding out a much more attractive way of professional living. Beleaguered as they are, even the thought should be attractive to many administrators. But the fundamental conception will be beyond the ken of some and not readily grasped by more. Implementation will require new skills as well as new orientations. Later, I shall have more to say about these, too.

First, however, let us review some of the concepts, each of which could be stated as a subhypothesis, which were developed in the League model to flesh out the working hypothesis, and some of the observations about them that appear reasonable or relevant in retrospect. At several points in this book, I have stressed limitations in the scope of the hypothesis and what we were about in exploring it. We did not encompass the whole of the public education enterprise; that would be impossible. But speculation on the elements we treated in relation to those we did not is neither impossible nor irrelevant. And so, following this review, I comment on other aspects—such as the larger system and teacher education colleges—in an effort to present a more comprehensive approach to educational improvement.

What I propose might be called a responsive model of change. The school becomes responsive to its needs and, increasingly, to resources relevant to these needs. Outside resources become increasingly responsive to the needs of the school and increasingly creative in devising ways to help. The accompanying processes of change require new orientations, knowledge, attitudes and skills on the part of everyone involved.

SOME POSTULATES PERTAINING TO SCHOOL IMPROVEMENT

First, the optimal unit for educational change is the single school with its pupils, teachers, principal—those who live there every day—as primary participants. The interactions of these people, the language they use, the traditions they uphold, the beliefs to which they subscribe, and so forth, make up the culture of the school. It is not necessarily a healthy ecosystem but it exists, often with surprising tenacity.

At the outset, although we found basic similarities among the eighteen schools, they were markedly different, too. They all had ways of doing things that appear to be quite common to schools: times of beginning and ending, pupil-teacher ratios, books and materials, etc. But they had different personalities. Some were depressing, tense, ready to explode. It was a relief to get into the car and drive quickly away. Another, in the same kind of building, was bright and bustling, open and friendly. About some of them I said, "I would like my children to be here."

It takes a bit of a twist from conventional thinking to conceptualize the school as all of a piece, with parts interacting with parts. It is much easier to focus on what the pupils are doing, or on the teachers (preferably just one), or on the principal. It took our staff a long time before most were able to think and talk of schools as entities— (Bell Street, Fairfield, Independence, Mar Villa, or Rainbow Hill), rather than only principals (Amanda, Ben, Duncan, Adam, or Gene), or only teachers (Ted, Phyllis, Audrey, George, or Susan). Even by the third year, some of us were prepared to give up on some of the principals and many of the teachers. That meant that we were ready to give up on the schools.

"The school as the organic unit for change" slips nicely off the tongue. But recognizing and acting upon the full meaning of the concept is quite another matter. Our experience and our data suggest that it is a concept worth taking seriously, but adapting and acting according to this orientation is not easy.

Second, schools change over the years—in appearance, internal organization, the curriculum, and so on (see Chapter 1). Presumably, then, *under certain conditions,* a school could change itself so as to be more satisfactory and satisfying to those who are part of its culture. This implies some change-oriented activity on the part of these primary participants.

At the outset, it was very difficult for us to know where each of the eighteen schools was with respect to its own evolution. But some rough estimates became possible relatively soon. Clearly, some were going no place but were simply trying to hold themselves together as collections of cells. Some appeared to have closed themselves off from the community, brooding in a somewhat resentful feeling of not being wanted. Others were at least trying some of the most popularized extant innovations. Change as a process of responding constructively to felt needs or problems was not a higly visible characteristic in any.

It is relatively rare to find schools with a sense of destiny.* They do change when prodded from the outside, the impetus for change falling off with the departure of the change agent or pressure. And they change under the leadership of an energetic, inspired person, change again falling off when he or she goes on to bigger and better things. But some continuing, productive movement to stay relevant or to meet newly defined expectations, in Eiseley's terms "a centrifugal dynamism," is rare, indeed. The concept of the self-renewing school seems to fade away before it begins.

It took us some months to hit on dialogue among members of the staff—simply talking together—as a critical initiating and sustaining element. In schools that are collections of cells, nobody talks with peers beyond casual greetings and trivial conversation about the weather or the past or coming weekend. Getting that dialogue going

---

* Throughout this section and elsewhere in this book, I refer to schools as though they had a life of their own. Personalizing them in this way is simply a convenient form of shorthand.

and working toward its greater salience, comprehensiveness, and relevance to significant regularities of schools is critical. But once under way, carrying forward from dialogue to decisions to action and to evaluation of the entire process, while demanding much group self-discipline, comes much more naturally and easily. Well-developed DDAE and other attributes discussed earlier, such as acceptance of and a rather relaxed attitude toward change, appear to go hand in hand.

We feel that one of the essential components of any comprehensive strategy of change in school settings is total group and small group DDAE, guided by criteria such as those developed in the League and reported in *Changing Schools: The Magic Feather Principle.*[8] External change agents, instead of trying to insert something into the school's culture, first should be trying to help that culture develop an awareness of and a responsiveness to itself. Something akin to DDAE as an ongoing regularity is essential.

Although a few schools do employ some such process as a way of conducting business, it is a rarity. Only a small fraction of faculties or faculty subgroups that meet together go about it in any organized systematic fashion. Our early visits to the League schools revealed lack of awareness of the potential significance of DDAE and, very soon, the primitive character of whatever group procedures existed. Likewise, we found little interest in or stimulation for such in the larger system, although one superintendent had a well-executed plan for bringing the principals together for regular dialogues, from which decisions and actions emanated. The hub of the League provided for this concern and, subsequently, some of the help needed to develop and refine the process.

Third, then, another element in a comprehensive model of educational change is something equivalent to our hub which views as important the initiation and refinement of the DDAE process. It probably does not much matter how this fits within the larger educational structure. It could be part of the function of the associate superintendent for curriculum and instruction; it could be the function of the so-called intermediate unit represented by the county as in California. The critical element is some continuing agency concerned about the internal decision-making processes of the school and capable of providing specific assistance, when called upon, in developing processes of group dynamics, securing relevant references on topics discussed by school staffs, conducting evaluations, and the like. This is just one of several functions of the hub or its equivalent; more will be added later.

Fourth, and closely related to the preceding, there must be a compelling, different drummer whose drumbeat somehow is picked up by the school's antenna. The sounds must be intriguing, challenging, countervailing, perhaps disturbing, but most of all they must be difficult to ignore.

This is a relatively unexplored realm. We have very few inquiries into what is most likely to trigger the fundamental interests or concerns of teachers. As presently conducted, teaching is an inordinately lonely vocation. Teachers are denied what office workers, for example, take for granted—lunch with a friend, perhaps over a glass of wine, and a little window-shopping going and coming. In one of our studies, we found teachers eager to find out what teachers in other parts of the country were doing, and they were especially pleased to get together for breakfast or dinner to discuss such matters.[9]

I am convinced that the majority of teachers (and, with a little encouragement, most of the others) want to do a better job and, above all, want teaching to be more satisfying, perhaps even fun. A drummer with an intriguing beat that reaches to these desires will be listened to. Our experience with the League schools reveals that our initial drumming got through; some shuffling occurred; clusters of teachers here and there began to tap their toes a little. The rhythm became contagious.

It is my belief that a drummer with an intriguing idea will be more compelling than a drummer with a process. And that the most compelling idea will be one that gets close to what teachers, in their most idealistic moments, think is their true calling, a calling now going unattended to in a cacophony of conflicting expectations. We need research to find out what is likely to get through. But just an idea is not sufficient. There must be a vehicle and an infrastructure to carry the idea, plant it and, subsequently, nourish it.

Fifth, not only must the alternative drummer be perceived as salient, there must be a perception, also, of longevity. A temporary, waxing and waning drumbeat will not suffice. School people have been badly disillusioned by the galloping hoofbeats of those itinerant educational peddlers who ride in and out again exhorting the latest elixir. Some presumably well-intentioned legislators cause even more damage because their bills often carry sanctions. It is one thing to allow alternative views to compete in the marketplace; it is quite another to favor one over another by putting it into the state education code. And too often, the ink is scarcely dried on the new bill before we are measuring its effects on pupil achievement. We conclude "no significant statistical differences" and impose some new scheme on weary teachers, now grown wary.

The fact that we signed a three-year agreement with the eighteen superintendents (who usually presented the proposal to their boards) and that we spoke of an engagement of at least five years communicated the idea of some longevity. In most school districts, even the superintendent is not around for that long! We went into the symbiosis with the expectation of assuring our own demise; our ultimate superfluity would be a mark of our success.

The continuing role of the alternative drummer and its permanence or mortality are questions for further exploration. Serendipity emerging from a successful symbiosis can be so seductive that the needed tension between the two dissimilar organisms steadily declines; in effect, the external agency gradually becomes a subsystem interacting smoothly with the other subsystems in an unwritten pact not to rock the boat.

In retrospect, I believe a viable solution to this problem depends on the degree to which the drummer-agency is independent and dissimilar. Consequently, I have some doubts about this role being performed successfully by the central district office. The natural drive of this office is maintaining the status quo, not tension. The role could be performed by some intermediate agency, perhaps at the county level, but a probable improvement would be the creation of intermediate units between the state and the local district, avoiding existing governmental units. Southern California, for example, might be divided into three such, rather than the present eight or nine counties, within which there would be a number of hubs serving consortia of schools.

|I|D|E|A|'s Change Program uses a wide range of intermediate agencies—county offices, colleges and universities, and hubs created especially for the purpose—to serve its network of schools exploring Individually Guided Education. A valuable body of experience is available but, unfortunately, there is not now any systematic documentation from which the effectiveness of various alternatives might be determined.

The dissimilar character of the hub is achieved and maintained best, I believe, through its research role. Beyond the gathering of some qualitative data about pupils and employees, research is not built into the functioning of schools and school districts, some rhetoric to the contrary notwithstanding. To keep studying the enterprise and feeding back to the participants data on DDAE, on how instructional time is spent, on values unconsciously embedded in ongoing regularities, on how pupils and teachers perceive what is going on, on how various groups feel about it, on community expectations, and the like is to assure a continuing tension of a sort that could be very constructive. Then, to provide some assistance in the interpretation and use of such data should assure a truly symbiotic relationship.

Our relationship to the League schools became more clearly defined and less ambiguous as we moved more and more towards a research function of the kind described above. Principals and teachers became increasingly aware of our clinical limitations and more appreciative of their own abilities. Our need for each other increased because of our differences. The blurring of these differences early on had only obfuscated the rationale for working together, creating unproductive tensions.

Although longevity of a proposed relationship between dissimilar organisms appears to be an essential element in getting a constructive change process under way, precautions must be exercised to assure a continued productive tension. The external agency must perform a unique function, needed by but not normally performed by the school. Those in the hub must be constantly alert to the danger of being seduced into doing for the schools what the schools ultimately must do for themselves.

Sixth, if change within the school is going to be significant and, therefore, probably to deviate from the established expectations and procedures of the system, the school will require a supportive peer reference group. Ideally, each school should enjoy the goodwill of the larger system, but it should not be too dependent on its continued approval. A school that changes beyond a little peripheral tinkering will attract attention. The superintendent may express concern—or may have to at least feign it to protect the school from hostile forces. Since the school is in many ways an isolated, fragile culture, often with tenuous relations within the larger ecosystem, even a little negative feedback may put an end to all innovative stirrings.

We put together eighteen schools in what we hoped would grow into a salient new social system. At the outset, it was simply a concept, perhaps understood by a handful of participants but not at all compelling. We deliberately fostered school-to-hub relations (fostered the drumbeat of the alternative drummer) while increasingly massaging the peer school structure. At first, for example, principals paid very close attention to our staff, waiting for our cues and seeking our approval. Increasingly, however, the approval of their peers became more important. The new social system of peer schools fostered and supported change in ways not easily assumed by the formal system which must answer to so many voices in the sociopolitical marketplace.

We chose to create this social system out of elements of differing ecosystems, each with its own set of restraints. This made it possible for one school faculty to realize that rules or conditions it took for granted did not prevail for a school in a neighboring district. Much of what school personnel accept as givens are simply matters of choice sanctioned by tradition and maintained through rule or habit. The opportunity to interact with peers from schools located in other districts clearly challenged old ideas and the comfortable cop-out that this is the way it always has been.

It is doubtful that an equally interesting mix would have occurred from schools within the same district. A promising adaptation, perhaps, would be clusters of schools from one district joining with clusters in two or three other districts. This, too, is an area for further inquiry.

The new social system did not eliminate the old one or, I think, the need for it. To make the League the only system would have replaced one bureaucracy with another. Instead, the League system created a certain tension with the eighteen old ones; in general, this was a productive tension, placing certain useful restraints on the new system and stimulating innovation in many of the old ones.

The new social system did not replace the need for the hub, either. But the role and activities of the hub changed. The ability of the hub to avoid establishing its own traditions and ways of doing things and to keep evolving appears to be a critical element in the self-renewing capability of the whole.

Seventh, although the growth of the new social system of schools reduces the vulnerability of each member school to attack from within its own ecosystem, the construction of communication networks with these larger systems is essential. These must include channels from individual schools to the rest of the district as well as from the League as an entity to all the districts.

League school principals and teachers were naïve, at the beginning, about how their innovative image would be received by peers. They were hurt when asked about their "funny farms," often responding defensively. We cautioned them about making presentations and speeches within their districts but urged them to do so in neighboring districts. By being "experts" elsewhere, news of what they were doing came back indirectly and was more acceptable.

The notion of diffusion from lighthouse schools employs the term "ripple effect," but "leapfrogging" is more accurately descriptive. Schools some distance away are more likely than one's neighbor to be interested initially. This concept argues once again for League membership to cut across school district lines—a non-League school may very well pay attention to a League school in another district. This whole area is still another begging for inquiry.

League principals, in particular, underestimated and often made erroneous predictions regarding the interest of the central office. Almost uniformly, they expected that office to support and, indeed, praise them for deviant activity. Some of them soon found out differently. They resented, for example, having to go before the board to get approval for special requests when they had expected approval from the superintendent or that the latter would carry the freight to the board. They resented, too, just being ignored—which might have been their best protection.

We held several discussion sessions designed to help them see the other side, why what they were up to might create problems for superintendents. Such thoughts had scarcely dawned on them. Undoubtedly, failure to see very far beyond the limits of one's own daily activities is a problem to be reckoned with in trying to help school personnel be more innovative. The systemic nature of real change in schools and school systems is not initially perceived.

It is clear, also, that we should have done even more to bring the superintendents into our thinking and planning. We provided them with a great deal of information, but they are busy people who tend to gain the data they need from people rather than documents. We did bring them together a couple of times each year but more for informational than involvement purposes. Probably, we should have conducted occasional seminars for superintendents designed to stimulate their thinking about problems of effecting change in schools and school systems.

Eighth, to respond to stimulation for change, even in relatively modest ways, is to require new knowledge, new skills, new patterns of behaving. Threat and insecurity are bound to be accompanying conditions. The overall process of strategy must anticipate both the need for training and the necessity of coping with tension, probably without knowing in advance what the specifics will be.

Initial League agreements anticipated a structure designed to take care of principals' needs. Their monthly meetings became, for most, an essential part of their lives. The fact that there was no long-term agenda assured flexibility and responsiveness to emerging problems. They did not provide for emergencies, but the availability of immediate help from the hub by telephone, although used rarely, provided a sense of security.

It is fair to say, I think, that the length of time required for principals to be comfortable with one another and to draw on their peer group for support always will be underestimated by change agents. Principals are accustomed to taking their cues from those higher in authority or from "experts." They are accustomed to being professionally alone and insecure. What the League structure provided by way of long-term support and collegial camaraderie is enormously significant. Its impact on the principals cannot be overestimated. It may be that cultivation of the role of the school principal, with accompanying provision of opportunities to acquire new knowledge and skills, is one of our least exploited avenues for school improvement.

The League structure provided less well for teachers initially but superbly later. At the outset, we overestimated the ability of principals to get things started in their schools and later underestimated the presence of some self-renewing activity in the schools. We inevitably found ourselves in some sort of direct consulting role, which became increasingly demanding and, at the same time, difficult to abandon. It was akin to trying to sort papers with just a little honey on one's fingertips.

From my point of view, in retrospect, the desired direction is to identify teacher strengths at the earliest possible opportunity and then try to bring together teachers at varying stages of expertise. We should have started such processes much earlier than we did, but we did not fully realize the potential power of teachers learning from teachers. By the time the project came to conclusion, the enormous teaching resources of the League were being unleashed for the conduct of a very meaningful in-service teacher education program involving hundreds of teachers at only the cost of traveling from school to school. The management costs also were minimal—merely those of gathering and disseminating information about ongoing activities and helping to bring teachers together. The next step would have been to create a somewhat more organized network of pedagogical service stations, about which I shall have more to say later in this chapter.

Coming back to the earlier remarks about the school as a self-renewing agency for change, my conclusion is that the school is a highly promising focal point for change. But it requires a process, at the heart of which is staff dialogue, by means of which it becomes responsive to its needs and to ways of fulfilling them better. To get started, it requires an alternative drumbeat, preferably coming from some stable source with sufficient prestige or a sufficiently successful, visible track record to legitimate ideas getting to the essence of teachers' concerns. This need and many later ones can be taken care of by an intermediate agency, such as the League hub, with no special axes to grind and with no potentially punitive authority over the schools.

Once started, a school group needs positive feedback from peers. The League provided a ready-made reference group of schools. Once embarked, teachers and principals need access to their counterparts in peer schools. This, too, the League provided. Then, the total system, once functioning, provided a good deal of the protection necessary for the most countervailing changes to take root and grow.

Under certain conditions, then, such as those described, a school can become an effective agent of and for change. Earlier, I cautioned the reader against equating the League and these conditions. The League simply served as a means of creating the conditions: there probably are many other ways to do so. Those seeking comprehensive strategies for change should look for alternative ways to implement the basic concepts and principles set forth here.

Also, more attention must be given to total school districts and their administrators, teacher education institutions, the creation of new institutions such as the hub serving the League, and to the potential of peer groups in the in-service education of school personnel. All these are part of the larger environment that must be responsive and supportive. To these matters I now turn.

THE SUPERINTENDENT AND THE LOCAL SCHOOL

As stated earlier, a change strategy focused on the individual school as key requires a fundamentally different administrative orientation on the part of district superintendents and their staffs and, indeed, a different kind of leadership style from that normally prevailing. Neither the conception nor the behavior stemming from it will be acquired easily. Prevailing patterns are well-established and have their own inner logic or rationale as well as a certain attractiveness for those already in office.

We need more data regarding the orientations of school superintendents, but, in recent years, their time has become more occupied with overall district matters pertaining to funding, budgets, and community affairs.[10] In one comprehensive study of a large city, it was found that the superintendent and his key subordinates spent an inordinate amount of time with the more than 150 sessions of the board held during the year of inquiry.[11] Admittedly, it would be difficult for a superintendent in a city of several hundred schools to perceive his prime task to be relating to these schools. But even in much smaller districts, such does not appear to be the orientation of very many superintendents.

The change strategy proposed here calls for such an orientation, suggesting that this can be done by decentralizing a great deal of programmatic authority and resources to go with it and assigning it to the principals. In effect, they are to be charged with the captaincy of their ships in reality as well as in name. This would be a dramatic departure from conventional practice.

It probably is rather comfortable for superintendent and principal alike if the principal's role and authority are vague and ambiguous. Unfortunately, such a situation fosters weakness. The principal is able to take shelter under claims of limited authority. By identifying principals with "administration," the expectation that they will lead and represent the school faculty is repressed. The principal remains in a kind of no-person's-land between the central administration and the teachers—perhaps one of the loneliest and least enviable situations in the entire education profession.

One of the most unfortunate accompaniments is a badly divided profession. Teachers have their association or union as do principals; and the superintendents see themselves as a group apart, with principals sometimes admitted but with second-class citizenship. The combined power needed for educational reconstruction is lost.

Today's superintendents would be well-advised to view themselves as a general manager of a shipping company with each principal responsible and accountable for his or her own ship. This means that key central staff members for curriculum, instruction, facilities, materials, and so on justify their existence on the basis of tending to the care of the 25, 95, or 250 ships "carrying the freight"—educating the children in their care. Bringing those ships along safely and well becomes the job of everyone in the central office. Unfortunately, much of what now goes on among central office personnel pertains to the care and feeding of the bureaucracy.

There are implications here that some central-office personnel will find distasteful—no doubt because they are threatening. The fact that they are threatening suggests insecurity, part of which stems from the way the jobs are defined by the people who occupy them and the fact that the jobs are poorly understood and often little appreciated by segments of the lay public and indeed, many teachers. These middle managers frequently shift about from assignment to assignment; neither the qualifications for the jobs they hold nor the criteria for successful performance are clear. Keeping things as they are may be the best assurance of survival. Since middle managers are close to the superintendent—are the superintendent's "people"—they can find his or her ear when an innovative principal cannot and frequently become exceedingly effective in blocking change.

I have grave reservations about many aspects of current supervisory roles. Specialized supervisors will argue that there would be little or no art or music or physical education in schools without them. Well, often there are no mathematics or English or biology supervisors but these fields are standard in the curriculum, nonetheless. There are other explanations for our neglect of the arts and emphasis on athletics which have nothing to do with the presence or absence of supervisors. If the arts are important, as I think they are, then we must have well-prepared arts teachers in the schools—and special resource personnel, without administrative or supervisory authority but simply the authority of competence, available through a hub or intermediate agency.

The term "captain of the ship" conjures up visions of absolute authority in the likes of Captain Bligh. But I am thinking here of a modernized merchant fleet, as exemplified by Norway, with a captain well versed in modern management skills, participating in a continuous program of personal updating, and a crew participating actively in all aspects of running the ship. Among other things, such a crew determines its own needs when a replacement is called for. Instead of some personnel officer remote from the scene sending the next applicant in line, the crew and captain write the specifications and choose from a pool of qualified candidates.

Clearly, considerable real authority and responsibility now centralized in the office of the superintendent are decentralized to the local school in a responsive change strategy. Much current interest in decentralization is more rhetoric than reality, more decentralization of responsibility than of authority. Humans do rise to the opportunity to be responsible if the necessary freedom and authority go with it. Resources now held in the central office must go to the schools which are, in most instances, better able to use them wisely simply because they are closer to the most important data. The size of the central office staff will be reduced accordingly; in my judgment, the operation of our schools will become more rather than less efficient. Some of the formerly centralized and bureaucratized human resources might go directly into the schools, some into intermediate helping agencies or hubs. But unless such people clearly have the skills necessary for working with children and teachers, the results could be disastrous. Most will require a vigorous program of updating in orientation, attitudes, knowledge, and skills.

Superintendents who are now frustrated with the complexities of running unnecessarily large bureaucracies should welcome an orientation and accompanying practices focused on supporting the capabilities inherent in local schools. Present orientations, focused as they are on the central office, call for them to be supermanagers, initiators, and the driving force behind change and innovation. However, although they do not like to admit it, the most today's superintendents can hope for is to keep the system clanking along. Leadership becomes a euphemism and not an attainable reality. An orientation toward releasing and fostering the centrifugal dynamism ready to go to work in most schools offers something beyond mere survival for the superintendent. Creating infrastructures involving leagues of cooperating schools is one way to proceed.

SCHOOLS OF EDUCATION AND LOCAL SCHOOL IMPROVEMENT

Schools of education have been markedly absent from the preceding discussion. It is difficult to define their role in any comprehensive approach to improving schools because they do not constitute a precise class of institutions. The overwhelming majority of those hundreds of colleges and universities involved in educating school personnel provide pre-service teacher education and in-service preparation for classroom teachers, principals, and various specialists through the master's degree. A much smaller number offer the doctorate, and most of these do so only in selected specializations. The emergence of research and research-oriented schools of education is a recent phenomenon. Perhaps only a dozen to twenty are recognized today as having inquiry-oriented faculties capable of offering first-rate preparation at the doctoral level in most of the subdivisions of the general field of education.

Most people think of schools of education as teacher-preparing institutions, and so, today, with a surplus of teachers and no indications of increased demand for years to come, they appear to be superfluous. But it is also generally recognized that there will be less turnover among teachers and that the average age of those teaching will increase, therefore, staff renewal becomes a potentially significant enterprise in which schools of education might be involved. Just how this involvement might best occur is not clear.

Meanwhile, there are strong signs that the practicing profession wishes to call the tune with respect to the conduct of their own in-service education—and, indeed, even the initial preparation of some personnel such as administrators. Job mobility is vastly reduced from what it was just a few years ago. Those who have jobs are unwilling to leave them while they secure advanced preparation for jobs not likely to be forthcoming. And the costs of taking leave for a year or more of university residence are high. The education profession wishes to bring in-service education to it, not to go away to get it.

The challenge is to find some point of meeting where the long-range needs of a young, insecure education profession and the resources and accompanying legitimatizing of our very best universities might come together. Several aspects and elements inherent in the responsive approach to educational improvement inherent in the League strategy suggest some possibly productive meeting points.

One of these is the reconstruction of pre-service teacher education. Currently, programs focus almost exclusively on the individual student in the college or university setting for most of the beginning preparation and, later, in the schools for practice. However, there is a discrepancy between the central values encountered in the two settings.[12] The former tends to stress emerging goals and values: inquiry rather than rote learning, questioning of conventional ways of doing things, personal autonomy more than the requirements of the system. The latter tends to stress conformity; indeed, those student teachers who learn well and do not challenge the pedagogical ways of their supervisory teachers tend to be marked high by those with whom they are placed.

It seems that the teacher-preparing program encourages divergent over convergent thinking on the part of the adults coming through it, whereas the schools, particularly the principals, tend to favor convergent thinking on the part of their staffs. For teacher-preparing institutions to develop students who value divergence is to place these young teachers in conflict with their employing institutions. This suggests the possibility of the two sets of institutions coming together in a symbiotic relationship. In effect, a school of education might join with a small network or league of schools in a quid pro quo relationship: the former helps the latter change; the latter provides team settings in which students preparing to teach become junior colleagues. The need to create these team settings where beginning teachers secure a proper internship or residency is itself a stimulus to changing the regularities of schooling, a venture in which a school and a school of education might profitably join. In the process, the normally sharp juncture between pre-service and in-service teacher education is blurred.[18]

In this relationship, the school of education might become the hub of a league of cooperating schools. Its library, media and materials center, and various other campus resources would become readily accessible to the schools. And it takes no great amount of imagination to envision the emergence of collaborative curriculum development ventures, with several campus departments participating.

What is suggested above probably will be seen as more appropriate for those many schools of education lacking a strong press for research than for those relatively few oriented primarily toward graduate teaching and research. Faculty in the latter group perceive the reward structure in the university as not favoring time-consuming involvement with schools. This is due in large part to their particular orientation toward research. The field of education has been dominated for thirty or more years by behavioristic psychology and the orderly research paradigms, usually involving small-scale simulations and experiments, that have tended to be derived from it. Studies have focused on individuals and small groups, with the pupil-teacher relationship paramount.

Education came late to what has been a long-standing line of inquiry. In Cronbach's words, "The aim of social and behavioral science, since Comte, has been to establish lawful relations comparable to those of the traditional natural sciences."[14] It borrowed heavily from disciplines already involved, especially from psychology, often without adequate reflection on the nature of the phenomena into which insight is required. Too remote from educational practice as the source of supplies, not surprisingly the field of educational research has become increasingly sophisticated methodologically while advancing very little substantively.

What has happened has happened and not without benefits. We should not completely abandon the testing of hypotheses and various manipulative experiments. But we must move on from our current perseverance with those short-term, small-sample experiments whose variables have already been examined again and again and whose results have been reported to small groups of like thinkers at educational conventions. We must turn to an examination of the phenomena where they exist, fashioning new methodologies as they are needed. Cronbach proposes:

> Instead of making generalizations the ruling consideration in our research, I suggest that we reverse our priorities. An observer collecting data in one particular situation is in a position to appraise a practice or proposition in that setting, observing effects in context. In trying to describe and account for what happened, he will give attention to whatever variables were controlled, but he will give equally careful attention to uncontrolled conditions, to personal characteristics, and to events that occurred during treatment and measurement. As he goes from situation to situation, his first task is to describe and interpret the effect anew in each locale, perhaps taking into account factors unique to that locale or series of events. As results accumulate, a person who seeks understanding will do his best to trace how the uncontrolled factors could have caused local departures from the modal effect. That is, generalization comes late, and the the exception is taken as seriously as the rule. . . .
>
> The special task of the social scientist in each generation is to pin down the contemporary facts. Beyond that, he shares with the humanistic scholar and the artist in the effort to gain insight into contemporary relationships, and to realign the culture's view of man with present realities. To know man as he is is no mean aspiration.[15]

And to know schools as they are is no mean aspiration. Even attempting to know them has been largely neglected in our attempts to reform them. Graduate schools of education need a research orientation toward the practice of education in the field. Through their teacher education programs, they might enter into collaboration with a network of schools as suggested above. Then, in return for access to studying the schools, they would agree to feed back relevant data to the schools as we did in the Study of Educational Change and School Improvement.

In effect, such schools of education would make a significant contribution to the efforts of the schools to change themselves. Knowledge about one's self alone can be a stimulant to change, a process worth studying in its own right. Surely schools of education, as *professional* schools, have an interest in improving the setting where members of the profession work. Consequently, they would become involved in change and, at the same time, have a unique, "inside" opportunity to study it. It has been said that one comes to understand something only as he seeks to change it. Given the circumstances proposed here, the prospects for coming to understand the schools would be promising, indeed.

No longer should there be a fear on the part of university personnel regarding the reward structure. Service is a criterion; contributing to the maintenance of a league of cooperating schools would be commendable, rewardable service. But, perhaps more important, unique opportunities would be created for pursuing the kind of research to which schools of education must turn if they are not to become anachronisms.

PEDAGOGICAL SERVICE STATIONS

Preceding chapters have stressed as part of the personal becoming of teachers in League schools their desire to help and be helped by peers. This is a largely untapped human resource for the continuous updating of teachers in-service. It became exceedingly important during the fourth and fifth years of SECSI, as our offices increasingly served as a kind of teacher service center, bringing together those who needed help with those who wanted to give it.

My recommendation, following these experiences, is that temporary pedagogical service stations staffed primarily by teachers become part of the infrastructure in a responsive model of educational change. They might take many forms. At first, we arranged to bring teachers together in the conference room of the hub. Increasingly, however, classrooms became the sites, with teachers visiting another teacher in the League throughout the day and then staying on in the afternoon for critiques and discussion of what they had observed, with the host teacher involved.

Another alternative would be to establish mobile units or teacher centers in sections of school buildings where enrollments are declining. These would be staffed on a rotating basis by teachers known to be skilled in the teaching of various subjects, individualizing instruction, constructing inexpensive learning materials, and so on. Sometimes, several members of a school staff might be involved if something requiring the cooperation of several teachers was on the agenda. Topics and activities would be widely publicized through a newsletter and continued until interest began to fall off.

Participation in a teaching or learning capacity would be regarded as part of one's work, with released time and substitute teachers provided as necessary. Actually, with team teaching established in the participating schools and all teachers being involved at some time or other, the need for substitutes probably would be minimal. In-service credits for salary purposes would be given for such participation, just as they are now for institute days or university classes.

As stated earlier, there is a resemblance here to the British teachers' centers.[16] After visiting many British centers, however, I have to ask whether the centers in England are too loosely defined and too eclectic in their functions to provide more than a somewhat related example. Some seek to introduce teachers to new materials. But we already meet many teacher needs in this regard, with well-supplied materials centers in county offices and instructional materials centers in many schools. Though many of these need improvement, we probably do not need to take care of this need, other than on a temporary, specialized basis, in pedagogical service stations. Some English centers give "courses," but this need is well taken care of here through highly developed systems of university-based programs for academic credit, extension programs, and the like.

What I see needed most in the United States and provided least in the English centers is the clinically oriented teaching of teachers by other teachers, if possible in the context of or immediately following a lesson. Teacher education here and elsewhere, pre-service and in-service, is not sufficiently "hands on." An analogy coming to mind is the physician-teacher with interns, residents, and colleagues in tow doing his morning rounds. Some parallel type of activity in schooling offers similar possibilities, it would seem. The collaboration of a theoretician from the university and a clinician in a classroom within a league of cooperating schools, with both student teachers and peer teachers in tow, offers intriguing possibilities.

My observation, admittedly from too small a sample, is that in attempting to be all things to all teachers, many of the British centers may be failing to perform well any particular set of functions. What is clearly needed in this country is a device whereby teachers wanting pedagogical help and teachers able to provide it are brought together, preferably close to the clinical setting. A pedagogical service station would attempt to do that and nothing more. In so doing, it would add to but not replace the rich array of services already available to teachers in many sections of the country. Clearly, we need studies to see what other needs teachers have which might be met through teachers' centers, perhaps similar to at least some of those now functioning in England.

INTERMEDIATE AGENCIES

Earlier, I indicated our initial view of the hub of the League as a temporary device, with a life span sufficient only to the task of creating a new social system of peer schools which would become increasingly salient. By the conclusion of SECSI, it was clear that the hub was more significant than we had surmised and that it should be conceived of as evolutionary but not ultimately expendable. Unfortunately, our initial view limited inquiry into it until it was almost too late, and so some of my observations here are merely speculation.

The League hub served initially as a legitimator. At the outset it was the alternative drummer, though, later, there were others. It served to get the several school cultures moving and to massage the social system of peer schools into a functioning reality. Throughout, it was a source of information about new ideas and materials. To some degree, it was a conscience, feeding back information that reinforced, raised questions, and, presumably, sometimes threatened. It sought to anticipate problems and needs for new skills and to respond to them as sensitively as possible. Toward the end, it became more and more a switching station for teachers seeking to get together with teachers.

All these functions and related activities appear to be appropriate for and within the scope of the administrative offices of school districts. But few such offices are performing them, perhaps because there are so many other functions to be performed: the care and feeding of the board, conducting campaigns for more funds, maintaining facilities, managing crises, and so on. Or it may be that the central office inevitably has an authoritarian image and, indeed, an authoritarian role to perform. It is exceedingly difficult for the office of ultimate responsibility to sanction the right to fail.

All these restricting, limiting conditions are amenable to change. The movement of collective bargaining from local to state levels could remove from the local district much of the tension now surrounding the process and could free time to be directed toward improving individual schools. For some years to come, however, these restraints will continue to prevail. In the meantime—and perhaps on a continuing basis—experiments in the creation of new institutions or the modification of existing ones probably will be necessary.

A significant component of a comprehensive, responsive change strategy could be an intermediate agency like the hub of the League, completely independent of but continuously advised by and advisory to the formal system of schools and schooling. The regional laboratories created by Title IV of the ESEA of 1965 were intended to serve somewhat as such intermediate agencies, but most of them went in another direction, usually caught up in the conventional role of the external change agent and linear R,D&D. The major failure of the regional laboratories was in the realm of tapping and coordinating the resources of their surrounding regions. A few used the right rhetoric but failed to match performance with that rhetoric. But it is not too late to try anew, with less money and on a less grandiose scale.

An intermediate agency serving as a hub would perform, probably, all of the functions performed by the hub of the League. But it is conceivable that it might serve also as a broker between several school districts and several universities existing in close proximity. It would have access to all the resources likely to be called upon in seeking to provide sustenance to schools in one or more networks. School districts and/or schools might pay a participating fee, which would be used both to employ a small coordinating staff and for the services of consulting and resource personnel to be located as needed. State colleges and universities might commit a specified amount of time counted as part of the service and teaching load of faculty members. In return, they would secure the services of teaching personnel to provide clinical enrichment for the teacher education program and access to the schools for the kind of research discussed earlier. The Atlanta Area Teacher Education Service described in Chapter 3, reconceptualized and revised in certain critical respects, provides a beginning model for the kind of intermediate agency envisioned.

What is needed will vary from locale to locale and particularly from urban to rural areas. Inquiry is needed in order to identify the missing links in existing constellations of institutions. The purpose should be to create an institution which is not subject to the whims or blandishments of any existing institution; which has no determining power over the careers of participants; which has only service and modest research functions to perform; which operates with a small staff, drawing most of its resources from other institutions; and which seeks to rotate most of the small staff it does have, frequently employing for a year or two persons who take leave from participating or other institutions. There are challenging possibilities here for creating interesting, productive, new human settings.

RESEARCH, DEVELOPMENT, AND DIFFUSION

On several occasions in this book, I have stated that the League model is not a complete model of change and that it is not a substitute for R,D&D. Rather, it represents an effort to treat a milieu different from that inhabited by persons involved in R,D&D—the milieu envisioned by the latter group as a target for their efforts. The intent was to reveal some of the complexities of the former and to pose some hypotheses pertaining to why the products of the latter failed, often, to penetrate the intended system.

Neither R,D&D nor the League model is adequate alone. Ideally, they are complementary parts of a change process, each needing the other. R,D&D needs a setting for its products but not an unreceptive one. Schools seek these products only as they become aware of their problems and what is available for dealing with them.

My bias, clearly, is in developing the responsiveness of the schools. What is needed is for responsive schools to reach out for whatever will help them, to select what appears to be useful, and to draw it into their field of control. All this represents a distinct shift in emphasis from what has prevailed, a different perspective, but not a rejection of R,D&D. Such would be a serious misinterpretation.

Nothing I have said eliminates the need for research, development, and diffusion. It is necessary to recognize that R,D&D means only what the letters stand for and is not a comprehensive change strategy. But it is an important part of a change strategy involving the development of a propensity toward change, on one hand, and the development of ideas, structures, and materials to meet changing needs, on the other.

R,D&D should proceed at full pace and not be confused with the task of providing insight into the operation of schools for decision-making purposes, the major function for research so far developed here. We need new insights into learning, teaching, and many other educational phenomena. This knowledge provides the basis for improved use of intelligence and, ultimately, has usefulness going far beyond research or evaluation oriented only to facilitating ongoing decisions in the realms of policy and practice.

The proper functioning of a responsive model of change necessitates the presence of and ready access to R,D&D. While R,D&D should be illuminated by practice, it should not be conducted merely to serve it. Researchers aware of and sensitive to their fields of work must follow their own insights, independent of the pleas of practitioners that their inquiries have immediate relevance.

The research role of the hub is to study what is happening in the schools it serves. It might serve as a center for R,D&D. But it also would draw upon research and related activities proceeding in universities and other centers. It serves as an intermediate agency between schools wanting help and places wanting to give it, more than as a production center in its own right. A major role of the hub is to bring together elements having something to offer each other—in this case, schools on one hand and the products of R,D&D on the other.

SUMMARY: THE RESPONSIVE MODEL

We have seen that the essential elements for educational change in the League model are the individual school with an internal process (DDAE) designed for sustained responsiveness to needs and relevant resources; strong links with a consortium of peer schools; a hub supporting both individual schools and the new social system; training programs sensitive to emerging needs for new attitudes, skills, and knowledge; various communication devices designed both to exchange information internal to the system and to bring in ideas from outside; and easy access to peers and other resource persons in order to secure assistance just as soon as the need for it is recognized. Both the inner drives and mechanisms for self-renewal and other stimulants to and support for such renewal are encompassed in the model. If there were nothing more to the schooling enterprise than individual schools, such a league of schools, as defined, would suffice as a responsive model for change and improvement.

But this, obviously, is not the case. We live in a large and complex society, with schools encompassed within large, complex bureaucracies. The press of these bureaucracies is so ever-present and so demanding that the several elements of a league soon would become subsystems seeking to operate smoothly and without countervailing, tension-producing characteristics. The league system would move rapidly toward a stable state, introducing only those modest innovations that do not arouse attention and, indeed, call for no significant changes on the part of personnel.

Consequently, though I have previously described the League as the outer agency in a productive inner-outer tension with the schools, it is also desirable to look at the league model as described here and in other volumes in this series as the inner agency in another context. After achieving a measure of smooth functioning, satisfaction, and perhaps even tranquillity, "it does not wait upon its environment, instead it intrudes farther and farther into it, experimenting on its own."[17] Unless there has been considerable previous communication with that environment, however, and perhaps even some preliminary agreements with it designed to facilitate ". . . the deliberate, temporary relaxation of rules in order to explore the possibilities of alternative rules,"[18] early encounters with this outer environment could be disastrous.

It is for this reason that I have discussed here the supportive stance of the district office most likely to sustain the precious, powerful "centrifugal dynamism" inherent in schools, once the human potential within them has stirred enough to create the beginnings of satisfying work places and to derive a sense of personal worth or potency in the process. The threats this process poses to external structures are more imagined than real because personal becoming involves self-transcendence and this, in turn, means a greater ability to identify with others. And so the superintendent who grasps this concept and seeks to meet the challenge will find that he has allies among principals and teachers who are willing to work with him in improving the places where the children are. If he cannot rise to such a challenge, he ought not occupy the office.

Also, I have endeavored to place in perspective the potential roles of schools of education as part of this larger environment. Currently, they are in danger of losing their way, just as the schools are in danger of cutting themselves off from this important source of intellectual supplies. Although they do not often act like they do, the two groups of institutions need each other—but for symbiosis, not stability. Their mutual relationship, too, must be one of sustained, productive tension.

What provides both the sense of direction for the required relationships and the glue to hold the pieces together is the concept of the single school, with its students, teachers, and principal as primary participants, as the key unit for change.

NOTES

1 Carl R. Rogers, *Freedom to Learn*, Charles E. Merrill, Columbus, Ohio, 1969, p. vii.

2 Harry S. Broudy, *The Real World of the Public Schools*, Harcourt Brace Jovanovich, New York, 1972, p. 227.

3 Daniel E. Griffiths, "Administrative Theory and Change in Organizations," in Matthew B. Miles (ed.), *Innovation in Education*, Teachers College, New York, 1964, p. 435.

4 Seymour B. Sarason, *The Creation of Settings and the Future Societies*, Jossey-Bass, San Francisco, 1972.

5 Wendell L. French and Cecil H. Bell, Jr., *Organization Development*, Prentice-Hall, Englewood Cliffs, N.J., 1973, p. 200.

6 James G. March, "Model Bias in Social Action," *Review of Educational Research*, vol. 42, no. 4, Fall 1972.

7 John Holt, *What Do I Do Monday?* Dutton, New York, 1970.

8 Mary M. Bentzen and Associates, *Changing Schools: The Magic Feather Principle*, McGraw-Hill, New York, 1974.

9 John I. Goodlad, M. Frances Klein, and Associates, *Behind the Classroom Door*, Charles A. Jones, Worthington, Ohio, 1970 (revised 1974).

10 New York [State] Office of Education Performance Review, *The Superintendent of Schools: His Role, Background and Salary*, Albany, New York, June 1974, p. 26.

11 Kenneth A. Tye, "A Conceptual Framework for Political Analysis, Public Demands and School Board Decisions," unpublished doctoral dissertation, University of California, Los Angeles, 1968.

12 In this regard, the studies of A. Garth Sorenson and his students are highly relevant. See, for example, A. Garth Sorenson, *Toward an*

Instructional Model for Counseling, Center for the Study of Evaluation, Report No. 4, University of California, Los Angeles, 1967.

13 I have addressed these matters at greater length in John I. Goodlad, "The Reconstruction of Teacher Education," *Teachers' College Record,* vol. 72, pp. 61–72, September 1970.

14 Lee J. Cronbach, "Beyond the Two Disciplines of Scientific Psychology," *American Psychologist,* February 1975, p. 121.

15 *Ibid.,* pp. 124–125, 126.

16 Stephen K. Bailey, "Teachers' Centers: A British First," *Phi Delta Kappan,* November 1971, pp. 146–149; Robert Thornbury (ed.), *Teachers' Centres,* Agathon Press, New York, 1974.

17 Loren C. Eiseley, "Alternatives to Technology," in Aaron W. Warner et al. (eds.), *The Environment of Change,* Columbia, New York, 1969, p. 166.

18 James G. March, "Model Bias in Social Action," *Review of Educational Research,* vol. 42, no. 4, p. 417, Fall 1972.

CHAPTER 8

NOTES ON THE ECOLOGY OF EDUCATION

For all living things the essence of a habitat is that it must be total, enduring and sustaining. In other words, a habitat must be habitable, not only in terms of food intake and reproduction but as an enfolding, protective, and satisfying world. It must offer resources and present challenges to which the species is capable of adapting its physiological and behavioral patterns in a meaningful and rewarding way. Insofar as the habitat itself is in course of change, such must be compatible, in its rate and direction, with that of which its users are capable.

—Max Nicholson (*The Big Change: After the Environmental Revolution*, McGraw-Hill, New York, 1973, p. 276)

Since my focus throughout this book has been on schools, readers might conclude that we need only to reconstruct them, difficult as this is, in order to achieve vital education. But dynamic schools alone will give us only an incomplete renaissance. It is difficult to conceive of schools being vital and at the same time detached in thought and practice from some more comprehensive conceptualization and functioning of educational institutions and agencies.

The school today, much more than a quarter-century ago, shares educational functions with agencies in addition to the family and the peer group. Television provides a striking case in point. In 1950, television sets were in about 5 percent of American homes; in 1975, they were in approximately 95 percent. By age seventeen, young people have spent about 9 percent of their lives before what was aptly called in *The One Hundred Dollar Misunderstanding* that "glass-faced bastard." By this age, they have been in schools just a little more than 8 percent of their present span of years—and television got to them first. For better or for worse, this electronic intrusion into our lives constitutes an educational revolution.

There have been studies into the effects of television, but these, like most of our studies of schooling, have been conducted along the lines of the narrow models of research and development criticized earlier. As with studies designed to get at the effects of various instructional treatments (with pupil aptitude a major factor in the design), these efforts closed out consideration of many significant dimensions. The responsive model of schooling developed in this volume recognizes the complexity of schools, identifies the realm of instruction as only one of several significant components, and opens up challenging frontiers of research, theory, and improvement. Similarly comprehensive models applied to the home and family, not just the television-individual relationship, would provide valuable insights into the impact of this medium—but only on family behavior and very closely related matters.

Just as instruction is only a part of school life and a television program only a part of home life, both the school and the home are only part of a still larger ecosystem which includes these two and other institutions. If our dialogue, decisions, actions, and evaluation are to be comprehensive from an educational perspective, then they must include consideration of all those institutions, agencies, and media performing educational functions. Each must be considered not only in its own right but also in its relations with all the rest. Television, for example, is not merely a component of home life, affecting it in a variety of ways. It has its own, virtually institutional existence, affecting children over and beyond the confines of parental control. But we know precious little about all of this. It is past time for us to begin to sort it out.

Putting together a more comprehensive picture of what already is and what potentially could be significantly educational in our society will require, first, a conceptual model going beyond those already available. The input-output model, which sets purpose before activity, is quite inadequate, although it has some use in testing limited experiments once some mapping of the terrain is well under way. The responsive model, which suspends some of the conventional rules of rational Western thought and which views activity as not necessarily guided by purpose, is useful for examining any given institution once identified. Also, its recognition and support of "centrifugal dynamism" in people and institutions suggest an eventual reaching out to find other people and institutions interested in education. But this reaching out by an institution serves to satisfy its own developing needs. Symbiosis between institutions and, subsequently, synergy result more from the mutual satisfaction of self-interests than from any recognition of oneness or unity and, therefore, of true independence.

What seems to be needed is an ecological model of education. It is difficult to describe what such might be; the term is only beginning to find its way into the educational literature. There are, of course, obvious parallels with the term and the concepts attached to it in speaking of our physical environment, and there is now considerable ecological work in several of the social science disciplines.

In popular usage, we have come to use the word "ecology" in referring to cleaning up the environment. There is an analogy here in thinking of schools. We have polluted our schools through ascribing to them an overload of functions. We have failed to look either at how these additional functions have affected the school's educational function or at other ways to fulfill them or at the extent to which other institutions also are fulfilling educational functions. In all probability, the entire ecosystem is now polluted by overlap, duplication, jangled communication lines, and the general dysfunctionality of institutional overload. The time has come to sort out the component parts and to determine what each is doing. Then, we need to explore the functioning of the entire system in order to determine the nature of a healthy condition and the nature of the pollutants and counterpollutants.

It becomes relatively easy to explore the use of this perspective in seeking to improve the functioning of schools within a larger family of institutions. First, we assume that we do not know what purposes (functions) the school is performing, and we suspend the tempting step of determining what functions it *should* fulfill. Rather, we seek to describe and, to the best of our abilities, understand what it now does. Presumably, following the tenets of the responsive model of schooling, this would be a joint effort of "external" researchers and "internal" inhabitants, each group interested in different things, presumably, and providing different perspectives. At present, we do not have the needed inquiries. Caught up in our pervasive, rational models we project what ought to be without knowing either what now exists or the consequences for the organism of what we propose to do. In fact, lacking an ecological view, we do not much concern ourselves with the potential effects of proposed changes in the habitat on those who live there or the reverse. Nor does it dawn on us that, from a different theoretical perspective, our behavior might be judged immoral.

Although some limited generalizations from studies such as these ultimately would be possible, they will be sharply limited; "...generalization comes late, and the exception is taken as seriously as the rule."[1] We probably need to work toward taxonomies of schooling, an activity long overdue in our field, wherein we endeavor to classify schools according not only to various differences such as size, location, socioeconomic status of parents, and the like, but also to the intensity of a given function being performed. Obviously, the needed studies cannot be guided by some single conceptualization or theory of what a school is or does or of what it should be or do. Schools in the United States do not belong to a single species, although most of our rhetoric seems based on the assumption that they do. It is likely that the so-called latent functions of a small school in rural Kansas are quite different from those in a large one in the Bronx.

In a conventional input-output model of schooling, once having identified these latent functions, we would seek to eliminate them in order to leave more time for those assumed to be educationally purposeful. But, from an ecological perspective, it might be perceived as wiser to legitimate some of these previously unrecognized functions simply because they are deemed important and no other agency for them currently exists. Seeking to make our schools more effective units in an ecosystem does not necessarily mean that we eliminate all the functions judged to be noneducational; nor does it mean seeking uniformity in functions for all types of schools. But it does mean that all functions being performed are to be raised to a level of visibility, scrutiny, and analysis in virtually a school-by-school process of description, analysis, and reconstruction.

We also need to examine other institutions from this same ecological perspective. Although we do not know which ones are now performing educational functions, we should be able to make some useful guesses while remaining alert to potentiality as well as to current activity. One useful way to proceed is by seeking to educate a group of children "from scratch," so to speak, with no school at all. Rusch's school-by-bus approach is promising.[2] Beginning with the problem of how best to construct school buildings, he concluded that no building is needed; in the environment of the city he discovered the necessary elements of a broad and varied educational program for several busloads of children. How all these might be put together in a smoothly functioning, healthy ecosystem for the education of all our people is, however, a much more complex and challenging task.

To assist us in this task, we need a variety of alternative scenarios regarding the essentials of what such an ecosystem, functioning within and as part of a highly complex society, might look like. Such scenarios must portray possible complementary roles to be played by the various component parts. The schools need not play just one role; it is possible and desirable to sketch several quite different ones.[3] Movement toward the deliberate sharing of educational functions and public funds by an array of institutions will not be easy. It begins with recognition that the schools do not now and simply cannot provide the mechanism for achieving all the goals of our society—not even all the educational ones. And this means setting aside a powerful part of the American dream and quite a few myths regarding our schools.

AN ECOLOGICAL VIEW OF EDUCATIONAL IMPROVEMENT

In the foregoing, I have used the word "ecosystem" several times. I have in mind an ecological community in which both living and non-living things constitute a system and interact within it. In this conception, man* is part of, not master or conqueror of, the environment. Things and sets of things, individuals and groups of people and the relationships among all these are seen as one, a unified whole.[4]

In this conception, there is nobody on the outside trying to do something to someone on the inside. All are part of the same systemic whole or ecosystem. Every person and every thing has consequences for all other persons and things. Nothing is inconsequential. Individuality and uniqueness exist but function and are understood in relation to the whole and to other parts of the whole.

This conception is not new to sociology and anthropology. Seminal sources were Emile Durkheim in France and Ernest W. Burgess in the United States, the latter perceiving juvenile delinquency in the context of ills in the larger social system and moving attention beyond treatment or incarceration for the individual. More recently, the ecological approach has influenced such fields as political science (Charles O. Jones), history (William H. McNeill), economics (Walter Isard), and urban planning (Harvey S. Perloff and Lowdon Wingo). Such little ecological thought as there has been in education has been very much

---

*Sexist denotations recognized, we still do not have an alternative word conveying the same connotations. "Humankind" sometimes serves, but not always; it does not quite serve here.

influenced by psychologists Kurt Lewin and Roger G. Barker, and the field of psychology is once again showing some signs of interest in the ecological perspective.

What all these approaches in the academic disciplines have in common is simply a concern with man and environment. They diverge with respect to the study of the individual organism in the environment (autecology), on one hand, and the study of population in its environment (synecology), on the other. Clearly, both branches are relevant to an ecology of education. But it is the latter that has been less pursued, is less understood, and has greater significance for perceiving a comprehensive educational ecosystem.

Although the ecological approach involves more than what goes on within a defined space, studies of specific locations are more amenable to research at this point in time. A great deal can be learned about an institution, for example, by studying it as an ecosystem within which relations to other parts of a larger ecosystem can be inferred. Linear thinking about schools concentrates on what is happening to the children, usually by measuring effects. The school is judged good or healthful, bad or unhealthful. Healthful and unhealthful are instrumental terms. Ecological thinking embraces the whole: the impact of pupils on teachers as well as the reverse; the impact of teachers on teachers; the use of resources; the relationship among all these. One then endeavors to determine the health of the whole. Healthy and unhealthy are organic terms. Viewed from the ecological perspective, it is difficult to conceive of an institution being good when any of its parts is not healthy. An institution must do more than produce products efficiently. It must provide good work for its inhabitants and conserve material resources simultaneously.

This is not an easy way to think. Traditionally, we have tended to view phenomena one at a time, separable and additive in their effects. Or, we have allowed the recognition of greater complexity to be encompassed by the so-called industrial model of input, productive and nonproductive responses, output, feedback loops, correction, repeat, etc. R,D&D, discussed earlier, follows such a model. The alternative involving variables interacting in a nonlinear fashion and functioning as an integrated system is now imbedded in both personality and social systems theory. But it has been scarcely considered in educational theory.

Models based on the traditional theory of the child as product and everything else as instrumental, according to Bronfenbrenner,

... seldom include the adjacent or encompassing systems which may in fact determine what can or cannot occur in the more immediate context. Such encompassing systems include the nature and requirements of the parents' work, characteristics of the neighborhood, transportation facilities, the relation between school and community, the role of television (not only in its direct effect on the child but in its indirect influence on patterns of family and community life), and a host of other ecological circumstances and changes which determine with whom and how the child spends his time: for example, the fragmentation of the extended family, the separation of residential and business areas, the disappearance of neighborhoods, zoning ordinances, geographic and social mobility, growth of single parent families, the abolition of the apprentice system, consolidated schools, commuting, the working mother, the delegation of child care to specialists and others outside the home, urban renewal, or the existence and character of an explicit national policy on children and families.[5]

One of the many advantages of an ecological theory is that it draws attention to what exists or is happening for purposes of information. What to do is not determined in advance but emerges out of diagnosis and consideration of alternatives. It may not be necessary to rip up the water system and replace it with another. Perhaps just a few leaks need to be repaired. Or, to use an analogy from schooling, it may not be necessary to install an entire new reading program; perhaps the teachers simply need more help with the present one.

Continuing inquiry into itself, then, is a condition necessary to the health of an educational ecosystem. Inquiry is enlightened by theory, and so the explanatory power of the theory is critical to the adequacy of the data generated by inquiry. In traditional studies guided by a simple ends-means theory of schooling, in which ends have been assumed and limited, the collection of data and, in turn, the conclusions about the adequacy of the school have focused on a limited array of pupil effects. Shifting the focus to include the nature of the means constitutes a first step toward a better theory of schooling. Enlarging the lens to include other educational activities in addition to those conducted in schools moves us toward a developing theory of education adequate to the requirements of social policy and planned change.

An educational ecosystem need not be without goals. But goals emerge out of virtually simultaneous consideration of two quite different sets of data: one descriptive, the other normative. The nature of descriptive data is quite clear. Such data describes existential conditions: 10 percent of the children constitute 90 percent of the daily absentees; 60 percent of the teachers wish they were doing something else; all the children watch television programs, X, Y, and Z from 8:00 P.M. to 11:00 P.M. The use of norms as data is less understood. Norms in an ecological sense constitute attempts to describe the healthy condition: absentees should be low and evenly distributed over the pupil population; teachers should be happy with their work; school-age children should get from eight to ten hours of sleep each night.

Traditional thinking tends to convert this second list directly into goals and to formulate activities designed to achieve or conform to them The most obvious solutions to the problems noted in the first set of data (if these data are secured at all), are to appoint more truant officers, select new teachers, and stop the children from viewing television at such late hours.

But an ecological perspective, guided by a more comprehensive view of education as a system, may lead to quite different conclusions and approaches. Nonattendance at school may be found to be related to both distance from school and parental circumstances. Perhaps the time of beginning school or the school transportation system is the component of the system to be manipulated. The unsatisfied teachers are found to be unhappy over conditions which do not seem to concern less-dedicated teachers—perhaps too many record-keeping and routine duties are preventing them from doing what they think is important. Their unhappiness may be warranted and the possibility of shunting these activities elsewhere can be examined. If the TV programs are to be judged outstanding, citizen action might get the viewing time changed or the normal schedules for going to bed and going to school could be temporarily revised.

The traditional, linear view of schooling seeks to make the school more productive, almost at any cost—the measure of effectiveness being certain effects produced in the pupil products. Failure to produce calls for more of something—money, time, materials—or some manipulations in classroom management or pedagogy. Usually, the proposed solution deals with a limited set of variables assumed to be modifiable. The results have been disappointing and we have become disillusioned with our schools.

By contrast, the ecological perspective encompasses a wide array of current and potential educational variables and assumes that all of them are modifiable. It assumes that the entire ecosystem can become something other than it is now. Solutions are not seen as necessarily calling for more. They may call for less—such as less time spent on reading at an early age and fewer functions to be performed by a single institution.

An ecological approach points to human engineering (a discredited term in recent years) to take care of those leaks and breaks in the system which require only repair and not the reconstruction of interacting parts. It turns to education as the appropriate way to discover how the system is functioning and to pose a never-ending series of scenarios regarding alternative functioning. How the gaps between reality and alternatives are perceived (or whether any are perceived at all) and acted upon provides the bases and directions for self-renewal. A static society will challenge little, will tend to seek the kind of functioning achieved in some earlier, more illustrious era, and will stress form over principle. A creative society will accept little or nothing as given or fixed, not even current visions of a healthy ecosystem.

I cannot accept the notion of a good society being one large production system serving preordained ends. Rather, it is one characterized by homeostasis (a *tendency toward* maintenance of a relatively stable environment), guided by a continuing search for what best sustains humankind. Just what this means is an important task for education and a prime function of educational institutions.

THE CONTEMPORARY USES
OF ALTERNATIVE EDUCATIONAL MODELS

It is now convenient to place in perspective three alternative models of education and to discuss their possible usefulness. They are not mutually exclusive, though for me the ecological is the all encompassing model within which the others play their appropriate roles.

The model identified first in this volume was characterized as the input-output model in which purpose precedes activity. It pervades Western civilization and the so-called industrial and military models stem from it. Likewise, the input, response (production or manufacture), output model has dominated curriculum development, teaching, and evaluation in education: goals are formulated and made precise (behavioral objectives), activities are designed to achieve the purposes, and attainment of purposes is evaluated. Applied to institutions and institutional behavior, especially efforts to change or reform, the theory has led to the linear R,D&D strategies described in Chapter 1, program-planning-budgeting systems (PPBS), statewide accountability plans, and competency-based training of teachers and administrators.

As Pace puts it, "The virtue of the model is that it guards against attributing to the environment a result that is predictable without any environmental intervention. The vice of the model is that it makes environmental influences hard to find."[6] Its virtue of rigorous control of the design elements forces a narrowness, excluding from consideration many important factors in the system. From the perspective of theory of change, it does not simply make environmental influences hard to find but sharply limits the array of variables manipulated. These problems merely reflect, of course, the general vices and virtues of sharply focused theories.

Bronfenbrenner is speaking to the central issue here when he observes that laborious statistical calculation was required to demonstrate that early intervention projects pertaining to the learning of young children had any effects whatsoever.[7] He argues for the necessity of manipulating many other factors in the child's environment—essentially for experimental human ecology.[8]

The more sharply defined the enterprise or activity and the more readily it can be separated from or viewed in isolation from other phenomena, the more useful the input-response-output model and its many relatives. The golfer suffering from a slice wants specific, technical help, propably involving adjusting the grip on the club. He does not want his psyche or life-style examined. Diagnosis, prescription, response, and practice produce a straight drive. Satisfaction comes from observing the effect of the revised stroke and from improved game and score. The same model could be used also to produce better golf balls and clubs. An ecological perspective is important (what are the implications of using the materials required for an adequately strong and flexible club shaft?), but it does not necessarily change or reduce the effectiveness of the model.

Clearly, then, the input-output model has usefulness with respect to improving certain specifics within a larger, ecological perspective, especially the quality of products made available to responsive schools. Likewise, it has much to contribute methodologically, although not as much, probably, as is attributed to it. More complex, comprehensive models usually stem from less sharply focused and clarified theories and, consequently, tend to suffer from less rigorous methodologies. But the reduced rigor of methodologies stemming from some alternative theories should be regarded less as a vice and more as a challenge to creativity.

Unfortunately, methodological difficulties with respect to the use of and inquiry into alternative models of education and change have contributed to overconfidence in and overcommitment to the input-response-output model, and it has moved into realms where it simply is overextended or quite inappropriate. For example, state-sponsored accountability plans for schools have a certain rational elegance that tends to close out arguments not grounded in criteria of efficiency.[9] Lack of a systemic view of the nature of things blinds one to the possible relationship between such approaches to teacher accountability and growing union membership on the part of teachers.

The strains on a schooling enterprise guided almost exclusively by the educational theory from which these models stem are now everywhere apparent. We counter students' drive for their rights with a demand that they be "responsible" without asking ourselves what in the environment of the school causes young people to conclude that they have little or no rights. Looking for such a relationship in no way detracts from the importance of their learning about both rights and responsibilities. We simply become aware of the fact that the relationships here may be more complex than we assumed and may call for a more powerful response that two 30-minute lessons a week on moral values and responsibilities.

Critical contemporary problems like this are symptomatic of a vastly overextended theory of education, change, and improvement which has, as we have seen, certain limited but important uses. Carried to its extreme abuse, the application of this theory to institutions elevates efficiency to the position of supreme criterion for their evaluation. Institutions and those in them are to be efficient servants (robots) of society. They are incapable of changing themselves, goes the rhetoric, and so change must come from without, be more or less forced on passive and only mildly resistant recipients. Means are good to the extent that they are seen as being instrumental to goal-oriented "progress." Man is master and, indeed, conqueror of his environment.

The necessary transition to what might be called a sustainable society, in contrast to a consuming one, involves reconstruction of our institutions. For this activity, the responsive model developed in this volume offers promise.

The responsive model assumes that purpose does not necessarily precede activity or action and that institutions, as conducted, are not necessarily goal-oriented. Institutions are in some degree self-conscious, which provides a beginning point for improvement since data regarding present status are potentially useful to the change process.

Stimulation, especially the stimulation of ideas, very often comes from without. Consequently, institutional antennas must be atuned to the larger environment. Resources from this external context are essential, as are encouragement and other forms of reinforcement. Our work suggests that reinforcement by peers and peer institutions is particularly important. There is, then, an inner and an outer in sustained processes of institutional improvement. A virtue of the responsive model is its fundamental appeal to people to improve their habitat, an appeal which has challenged humankind down through the centuries. Consequently, its usefulness is in reconstructing the institutions we already have. "To make this a better place for those of us who live and work here" becomes a rallying call. The relationship between effort and reward is reasonably clear. We often are asked about the motivations and rewards inherent in the League. The questioner usually has in mind material rewards, and the assumption implied is that, without new material incentives, teachers "won't play." We feel quite comfortable in replying to the effect that teachers are motivated, given the freedom, simply by the opportunity to redesign their work places.

A difficulty lies in the words "given the freedom." As we have seen, the pervasive model of schooling and change is quite different from the responsive one, and so those aspiring from within soon perceive themselves to be in a harsh and abrasive world which is quite unsympathetic to their aspirations and efforts. And so, I have given considerable attention in previous chapters to the inherent fragility of this approach and the support systems necessary to its sustenance. Because of the complexity inherent in developing and maintaining these systems, a certain amount of failure is almost certain to occur—failure which can be shattering and which usually leads to more excessive utilization of efficiency-oriented processes from without. But this simply is an unavoidable part of the necessary transition. It does not deny the usefulness of the model but simply points to the need for careful nurturing of efforts derived from it.

A conceptual and operating weakness of the model stems from a certain parochialism inherent in the rallying call and all that it implies. The challenge is readily converted (and perhaps perverted) into a drive to be "first" or "best" at any cost rather than healthy. This, in turn, could lead to a sort of self-induced instrumentalism. A major danger is that those in the institution may not ask themselves whether or not they are doing the "right" things but merely whether they are doing well whatever it is they do.

It seems to me that this possible weakness, more apparent just as institutions are about to decline than at any other time, can only be offset by that "... healthy relativism, which should prevent us from idolizing ourselves and our nation, our creeds, our truths, and our little knowledge."[10] This relativism, in turn, arises out of an ecological perspective, wherein the interdependence of all and the relative significance of each institution are perceived. Nonetheless, this perspective does not detract from the responsive model, nor the long-standing humanistic theory from which it is derived, as a useful guide to institution-building. In fact, the responsive model helps us to move conceptually and operationally to the more encompassing ecological one.

As we have seen, an ecological model of education goes far beyond schools in seeking to embrace people, things, and institutions in a systemic, interrelated whole. It encourages awareness of much more than the effects of a stimulus on the organism for which it is intended. It looks for effects on far-distant elements of what is seen as an interacting system, within which what is consequential for one organism is consequential for any and all others. This also means that the model seeks to direct attention to malfunctioning which may have its roots some distance away from where the symptom manifests itself.

Guided by an ecological model, one suspends value judgments until one has a data-based perspective regarding the function of what might otherwise be prejudged to be bad or an illness. One seeks to find out what an identified condition appears to be doing for the system just as Freud asked what the condition does for the person. Thus, the small local high school defies any reasonably comprehensive exemplars of "good" educational programs but contributes to community solidarity. What will be lost in consolidating this school with another twenty miles distant? Instead of ignoring or effectively terminating this normally unlegitimated social function, perhaps efforts should be made to help this school perform it more effectively.

This ecological perspective encompasses the other two models. It is discovered, for example, that a community college is not reaching a large portion of those viewed as appropriate clients even though some live closer than many who are attending. It may not be necessary to build still another institution, the usual galvanic response. A better response might be to provide courses in homes via television. Much of the subsequent development of software is then guided by the tenets and techniques of good R&D.

The ecological model is not entirely goal-free with respect to activities and evaluation, even though the inherent value structure favors homeostasis (and homeostasis is a far cry from rigor mortis!) rather than continuous progress toward some externally derived goal. Goals emerge out of relating a defined condition to some envisioned model of improved health. Consequently, they are situational, temporary, and emergent.

Whereas the input-output or ends-means-effects model is oriented very much to the present (what works) and the responsive model to the present and future (where we are and what we might become), the ecological model seeks constantly to keep past, present, and future in perspective. What did we once do that would now be relevant and appropriate? What does what we are now doing destroy? What will be the effects on the unborn of what we are doing now or contemplate doing? Each person shares in the history of humankind, bears a relationship to people and places elsewhere, and is father or mother of what is yet to be. A major use of an ecological model of education is to develop such an awareness and accompanying sense of identity among those who inhabit the ecosystem.

CONCLUSION: THE CREATING OF WALDENS

Boyer has stated neatly the problem confronting us: "... a society without control over change is a society with its future out of control."[11] If we are to gain some reasonable measure of control over change, we must think in ecological terms regarding our lives and institutions. The development of such thinking is an appropriate central educational activity.

But this is not sufficient. Social planning and social engineering, too, must be guided by an ecological perspective, with an awareness of the interrelatedness of things, people, and institutions. Margaret Mead states succinctly what is required in addressing the problem of the modern family:

> In the 30's medicine reduced a patient to an organ. If a patient had kidney trouble, that's what we treated. Twenty years later we remembered that a patient was more than a kidney. ... We remembered that he had a heart, a brain, and we began to treat the whole patient.
>
> It took another 10 years to get the patient back in the family, then the family back in the community. Now we must put the community back in the nation and the nation back in the world. You can't save the family all by itself.[12]

You can't save the school all by itself either. It is not a self-contained entity, with all the necessary ingredients for a full self-renewing culture. "The school as a culture" is merely a convenient metaphor, though it is an enormously useful one for coming to understand schools better and in seeking to improve them. It helps to remind those of us who do not live in schools each day but who want to improve them that the learning involved in changing a school will contribute to our own understanding of schools as well as to school improvement—at least if we can forget the missionary role long enough to become learners.

While an ecological perspective is now essential to education and to social engineering, few of us have the opportunity or perhaps even the inclination to become engaged in societal reconstruction much beyond the daily sphere of our lives of family, work, and leisure. But the complexity of our industrialized society and the shock of its rapid change confound this daily existence, frequently leaving us numb. We come to suffer from a profound ennui, seeming to have little control over our daily lives and our personal futures, to say nothing of the whole of society. What the League offered most to those inhabiting the schools as a workplace was an opportunity to re-create their habitats and in the process to gain a sense of personal worth and potency.

The concept of reconstructing our places of work gives us a place to catch hold, a place to begin, even the promise of a new sense of community. Relatively few workers have any sense of communion with their fellow workers. Joseph Heller, early in his book *Something Happened,* has his narrator say the following:

> In the office in which I work there are five people of whom I am afraid. Each of these 5 people is afraid of 4 people (excluding overlaps) for a total of 20, and each of these 20 people is afraid of 6 people, making a total of 120 people who are feared by at least 1 person. Each of these 120 people is afraid of the other 119 and all of these 145 people are afraid of the 12 men at the top who helped found and build the company and now own and direct it.[13]

At first intrigued and amused by the novel's antiheroic central character, we come more and more to understand him and, then, chillingly, to sympathize and identify with him. He is comfortable with neither his family nor his fellow workers, the two little social clusters within which he spends almost all his life. These are the two centers of gravity for most of us and for which no very satisfactory substitutes seem to be available.

A major part of our trouble is that, for most people, work is merely a job replaceable by another job. We carry from our traditions the notion that a job provides the money to do other things and has little value in its own right; it is instrumental to something else. Retirement lies at the end of the rainbow. How wrong a view this is! Hasn't the time come to make work a satisfying place to be so that the job is no longer just a job but is, instead, good work?

For teachers, principals, and pupils in the schools, the opportunity appears to be most obvious. But perhaps this is because, as an educator, I view all our educational institutions from the perspective of one who has found so much good work in them. And, of course, I view schools in the responsive mode and not in the industrial model. Schools are not factories. Their worth is found in the quality of life sustained there. The criteria used to evaluate both ends and means are essentially the same, simply because the ends (or, better, the values) are found in the means.

Our data show that use of the responsive model as exemplified by the League stimulated progress toward more satisfying work in the schools. Perhaps two examples are more useful here than a recitation of the data reported elsewhere.[14] Early in the project, Steve, one of the principals, confided in me he could hardly wait each week to get out of his school to his special Walden Pond—a small lake in southern California. He stayed there for just as long as he could each weekend, returning reluctantly to the school each Monday morning. Several years later, no less enthusiastic about his Walden, he talked about his present satisfaction with school, his new-found Walden of work.

Our films document a somewhat euphoric principals' session recounting what the several years of experience in the League had done for them. Ben, half-laughing and somewhat embarrassed, is speaking. "An interesting thing happened as far as my wife is concerned.... Somewhere last school year, maybe about in January, she said, 'You know, Ben, you are working much harder than you ever have, but you are a lot happier.' And, you know, we've heard the same thing about teachers." We are back to the ecological again. What goes on in the school affects home and family, just as the reverse is true. One cannot be saved by itself, but perhaps the two can be saved together.

Because of the complexity of our daily lives and, for far too many, limited satisfaction in places of work, probably all of us want to escape from time to time a place like Walden Pond. But such ponds are

becoming harder to find and they reflect, in varying degrees, the ecological problems from which we want to escape. Whether or not we
agree with his concepts of environmental contingencies and rein-
forcers, Skinner, in *Walden II,* offered a more viable solution—the creation of Waldens as places of full-time residence by those who inhabit
them. Of course, Skinner was not speaking of some retreat deep in the
woods or cut off from the rest of society by a moat. *Walden II* is alle-
gorical; it is a symbolic representation of our society and how we might
redesign it.

For those who spend a large part of their lives in schools, or banks
or post offices, or other institutions, some combination of the reality
of Thoreau's *Walden* and Skinner's *Walden II* is called for in creating
there a Walden III or XV or LXI. Skinner places human destiny in the
hands of humans and the society they create and, while not simplifying
or underestimating the complex tasks of creating "a habitat that is total,
enduring and sustaining," challenges us to do so. There is no human
future in seeking idyllic ponds as places of enduring satisfaction. Our
future is in our institutions, "the bones of our civilization." And so
it is in and with our institutions that each of us must proceed to create
satisfying work.

The lesson from Walden is in Thoreau's actual experience, not in
the myth that so effectively obscures the reality. Thoreau lived—more
or less—for a year beside the pond. He contemplated and described
it in all its seasons. But he did not regard the cabin as his permanent
home nor his brief residence there a way of life. "Walden was a ges-
ture."[15]

Walden Pond was only two miles from Concord and Thoreau's
family house was just a mile away. Edel's research is fascinating:

> ...we come upon curious information: the diary of the Boston hostess,
> Mrs. J. T. Fields, for example. Thoreau, she records, was a good son; he
> loved his mother and, she adds, "even when living in his retirement at
> Walden Pond, he would come home every day." We find confirmation
> in the first important biography of Thoreau written by his fellow towns-
> man...Frank B. Sanborn, in 1882. He says Thoreau "bivouacked" at
> Walden, adding that he really lived at home, where he went every day.[16]

Edel's often hilarious report tells us also that the Fitchbury Rail-
road steamed regularly past the opposite end of the pond (and it is a
pond, no way deserving to be called a lake); his mother and sisters
made a special trip out to the pond every Saturday; he raided the

family cookie jar on his frequent visits home; and he frequently enjoyed dinner in the homes of friends, as he had before his sojourn at Walden. Thoreau biographer Walter Harding gives us the punch line: "Rumor had it that every time Mrs. Emerson rang her dinner bell, Thoreau came bounding through the woods and over the fences to be first in line."[17]

A picture of life at the side of the pond is equally myth-shattering. Edel quotes Harding again:

> Occasionally whole groups of Thoreau's friends came out together to the pond and swarmed into his little cabin. It became quite the fashion to hold picnics on his front doorstep. When it rained, his visitors took refuge inside. He had as many as twenty-five or thirty people inside the tiny cabin at one time. On August 1, 1846, the antislavery women of Concord held their annual commemoration of the freeing of the West Indian slaves on his doorstep, and Emerson, W. H. Channing, and Rev. Caleb Stetson spoke to the assembled group. Afterward, a picnic lunch was served to all the guests.[18]

It is no small irony that Thoreau did not construct his hut out of his surrounding, temporary habitat. It was a kind of prefab, bought elsewhere and reassembled. Earlier, on a fishing trip near Walden Pond, on Fairhaven Bay, Thoreau and a friend burned a large section of woods in a careless act. Thoreau cooked his fish over a fire in a stump and, soon, the brush and weeds were aflame. "While help was coming he climbed to the highest rock of Fair Haven Cliff. 'It was a glorious spectacle,' the excited fisherman wrote in his journal much later, 'and I was the only one there to enjoy it.' "[19]

There is much more to be learned, obviously, from this picture of life at Walden than from the myth. Thoreau only encroached on the wilderness—if the site of his contemplations might be called that. He did not live there in any sense of creating a habitat. Unfortunately, this is the way a very large segment of humankind views the workplace and its setting. And Thoreau bivouacked for only a year; the average worker bivouacks in a number of workplaces for about forty years. Is it not time to convert the tragic myth of a job as instrumental to life into a reality of meaningful work and a satisfying ecological relationship with family and leisure? Freud was close to truth in saying that the two central elements of life are love and work.

Thoreau's carelessness with his cooking fire is symbolically repre-

sentative of our neglect of our cities and of our "throw-away" culture.*
Friends and neighbors are throw-away, too. There will be more to replace them. And if we don't like any of them, we can go off to Walden
Pond. But then people would encroach on us again, and there would
have to be flight to still another wilderness. Wildernesses, too, are
throw-away, even by those who seek in them some personal salvation.

The Walden myth is useful for the reconstruction of schools according to the responsive model because it suggests not merely the
finding of a retreat but the possibility of creating a human setting unlike those against which Thoreau railed: "Wherever man goes men will
pursue him and paw him with their dirty institutions and if they can,
constrain him to belong to their desperate oddfellow society," he said
in *Walden*. Skinner's *Walden II* is useful because it tosses aside the
idea of a wilderness retreat and confronts us with all the tasks of reconstruction and the folly of trying to run away. Doing away with our
schools or burning down the banks are nonanswers to our problems.

The myth tells us little about Thoreau confirmed in his sojourn by
the pond. Five years before *Walden* (1854) appeared, he wrote in
A Week on the Concord and Merrimack Rivers (1849): "It takes two
to speak the truth, one to speak and the other to hear." And Ekstein
observes:

> Even in Walden he noted, "I have three chairs in my house: one for
> solitude, two for friendship, three for society." He had discovered that
> individualism, in the sense of being alone and isolated like a Robinson
> Crusoe, could not be maintained nor achieve inner change. He had
> discovered that one needs friendship, love and a functioning society.[20]

The Walden reality is useful because it reminds us of those parts
of the ecosystem lying beyond the pond which those in schools can
neither leave behind nor ignore. The school is too interdependent with
its larger ecosystem to be a clearly identifiable self. The people in a
school make up only a temporary culture; for part of the time they
occupy other roles (some of them perceived to be more important) in
the same ecosystem. If the culture of the school is to become dynamic,
to the point of enjoying the hyperbolic description, "self-renewing,"
those in it must perceive their roles, activities, and rewards there as
significant. This is what happened, I think, to a gratifying degree in

---

* In fairness to Thoreau, he did not regard his pond as disposable; he respected its
ecological fragility. But he, of all people, should have known better than to set a fire
in a tree stump.

the League. But we must take care not to deceive ourselves into thinking that the concept of a self-renewing school, or of the culture of a school, is anything other than a metaphor.

The culture of the school is an exceedingly useful metaphor for conceptualizing and testing appropriate decision-making roles in the ecosystem of which the school is a part. The new dogma in schooling, as in many other things, is "citizen participation." There is a myth abroad in the land that if we simply get lay citizens into the act, all good things will follow. But experience suggests otherwise. Though the idea has a great deal of merit and obvious potential benefits, we need a variety of social experiments designed to work out the respective decision-making roles and the logistics before we go plunging into still one more deep, dark pool of disillusionment. We already should have enough experience and evidence to know at the outset that some kinds of intervention by those who are not primary participants imperil certain fragile and exceedingly important elements of a school's ecosystem—those elements out of which those living there might create satisfying habitats.

We must understand, too, that the concept of a school-community ecosystem also is only a metaphor, useful for some understandings but not as a comprehensive model of assumed reality. Currently, "community" is a much abused concept. It is being redefined so as to have only the most parochial of connotations—my neighborhood, my class, my race, my school.[21] There is a much larger community and it, too, has a stake in those "community schools." Likewise, a child has a right to be educated in and for a community going much beyond what he can see and touch and smell. It is the school's responsibility to conceive of itself as part of the nation's and, indeed, humankind's ecosystem and to educate in those inalienable rights for which unseen and unknown citizens have fought and died. Some of them had better ideas than each child's parents have about how and in what to educate.

Each of us owns an interest in every school. And so there must always be both an inner and an outer force in changing schools. The problem is to create and maintain a productive state of tension between the two. The League of Cooperating Schools represents a modest contribution to the understanding of what is required. It promises no easy, instant, rose gardens, only the planting and caring thereof, accompanied by many hours of satisfaction in watching the bushes grow and bloom. In the process, one discovers and creates one's own special Walden.

NOTES

1   Lee J. Cronbach, "Beyond the Two Disciplines of Scientific Psychology," *American Psychologist*, February 1975, p. 121.

2   Charles Rusch, "MOBOC: A Mobile Learning Environment," in Gary Coates (ed.), *Alternative Learning Environments*, Dowden, Hutchinson, Ross, Inc., Stroudsburg, Pa., 1974.

3   See, for example, John I. Goodlad et al., *The Conventional and the Alternative in Education*, McCutchan Publishing Corporation, Berkeley, Calif., 1975.

4   This is the idea of mankind (or, sometimes, humankind). See Gerhard Hirschfeld, *An Essay on Mankind*, Philosophical Library, New York, 1957; and W. Warren Wagar, *The City of Man*, Houghton Mifflin, Boston, 1967.

5   Urie Bronfenbrenner, "Experimental Human Ecology: A Reorientation to Theory and Research on Socialization," presidential address, Division of Personality and Social Psychology, American Psychological Association, 1974.

6   C. Robert Pace, "A Contextual Model for Evaluating the Impress of College on Students," unpublished paper (mimeo).

7   Urie Bronfenbrenner, *Is Early Intervention Effective?* Department of Health, Education, and Welfare, Office of Child Development, Washington, D.C., 1974.

8   Bronfenbrenner, "Experimental Human Ecology."

9   John I. Goodlad, "Perspective on Accountability," *Phi Delta Kappan*, (in press).

10   Robert Ulich, "The Ambiguities in the Great Movements of Thought," in Robert Ulich (ed.), *Education and the Idea of Mankind*, Harcourt, Brace & World, New York, 1964, p. 23.

11   William H. Boyer, "Education for Survival," *Phi Delta Kappan*, vol. 52, p. 258, January 1971.

12   Ursula Vils, "Distilling 50 Years of Family Needs," an interview with Margaret Mead, *Los Angeles Times*, May 4, 1975.

13   Joseph Heller, *Something Happened*, Knopf, New York, 1974, p. 13.

14   See Mary M. Bentzen and Associates, *Changing Schools: The Magic Feather Principle*, McGraw-Hill, New York, 1974.

15   Leon Edel, "Walden: The Myth and the Mystery," *American Scholar*, Spring 1975, p. 273.

16   Ibid., p. 274.

17   Quoted in ibid.

18   Ibid., pp. 274–275.

19   Ibid., p. 277.

20   Rudolf Eckstein, "Towards Walden III," *Reiss-Davis Clinic Bulletin,* vol. 2, no. 1, p. 17, Spring 1974.

21   Robert M. Hutchins, "The Great Anti-School Campaign," in *The Great Ideas Today,* pp. 154–227, Encyclopaedia Britannica, Inc., Chicago, 1972.

A SELECTED BIBLIOGRAPHY ON EDUCATIONAL CHANGE

Compiled and Annotated by Lillian K. Drag

This selection of readings is an extension of the listings entitled "A Bibliography on the Process of Change," in Carmen M. Culver and Gary J. Hoban, eds., *The Power to Change: Issues for the Innovative Educator* (McGraw-Hill, 1973). A few of the basic references contained in the earlier bibliography are retained in the present listing in order to provide a more balanced and broader picture of the state of the field. For the most part, however, the present selection relates more directly to the development of Goodlad's thesis in the text of this volume and includes the substantial body of references from which he draws, not all of which were cited in his end-of-chapter notes.

The bibliography is arranged in four parts. Part I broadens perspectives with material on building theories of change, constructing models, and dealing with issues involved in educational change. Materials in Part II offer strategies and tactics for implementing the strategies. Inherent in the writings is discussion of structures for changing schools. Part III deals with actual practice. First, titles describing aspects of the |I|D|E|A| Study of Educational Change and School Improvement (SECSI) and the vehicle used for the study, the League of Cooperating Schools, are listed. These are followed by descriptions of other case studies. Part IV lists reviews of the literature on change for those who would pursue more rigorously historical and current developments in the field.

PART I.   BUILDING THEORIES, CONSTRUCTING MODELS, AND BROADENING PERSPECTIVES

Abbott, Max G.: "Programmatic Research and Development on Innovativeness and the Organizational Attributes of Schools." Paper presented at the Annual Meeting of the American Educational Research Association, Los Angeles, February 1969.

Problems of organization are seen as (1) coordination in the educative process, (2) maintenance of the enterprise through time, (3) efficient distribution of decision-making responsibilities, (4) effective connection with institutions on which the enterprise depends, and (5) retention of an optimum level of flexibility so that the organization may continue to innovate. Three dimensions of analysis are used: structural, sociocultural, and sociopsychological. See also his article entitled "The School as Social System: Indicators for Change," in *Socio-Economic Planning Services,* vol. 2, 1969, pp. 167–174.

Argyris, Chris, and Donald A. Schön: *Theory in Practice: Increasing Professional Effectiveness,* Jossey-Bass, San Francisco, 1974.

Encompasses professions that serve in the fields of health, justice, education, organizational management, urban planning, and social welfare and addresses the questions: What is professional competence? How is it acquired? How can professional education be redesigned? Uses the field of education in examples of incongruities between espoused theories and theories-in-use and, again, in describing field experience.

Baldridge, J. Victor: "The Impact of Individuals, Organizational Structure and Environment on Organizational Innovation." R&D Memorandum No. 124, Stanford Center for Research and Development in Teaching, Stanford University, Stanford, Calif., 1974.

Reports on studies of organizational change in two school districts, one in Illinois, the other in California. Found that complex organizations with heterogeneous environments are more likely to initiate and sustain innovations than simple organizations in more homogeneous environments. Concludes: "We must be in the business of creating organizations with built-in capacities for assessing their needs and creating viable alternatives."

————, and Terrence E. Deal (eds.): *Managing Change in Educational Organizations: Sociological Perspectives, Strategies, and Case Studies,* McCutchan Publishing Corporation, Berkeley, Calif., 1975.

Contributors from the social science research fields and educational practitioners provide a balanced compilation of readings, identifying exemplary work in educational innovation. Introductory section deals with invention and diffusion of educational innovation and organizational subsystems. Part two presents strategies for change agents, leadership dynamics, and political aspects of change. Part three provides case studies over half of which emanated from research and development centers. This is a useful source book to provide an overview of the field.

Bennis, Warren G.: *Changing Organizations: Essay on the Development and Evolution of Human Organization,* McGraw-Hill, New York, 1966. Reviews action, writings, and thinking in this field. Chapter 3, "Toward a Truly Scientific Management: The Concept of Organizational Health," offers a helpful analysis applicable to any organization. Part 2 describes attempts by behavioral scientists to apply their sociological and psychological knowledge toward improvement of organizations through planning and controlling organizational change. Includes discussion of planned change and "operations research," change agents, change programs, and strategies.

Bhola, Harbans S.: "Limitations and Possibilities of Educational Diplomacy —A Theoretical Framework." Paper presented at the Sesquicentennial Seminar in Comparative Higher Education, School of Education, Indiana University, Bloomington, October 1970.
Suggests that change agents can use the author's configurational theory of innovation diffusion: (1) the configurational relationship between the initiator of change and the target of change, (2) the linkages within and between them, (3) the environment surrounding the initiator and the target, and (4) the available resources.

Carlson, Richard O., et al.: *Change Process in the Public Schools,* Center for the Advanced Study of Educational Administration, University of Oregon, Eugene, 1965.
Report of a seminar of school officials and social scientists. Contains "Barriers to Change in Public Schools," by R. O. Carlson; "Planned Change and Organizational Health: Figure and Ground," by Matthew Miles; "The Place of Research in Planned Change," by R. J. Pellegrin; and "Directed Change in Formal Organizations: The School System," by Art Gallaher. Clinic sessions give attention to specific change problems encountered by school officials.
See also his book entitled *Adoption of Educational Innovations* (Center for the Advanced Study of Educational Administration, University of Oregon, Eugene) and his article "Environmental Constraints and Organizational Consequences: The Public School and Its Clients," *Behavioral Science and Educational Administration,* Sixty-third Yearbook, Part II, National Society for the Study of Education, University of Chicago Press, Chicago, 1964, pp. 262–276.

————: "Summary and Critique of Educational Diffusion Research." Paper presented at the National Conference on the Diffusion of Educational Ideas, East Lansing, Mich., March 26–28, 1968.
Delineates the diffusion process as (1) acceptance, (2) over time, (3) of some specific idea or practice, (4) by individuals, groups, or other adoptive units, linked to, (5) specific channels of communication, (6) to a social structure, and (7) to a given system of values or culture.

Cartwright, Dorwin, and Alvin Zander (eds.): *Group Dynamics: Research and Theory,* 3d ed., Harper & Row, New York, 1968.
A comprehensive collection of readings providing a thorough back-

ground for understanding the group dynamics movement. Shows the development of ideas and processes, describing the various forms the movement took, such as techniques of group leadership, management, analysis, sensitivity training, "T" groups, etc. These techniques developed to change behaviors are still very much alive and well in the change process.

Charters, W. W., Jr., and John E. Jones: "On the Risks of Appraising Non-Events in Program Evaluation," *Educational Researcher,* vol. 2, November 1973, pp. 5–7.
Observes that some innovations have been discredited which have never really been implemented. Suggests appraisal based on four possible levels of innovation and implementation: (1) institutional commitment—a public announcement, (2) structural context—changes in formal arrangements and physical conditions, (3) role performance—changed behavior patterns of teachers, and (4) learning activities—students' behavior, activities, experiences, and performance consistent with the intent of the innovation.

Chase, Frances S.: "Educational Research and Development in the Sixties: A Mixed Report Card," *Curriculum Theory Network,* Monograph Supplement, 1971, pp. 142–163.
A background paper submitted to the Select Subcommittee on Education, U.S. House of Representatives, April 1971. Cites major achievements of R&D and obstacles as viewed by R&D personnel and non-R&D people. Lists ten major lessons learned from the R&D experience of the sixties.

Clark, David L., and Egon G. Guba: "An Examination of the Potential Change Roles in Education," *Rational Planning in Curriculum and Instruction,* National Education Association, Center for the Study of Instruction, Washington, D.C., 1967, pp. 111–133.
Develops a logical structure for examining change roles in education. Divides the innovation process into four parts: research, development, diffusion, and adoption. Describes each stage in detail with recommendations for action.

Conant, James B.: *Two Modes of Thought,* Trident Press, New York, 1964.
Discusses advances in the natural sciences resulting from collaboration of scientists with two perspectives: the empirical-inductive method of inquiry and the theoretical-deductive. *Note:* Goodlad pursues the interweaving of these modes in developing his own model for the improvement of schooling.

Ford Foundation: *A Foundation Goes to School: The Ford Foundation Comprehensive School Improvement Program,* The Foundation, New York, 1972.
Report of a large-scale project which suggests that most of the so-called innovations were installed only partially or not at all, despite concerted efforts and support of the foundation.

Getzels, Jacob W.: "Creative Administration and Organizational Change:

An Essay in Theory," in *Frontiers in School Leadership*, Louis J. Rubin (ed.), Rand McNally, Chicago, 1970, pp. 69–85.

Distinguishes several types of change: enforced change, expedient change, essential change (voluntaristic), and extruded change. Feels that the administrator must take these into account if obstacles to change are to be overcome. Stresses the challenge of the problematic, the need for variation.

Getzels, Jacob W., James M. Lipham, and Roald F. Campbell: *Educational Administration as a Social Process: Theory, Research, Practice*, Harper & Row, New York, 1968.

Chapter 4 presents the general model developed by Getzels and Egon Guba providing a framework for the study of administrative behavior. The relationship between the normative (institutional) dimension and the personal (individual) dimension of social behavior within the cultural sphere is graphically represented. The point that observed behavior in a social system is always a function of the interaction between these dimensions is emphasized. This model was explored in part of the League study.

Goldhammer, Keith: *Issues and Strategies in the Public Acceptance of Educational Change*, Center for the Advanced Study of Educational Administration, University of Oregon, Eugene, 1965.

Delineates the factors affecting public acceptance of change. Categories of factors are (1) the public's image of the advocate of change, (2) the public's image of the organization and the ends which it serves, (3) the public's view of the proposed changes, (4) the consequences of the proposed change with generally accepted values and recognized needs, and (5) situational factors which facilitate or impede the acceptance of change.

Goodlad, John I., and M. Frances Klein: *Looking Behind the Classroom Door*, 2d ed., Charles A. Jones, Worthington, Ohio, 1974.

After a report on the condition of schooling, recommendations follow for continuous reconstruction of schooling to meet the changing conditions of society: each school faculty identifies its most critical problem, engages in sustained dialogue regarding alternative courses of action, takes action on one or more of these alternatives, and periodically appraises the results ("a self-renewing school").

Guba, Egon G., et al.: *The Role of Educational Research in Educational Change, The United States*. Conference on the Role of Educational Research in Educational Change, UNESCO Institute for Education, Hamburg, Germany, July 19–22, 1967, The National Institute for the Study of Educational Change, Bloomington, Ind., 1967.

Guba collects and describes the trends in the United States on the basis of authorities in various aspects of research: (1) institutional setting of research, by Sam Sieber, (2) problems in organizing research institutes, N. L. Gage, (3) trends in recruiting and training staff for research, Johns Hopkins, (4) dissemination of research results, Thomas

Clemens, and (5) role of research in the innovation process, Henry Brickell. Guba presents a model for change including research, information, development, diffusion, and utilization—a rational sequence from invention to dissemination.

Hage, Jerald, and Michael Aiken: *Social Change in Complex Organizations*, Random House, New York, 1970.

Presents the organizational factors that may influence change in school: complexity, centralization (power in hands of few), formalization of staff procedures and regulations, stratification, production (quantity versus quality), efficiency, and morale. Perceives the organization as a social system, contrasting and comparing the dynamic and the static style. Change within the system, change of the system, and the process of change are examined. Includes case studies.

Halprin, Lawrence: *The RSVP Cycles: Creative Processes in the Human Environment*, George Braziller, Inc., New York, 1969.

An ecologically oriented way of looking at change:

R = Resources, what you have to work with, human and physical, and their aims and motivations.

S = Scores, symbolization of processes, allowing communication over time and space to other people including participation and feedback.

V = Valuation, analysis of the results of action, selection and decision.

P = Performance, the result of scores, is the style of the process.

Herriott, Robert E., and Benjamin J. Hodgkins: "Social Context and the School: An Open-System Analysis of Social and Educational Change," *Rural Sociology*, vol. 34, June 1969, pp. 149–166.

Argues that the community probably permits the school to be a change agent only to the extent that community wants it to be changed. Until the local environment which supports, maintains, and controls the American public schools can be changed, little widespread change can be made in the structure of the school.

Interchange, Michael Fullan (ed.): "Innovations in Learning and Processes of Educational Change," The Ontario Institute for Studies in Education, Ontario, Canada, vol. 3, nos. 2–3, 1972.

This special edition deals with causes for success and failure at the implementation phase of innovation. Looks at changes in structure and organization, instructional and curriculum change, and participative decision making. Fullan's introductory article "An Overview of the Innovative Process and the User" elaborates on the premise that in order to understand school change, it is necessary to examine the social relations among all major groups of people who are involved in or affected by the process.

The Journal of Applied Behavioral Science, "Power and Social Change," Mark Chesler and Orian Worden (eds.), vol. 10, no. 3, 1974.

A special issue emphasizes the roles and values of social scientists as creators, organizers, and disseminators of social knowledge and beliefs about social systems, power, and change. Examines the goals and activities of practitioners of social change. Henry Levin, "Educational Reform and Social Change," argues that school will always be used to reproduce society rather than to modify it.

Katz, Daniel, and R. L. Kahn: *The Social Psychology of Organizations,* Wiley, New York, 1966.
Discusses the behavior of people in organizations based on "open-system theory," which is carefully defined. In Chapter 13, seven approaches to organizational change are considered: information, individual counseling and therapy, peer-group influence, sensitivity training, group therapy, survey feedback, and direct systematic change.

Lippitt, Ronald, Jeanne Watson, and Bruce Westley: *Dynamics of Planned Change,* Harcourt, Brace & World, New York, 1958.
Discusses aspects of change and various types of professional workers concerned with it: change agents, the client system, change forces, phases of change, and methods of change. Still a basic reference.

McGregor, Douglas: *Leadership and Motivation,* The M.I.T. Press, Cambridge, Mass., 1966.
Provides a theory ("X"/"Y" theory) for dealing with the concept of organizational health. Use of the theory in schools would broaden school objectives from student learning outcomes to dealing also with the social, egoistic, and self-fulfilling needs of the individuals in the organization: principals, teachers, and pupils. Tye and Novotney in *Schools in Transition* (see Part 3 of this bibliography) apply the "X"/"Y" theory to schools.

March, James G. (ed.): *Handbook of Organizations,* Rand McNally, Chicago, 1965.
A comprehensive reference work which examines specific institutions such as schools in their organizational context. It includes such chapters as "Decision Making and Problem Solving," "Influence, Leadership, Control," and "Changing Interpersonal and Intergroup Relationships in Organizations." Charles Bidwell's chapter, "The School as a Formal Organization," is fundamental to understanding changing schools.

March, James G.: "Model Bias in Social Action," *Review of Educational Research,* vol. 42, no. 4, Fall 1972, pp. 413–429.
Examines a relativist and a rationalist bias in models of social policy, both of which accept choice as appropriately consequent upon purpose, resulting in a static interpretation of human goals. Suggests supplementing the technology of reason with a technology of playfulness, or "sensible foolishness": treating goals as hypotheses, intention as real, hypocrisy as a transition; memory as an enemy, and experience as a theory. Result: stimulating change which might develop unusual and more interesting people, organizations, and societies.

Marrow, Alfred: *The Practical Theorist: The Life and Work of Kurt Lewin,* Basic Books, New York, 1969.
Refers to Lewin's belief that theories and methodologies of psychology should be applicable to the "real world" which led to his development

of the concepts of action research and group dynamics. These concepts became a solid part of the thinking, actions, and techniques of social psychologists of the sixties.

Miles, Matthew B. (ed.): *Innovation in Education,* Bureau of Publications, Teachers College, Columbia University, New York, 1964.
A basic reference for the study of change, especially these chapters: "Educational Innovation: The Nature of the Problem," by Matthew Miles; "Curricular Change: Participants, Power, and Processes," by Gordon Mackenzie; "Administrative Theory and Change in Organizations," by Daniel E. Griffiths; and "On Temporary Systems," and "Innovation in Education: Some Generalizations," by Matthew Miles.

Moos, Rudolph H., and Paul M. Insel (eds.): *Issues in Social Ecology: Human Milieus,* National Press Books, Palo Alto, 1974.
Collection of articles on ways environmental factors influence man and his behavior. Part V, "Behavior Settings and Psychosocial Interactions," includes Roger Barker's "The Ecological Environment" and Paul Gump's "Big Schools—Small Schools." Also pertinent is Ronald Corwin's "Patterns of Organizational Conflict."

Nagi, Saad Z., and Ronald G. Corwin (eds.): *The Social Contexts of Research,* Wiley, New York, 1972.
The final chapter by the editors, "The Case of Educational Research," shows how the issues discussed in the book converge. Issues are drawn within the contexts of values and ideologies, control, organization, operation, and ethics. James McNaul's "Relations between Researchers and Practitioners," is especially pertinent.

National Institute of Education: *Building Capacity for Renewal and Reform: An Initial Report on Knowledge Production and Utilization in Education,* by Marc Tucker and others, National Institute of Education, Washington, D.C., December 1973.
This position paper on the acquisition of knowledge shows that the R,D&D model of the 1960s failed to realize actual change in the schools. Suggests that project grants be designed to include provision for studying the process of innovation.

Orlosky, Donald, and B. Othanel Smith: "Educational Change: Its Origins and Characteristics," *Phi Delta Kappan,* vol. 53, March 1972, pp. 412–414.
Report of a study made for the U.S. Office of Education charting the major change efforts of the past 75 years according to date of origin, source, rating of success, and focus of change. Implications of origin (whether outside the school setting or within the field of education) and the focus of change (instruction, curriculum, organization, and administration) are listed in fourteen concluding points.

Reynoldson, Roger L.: *The Interrelationships between the Decision-Making Process and the Innovativeness of Public Schools,* U.S. Office of Education, Washington, D.C., 1969.
Study of forty-nine public schools indicates that there is more innova-

tion in schools with more open organizational climate. The characteristics and style of leadership of the principal as well as the communication networks were found to be critical factors.

Rogers, Everett M., and F. Floyd Shoemaker: *Communication of Innovations: A Cross-Cultural Approach,* Free Press, New York, 1971.
In this second edition of Rogers's book *Diffusion of Innovations,* the focus is on the informal social group and the formally organized system rather than the individual as an innovator. Relates concepts of diffusion research to those of organizational change, stating that "social change is an effect of communication." Adopter characteristics and innovations are seen as related to adoption patterns and rates of diffusion.

Sarason, Seymour B.: *Creation of Settings and the Future Societies,* Jossey-Bass, San Francisco, 1972.
Examines the processes and problems common to the creation of settings ("any instance when two or more people come together in new and sustained relationships"). Draws upon personal participation in the creation of new settings in education and other fields to describe and analyze failures and successes. Social systems, socialization, and leadership are examined.

————: *The Culture of the School and the Problem of Change,* Allyn and Bacon, Boston, 1971.
The author uses the ecological approach to describe the school setting, examining the set of beliefs that emerges as individuals interact within the organization. He feels that the study of the "regularities" of behavior and programs to determine patterns is more significant in trying to effect change than the imposition of an innovation. Two detailed case reports of the processes of change indicate that lack of vehicles for discussion and communication in the school blocks efforts to change.

PART II. STRATEGIES AND TACTICS

Argyris, Chris: *Management and Organizational Development: The Path from XA to YB,* McGraw-Hill, New York, 1971.
Focuses on human resources to: solve problems, make effective decisions, and generate commitment to implementation. Assumes "man can be more of an active contributor to his and his organization's well-being."

Baldridge, J. Victor, and Rudolph Johnson: *The Impact of Educational R&D Centers and Laboratories: An Analysis of Effective Organizational Strategies,* Stanford Center for Research and Development in Teaching, Stanford University, Stanford, Calif., 1972.
Gives some examples of successful implementation indicating the organizational arrangements which seem to help or hinder success. Offers

recommendations for improving the dissemination process, the weakest link in the change process.

Barry, Elizabeth F.: "The Relationship between Propensity toward Self-Directed Change in School Faculties and Selected Factors in the School's Subculture," unpublished doctoral dissertation, University of California, Los Angeles, 1974.

Extends the |I|D|E|A| Study of Change in the League of Cooperating Schools (1965–1971) investigating whether a school staff's problem-solving process indicates the school's propensity toward self-directed change. Includes an analytical review of the literature dealing with the history and development of change strategies and the current state of the field.

Becker, James: "Organizing for Change: The Individual in the System," *Social Education,* March 1973, pp. 193–196.

Lists seven factors indicating flexibility and responsiveness to change of a school faculty and presents practical guidelines for implementing change.

Becker, James M., and Carole L. Hahn: *Wingspread Workbook for Educational Change Agents,* Social Science Education Consortium, Inc., Boulder, Colo., 1975.

The experienced participants in the National Seminar on the Diffusion of New Instructional Materials and Practices, held in June 1973, contributed the practical suggestions in this workbook for people working for change in schools. Details effective and appropriate ways of introducing and maintaining new products, practices, and programs.

Beckhard, Richard: *Organizational Development, Strategies and Models,* Addison-Wesley, Reading, Mass., 1969.

Organization development is defined as an effort to increase effectiveness and health through planned interventions in the processes of the organization, using behavioral-science knowledge. Strategy requires diagnosis of the various subsystems and the processes that are occurring. Uses and defines the terms "change manager" and "change agent." Describes alternative arrangements for linking organizations and outside resources. "Change" means change in organizational climate.

Bennis, Warren G., Kenneth D. Benne, and Robert Chin (eds.): *The Planning of Change,* Holt, New York, 1967.

A volume of readings stressing two aspects of planned change: the change agents' and the clients' systems. The relationship established between the giver and receiver of help is considered basic to the outcome. "How well the process is understood by each and what degree of openness for examination and for possible reconstruction exists for both parties are, therefore, of central importance."

————: *The Planning of Change,* 2d ed., Holt, New York, 1969.

"Brings together some of the best current conceptualizations of different aspects of application and change process." Discusses and evaluates a growing body of change technologies. About nine-tenths of the readings in this edition are new.

Bentzen, Mary M., and Kenneth A. Tye: "Effecting Change in Elementary Schools," in *The Elementary School in the United States,* Seventy-second Yearbook, Part II, National Society for the Study of Education, John I. Goodlad and Harold G. Shane (eds.), University of Chicago Press, Chicago, 1973, Chapter 14.
Reviews and synthesizes the accumulation of knowledge about the nature and use of change strategies. Despite these developments, the authors find few satisfying solutions to the problem of changing schools. Proposes that schools be viewed as a social system, that they become self-renewing, and that they "will either do it themselves or it won't get done."

Brickell, Henry M.: "Two Change Strategies for Local School Systems," *Rational Planning of Curriculum and Instruction,* National Education Association, Center for the Study of Instruction, Washington, D.C., 1967, pp. 135–153.
Elaborates on two strategies, one based on decision to invent a new instructional process, the other to adopt one invented elsewhere. Delineates sets of conditions for each strategy which are practical enough to be put into use in any school committed to change.

Center for Coordinated Education, University of California, Santa Barbara: *Synergetics and the School: Strategies for School Improvement,* The Center, Santa Barbara, Calif., 1966.
Characterizes synergetics as cooperative interaction of various elements of a system. Takes the position that coordinated, participative action results in greater gains than separate unit efforts.

Charters, W. W., Jr., et al.: *Contrasts in the Process of Planned Change of the School's Instructional Organization,* Program 20, Center for the Advanced Study of Educational Administration, University of Oregon, Eugene, 1973.
A symposium prepared for the 1973 AERA Annual Meeting in New Orleans. Summarizes some of the findings of attempts made to implement staff organization plans at the grass roots level of school and school district. Identifies factors that served to hinder or facilitate implementation of innovations. Process view of change emphasized.

Chesler, Mark A., et al.: *Planning Educational Change,* vol. 2, *Human Resources in School Desegregation,* U.S. Department of Health, Education, and Welfare, Washington, D.C., 1969.
Though addressing a specific problem (desegregation) and specific personnel (school superintendents), this manual outlines a process using planned steps: identification of goals, diagnosis of the situation, development of plans, feedback and evaluation, and a recycling step in which further goals are established for continuing change efforts.
Planning Educational Change, vol. 3, *Integrating the Desegregated School,* U.S. Department of Health, Education, and Welfare, Washing-

ton, D.C., 1970, chaps. 6–9, discusses the principal as leader in the change process. See also his chapter entitled "Change-through-Crisis Model," in Ronald G. Havelock and Mary Havelock, *Training for Change Agents,* Center for Research Utilization of Scientific Knowledge, Institute for Social Research, University of Michigan, Ann Arbor, 1972.

Corey, Stephen M.: *Action Research to Improve School Practices,* Teachers College, Columbia University, New York, 1953.
Action research is used here as it is defined by Kurt Lewin: research done in an actual problem context and which would be socially ("educationally") useful as well as theoretically meaningful.

Dalin, Per: *Innovation in Education: A Systemic View.* Paper prepared for the IMTEC course "The Management of Educational Change: Secondary Education," Norway, October 1973, Centre for Educational Research and Innovation, OECD, Paris, 1973.
Defines key terms, describes various strategies, and identifies stages of innovation. Delineates four categories of barriers to educational innovation: value barriers, power barriers, practical barriers, and psychological barriers. Combines them in a framework for comparison of innovation in an international setting.

————: "Planning for Change in Education: Qualitative Aspects of Educational Planning," *International Review of Education,* vol. 16, no. 1, Special Number, pp. 436–449, 1970.
Describes briefly some major strategies for change (from Havelock). Indicates that change in schools occurring as a result of cooperative planning is more likely to be effective than mandated change and points out the need for constant interchange between components. Suggests international collaboration.

————: "Strategies for Innovation in Education," *Case Studies of Educational Innovation,* vol. 4, Centre for Educational Innovation, OECD, Paris, 1973.
A summary report which draws conclusions and implications based on the three earlier volumes of case studies. Focuses on the dynamics of change stressing participative decision making, the role of leadership at the various levels, and relationships between research and political decision making.

Education and Urban Society, C. Brooklyn Derr (ed.), vol. 6, no. 2, February 1974.
This issue is devoted to "organization development," indicating present state of the field and its application to education, especially to urban school systems. Richard Schmuck's article "Bringing Parents and Students into School Management" and the descriptive article "An Inner-City School that Changed—and Continued to Change," by Arthur Blumberg et al., are pertinent.

Eidell, Terry L., and Joanne M. Kitchel (eds.): *Knowledge Production and Utilization in Educational Administration,* University Council for Edu-

cational Administration and Center for the Advanced Study of Educational Administration, University of Oregon, Eugene, 1968.
Contributing authors Goldhammer, Guba, Havelock, and Schmuck focus on strategies for implementing change in educational organizations.

Fox, Robert S., et al.: *Diagnosing and Improving the Professional Climate of Schools,* NTL Learning Resources Corporation, Fairfax, Va., 1973.
Describes first the improvement program including concepts and theories about the school as a social system. Part 2 is a compilation of instruments designed to serve as a manual for defining and solving problems; developing plans for change; and determining who's responsible for what, how things get done, and how to use one another's resources through better internal communication.

French, Wendell L., and Cecil H. Bell, Jr.: *Organization Development: Behavioral Science Interventions for Organization Improvement,* Prentice-Hall, Englewood Cliffs, N.J., 1973.
Offers definition, history, characteristics and foundations, illustrative cases, and the most thorough review of theory and practice of organization development to date. Includes chapters on action research; team interventions; and personal, interpersonal, and group-process intervention.

Giacquinta, Joseph B.: "The Process of Organizational Change in Schools," *Review of Research in Education,* vol. I, Fred N. Kerlinger (ed.), F. E. Peacock, Publisher, Itasca, Ill., 1973, pp. 178–208.
Discusses three basic stages in the process of organizational change: initiation of the innovation, implementation, and incorporation as a stable part of the organization. Develops a theoretical framework for the study of change with procedures for collecting and analyzing data. See Gross et al., cited below, for a more comprehensive related work.

Goodlad, John I.: "Educational Change: A Strategy for Study and Action," *The National Elementary Principal,* vol. 48, January 1969, pp. 6–13.
Describes the creation of the League of Cooperating Schools in southern California as an effort by the |I|D|E|A| Research Division to study educational change and improve schools. He develops the rationale behind it and the research effort accompanying it. See also entries in the section entitled "The Study of Educational Change and School Improvement and Other Case Studies."

Havelock, Ronald G., *The Change Agent's Guide to Innovation in Education,* Educational Technology Publications, Englewood Cliffs, N.J., 1973.
Discusses the role of the change agent, giving four examples of change agents in action. Delineates six stages of planned change and their interrelationships. Translates research finding for the novice and practicing change agent in schools and offers suggestions for choosing the best strategy for changing schools. Provides a list of the major information sources in education in the United States.

————, and Others: *Planning for Innovation through the Dissemination and Utilization of Knowledge,* Center for Research on the Utilization of Scientific Knowledge, University of Michigan, Ann Arbor, 1971.

A comprehensive analysis of the literature in the fields of mental health, agriculture, medicine, public health, law, business, and especially education. The authors draw upon social psychology, sociology, and communications science for their analytic framework advocating more linkage roles to effect better dissemination and utilization of knowledge. They suggest other significant factors: degree of structure and openness of user and resource systems, capacity to marshall diverse resources, reward, proximity to resources and others users, and synergy.

Hemphill, John K., and Fred S. Rosenau (eds.): *Educational Development: A New Discipline for Self-Renewal,* Center for the Advanced Study of Educational Administration, University of Oregon, Eugene, 1973.

Contributors' work at the Far West Laboratory for Educational Research and Development provided the background of experience necessary to write about the basic conception of development as part of educational R&D. Examples of development efforts, including planning, evaluating, and disseminating and installing products and practices are offered. Some of the major barriers to implementing research findings are discussed.

House, Ernest R.: *The Politics of Educational Innovation,* McCutchan Publishing Corporation, Berkeley, Calif., 1974.

Experiences with two major innovations lead the author to believe that the political and economic structure of the school allows certain types of activities and prohibits others; that an advocate working within the system is needed to overcome rigid internal structure if innovation is to succeed; and that most innovations depend on face-to-face personal contacts. He suggests reasons for persistence of government policies (the "R" and "D"), despite repeated failures (in the second "D"—diffusion), pointing out that the practitioner operates in a context foreign to the developer.

————, Joe M. Steele, and Thomas Kerins: *Development of Educational Programs: Advocacy in a Non-Rational System,* Center for Instructional Research and Curriculum Evaluation, University of Illinois, Urbana, 1970.

Report of a study to ascertain success and quality in program development. Variables (interacting) found to be most powerful: (1) size of the developing unit, (2) norms of the unit toward the innovation, (3) opinion leadership exerted on behalf of the change, (4) status of the advocate within the system, and (5) contact of the system with the outside world.

Huberman, A. M.: *Understanding Change in Education: An Introduction,* Experiments in Innovation in Education, no. 4, UNESCO, International Bureau of Education, Paris, 1973.

Discusses change agents, resistors, innovators, and traits and functions of innovative institutions. Gives basic models of planning and executing change. Finds that the majority of studies done on change in education come from America and draws implications.

Immegart, Glenn L., and Francis Pilecki: "Assessing Organizational Output: A Framework and Some Implications," *Educational Administration Quarterly,* vol. 6, Winter 1970, pp. 62–76.
Emphasizing that organizational output analysis suggests a change orientation, the authors propose criterion measures: (1) productivity—product utility and services utility, (2) integration potential—self-actualization, group decision making, and an individual's flexibility to change, (3) organizational health—adaptability, sense of identity, and capacity to test reality, and (4) feedback—desirability and penetration.

Kimbrough, Ralph B.: *Administering Elementary Schools: Concepts and Practices,* Macmillan, New York, 1968.
The author thinks that many principals do not feel that the consequences of initiating instructional change are worth the effort because of difficult social problems. He proposes a mode of thinking about human behavior that is fused with knowledge of operational management. He sees each elementary school as a social system that is unique and suggests ways of thinking about particular administrative setups, describing types of community power structures, organizational climates of individual schools, and varying personnel characteristics.

Lawrence, Paul R., and Jay W. Lorsch: *Developing Organizations: Diagnosis and Action,* Addison-Wesley, Reading, Mass., 1969.
Focuses on (1) the organization—environment interface, (2) the group—group interface, and (3) the individual—organization interface. Behavioral science tools and concepts to deal with problems of each of three interfaces form the basis for a model of organization development consisting of four stages: (1) diagnosis, (2) action planning, (3) implementation, and (4) evaluation. Views such variables as structure, conflict, goals, and outcomes within different environments and shows that different conditions call forth different organizational forms.

Morphet, Edgar L., and Charles O. Ryan (eds.): *Planning and Effecting Needed Changes in Education,* Third Area Conference Report of Designing Education for the Future: An Eight-State Project, The Project, Denver, 1967.
Useful papers include Kenneth Hansen's "Planning for Changes in Education"; Robert Chin's "Basic Strategies and Procedures in Effecting Change"; Robert Howsam's "Effecting Needed Change in Education"; Ralph Kimbrough's "Power Structures and Educational Change"; and Don Glines's "Planning and Effecting Needed Changes in Individual Schools."

Novotney, Jerrold M., and Kenneth A. Tye: *The Dynamics of Educational Leadership,* 2d ed., Educational Resource Associates, Inc., Los Angeles, 1973.

Discusses the concept of leadership, its dimensions, various styles of leaders, the tools of leadership, and relationships in working with groups. Develops the conceptual framework for such work emphasizing the importance of knowledge of human beings and principles of human interaction.

Owens, Robert G.: "Conceptual Models for Research and Practice in the Administration of Change." Paper presented at the American Educational Research Association Annual Meeting, New Orleans, La., 1973.

Concisely identifies overall strategies of organizational change, indicating tactics explicitly useful with each of the strategies. Implications for administrative practice and research are clearly drawn, strongly suggesting the use of repertoire of strategies and tactics geared to the dynamic interrelationships of the organization. Stresses decision-making processes, indicating that organizational change means more than just the adoption of some innovation; it means totally reconstructing the school organization to create a self-renewing organism.

————: *Organizational Behavior in Schools,* Prentice-Hall, Englewood Cliffs, N.J., 1970.

Attempts to provide the school administrator with information to enable him to gain new behavioral knowledge and use it in coping with professional problems; Chapter 5, "Decision Making"; Chapter 6, "Leadership in the School"; and Chapter 7, "Change in an Organizational setting."

Prescott, Daniel A.: *The Child in the Educative Process,* McGraw-Hill, New York, 1957, chap. 13.

Describes the Child Study Program, its structure, substantive elements, and purposes in attempting to change teachers by helping them better understand children and themselves. It uses nondirective techniques of group leadership, management, and analysis.

Rand Corporation: *Federal Programs Supporting Educational Change: A Model of Educational Change,* vol. 1, by Paul Berman and Milbrey Wallin McLaughlin, Rand Corporation, Santa Monica, 1975 (#R1589/1).

————: *Federal Programs Supporting Educational Change: Factors Affecting Change Agent Projects,* vol. 2, by Paul Berman and Edward Pauley, Rand Corporation, Santa Monica, 1975 (forthcoming, #1589/2).

————: *Federal Programs Supporting Educational Change: The Process of Change,* vol. 3, by Peter W. Greenwood and Dale Mann, Rand Corporation, Santa Monica (forthcoming, #R1589/3).

————: *Federal Programs Supporting Educational Change: The Findings in Review,* vol. 4, Rand Corporation, Santa Monica (forthcoming, R1589/4).

Schein, Edgar H.: *Process Consultation: Its Role in Organization Development,* Addison-Wesley, Reading, Mass., 1969.

Tests interventions which a process consultant might make, contrasting them with standard consultancies where expert advice is given on particular problems. In process consultation, it is assumed that the organization does not know how to use its own resources effectively, and the process consultant shares his own skills and values to help the organization develop.

Schmuck, Richard A., et al.: *Handbook of Organization Development in Schools.* Prepared at the Center for the Advanced Study of Educational Administration, University of Oregon, Eugene, 1972.
"This handbook is a guide to planned actions for facilitating human responsiveness and adaptability in school organizations."—Preface. A manual developed to facilitate use of ideas presented below.

————, and Matthew Miles (eds.): *Organization Development in Schools,* National Press Books, Palo Alto, Calif., 1971.
Presents the rationale behind OD, the problems encountered in OD research, and the effects of OD on specific organizations where it has been employed. Examines how change agents are organized, trained, enter, and work in schools.

Sieber, Sam D.: "Images of the Practitioner and Strategies of Educational Change," *Sociology of Education,* vol. 45, Fall 1972, pp. 362–385.
Discusses three basic strategies of change and shows how they are rooted in particular "images of the practitioner" (e.g., as "the rational man" he is conceived as a person basing decisions on the best information available; therefore the focus of change is on intellectual processes).

Takanishi-Knowles, Ruby: *Collaboration between Educational Researchers and School Personnel: Some Reflections and Proposals for Reducing the Research-to-Practice Gap,* Stanford Center for Research and Development in Teaching, Stanford University, Stanford, Calif., 1973.
Three principles were considered important in reducing the research-to-practice gap: (1) communication of research results to teachers involves the individual's feelings of competence, (2) direct teacher involvement is necessary for planning and carrying out changes in teaching, and (3) attention to individual differences in research on teaching increases success. The author considers "improvement" dependent upon a reciprocal and continual process of interaction between researchers and practitioners. Collaboration process should take into account: (1) the need to institutionalize the process to assure continuity and renewal and (2) the authority structure of school organizations, or the need for administrative sanctions and participation in collaboration.

Temkin, Sanford (ed.): *What Do Research Findings Say About Getting Innovations Into Schools: A Symposium,* Research for Better Schools, Inc., Philadelphia, 1974.
Includes pertinent papers by Ronald Havelock, "Locals Say Innovation Is Local"; Richard Miller, "What We Can Learn about Change Processes from ESEA, Title III"; J. Victor Baldridge, "Political and Structural Protection of Educational Innovations"; and Matthew Miles, "A Matter

of Linkage: How Can Innovation Research and Innovation Practice Influence Each Other?"

Tye, Kenneth A.: "The Political Linkage Agent," in Ronald G. Havelock and Mary Havelock, *Training for Change Agents,* Center for Research Utilization of Scientific Knowledge, Institute for Social Research, University of Michigan, Ann Arbor, 1972, pp. 143–150.

Develops a program to effect political and structural changes in school systems using a political linkage agent who would act as process helper, catalyst, and solution giver until an equitable balance of power is achieved.

————, Charles C. Wall, and Judith S. Golub: "The Principal as a Change Agent: A Concept Revisited," *The National Elementary Principal* (forthcoming).

Discusses in depth two sets of leader behaviors crucial in attainment of school goals, institutional and personal, and four dimensions of programs aimed at fostering those behaviors. Based on findings of the |I|D|E|A| Study of Educational Change and School Improvement relating to the role of the principal as a change agent.

Watson, Goodwin (ed.): *Change in School Systems,* National Education Association, Washington, D.C., 1967.

Papers published for the Cooperative Project for Educational Development by National Training Laboratories, NEA, which focus attention on processes of the schools and on strategies designed to test and develop the core ideas outlined in the companion volume *Concepts for Social Change.* Includes Matthew Miles, "Some Properties of Schools as Social Systems" and Charles C. Jung, Robert Fox, and Ronald Lippitt, "An Orientation and Strategy for Working on Problems of Change in School Systems."

————: *Concepts for Social Change,* National Education Association, Washington, D.C., 1967.

Working papers which develop core ideas about planned change to give direction to the Cooperative Project for Educational Development (COPED). Paul C. Buchanan, "The Concept of Organizational Development, or Self-Renewal as a Form of Planned Change"; Goodwin Watson, "Resistance to Change"; Donald Klein, "Some Notes on the Dynamics of Resistance to Change: The Defender Role"; and Matthew Miles and Dale Lake, "Self-Renewal in School Systems: A Strategy for Planned Change."

Willower, Donald J.: "Educational Change and Functional Equivalents," *Education and Urban Society,* vol. 2, August 1970, pp. 385–402.

"Approaches to innovation direct attention away from social system considerations." Contends that the school displays an array of structures that are functional for the organization and its adult personnel but dysfunctional or neutral for pupils. Functional equivalents or alternatives are suggested after analysis of social structures, roles, and social norms.

Zaltman, Gerald, et al.: *Processes and Phenomena of Social Change,* Wiley, New York, 1973.

Although this collection deals with a field broader than educational change, it includes several chapters directly related to education: James S. Coleman, "Conflicting Theories of Social Change"; Goodwin Watson, "Resistance to Change"; Lindley J. Stiles and Beecham Robinson, "Change in Education"; Charles A. Kiesler, "Evaluating Social Change Programs"; and Alan E. Guskin and Mark A. Chesler, "Partisan Diagnosis of Social Problems."

PART III.   THE STUDY OF EDUCATIONAL CHANGE AND SCHOOL IMPROVEMENT AND OTHER CASE STUDIES

A.   The Study of Educational Change and School Improvement (SECSI)

Bentzen, Mary M., and Associates: *Changing Schools: The Magic Feather Principle,* McGraw-Hill, New York, 1974 (|I|D|E|A| Reports on Schooling).

Describes in detail the intervention strategy, the processes, successes, failures, and outcomes of the Study of Educational Change and School Improvement (SECSI). Emphasis on staff development processes in the League of Cooperating Schools includes description of the use of DDAE (dialogue/decision making/action/evaluation). Attends to factors suggesting self-renewing capacity of schools. Includes case studies as well as appendixes of instruments used and statistical tables.

Culver, Carmen M., and Gary J. Hoban (eds.): *The Power to Change: Issues for the Innovative Educator,* McGraw-Hill, New York, 1973 (|I|D|E|A| Reports on Schooling).

Contributors to this collection of readings were members of the |I|D|E|A| Research Division from the Elementary School Appraisal Study and the Study of Educational Change and School Improvement. They focus on changes to be made in the school as an organization, in the working relationships of principals and teachers, and in the functions of principal leadership. They describe with anecdotal material the stages of change in elementary schools, the peer-group strategy developed in the League, an institutional evaluation system, and a plan for accountability.

Goodlad, John I.: *Educational Change: A Strategy for Study and Action,* Institute for Development of Educational Activities, Inc., Melbourne, Fla., 1968.

Lists a number of potential changes which have failed to work in schools and describes a new strategy, "The League of Cooperating Schools," a consortium of principals and their schools which attempted to improve. See also his "The League of Cooperating Schools," *A Setting for Change,* |I|D|E|A|, 1968.

————: "The League of Cooperating Schools," *California Journal for Instructional Improvement,* vol. 9, no. 4, December 1966, pp. 213–18.
Describes the purposes and formative stages of the strategy for change in the League model.

————: "Staff Development: The League Model," *Theory Into Practice,* vol. 11, October 1972, pp. 207–214.
Discusses the factors to be taken into account in effecting educational change, stressing the "culture of the school." Describes the League model to illustrate how it supports the change process and how research into the change process helps schools improve their practice.

Lieberman, Ann (ed.): *Tell Us What To Do! But Don't Tell Me What to Do!* |I|D|E|A|, Dayton, Ohio, 1971.
"Changing teachers talk about themselves" as participants in the League of Cooperating Schools' Study of Educational Change conducted by the |I|D|E|A| Research Division. Frustrations and feelings of accomplishment are spelled out from the planning stages through the five years of the project to the final stages.

Novotney, Jerrold M. (ed.): *The Principal and the Challenge of Change,* |I|D|E|A|, Dayton, Ohio, 1968.
Contributors are members of the |I|D|E|A| Research Division involved with the League of Cooperating Schools. Kenneth Tye discusses eqilibrium, resistance, and strategies within the context of system models followed by Mary Bentzen's look at the conflicting roles of the principal. Robert Sinclair examines leadership concerns, Jerrold Novotney explores staff involvement, and Donald Myers, "The Art of Decision Making."

Shiman, David A., Carmen M. Culver, and Ann Liebermann (eds): *Teachers on Individualization: The Way We Do It,* McGraw-Hill, New York, 1974 (|I|D|E|A| Reports on Schooling).
Written by teachers in the League of Cooperating Schools for other teachers wishing to initiate a program or improve in individualizing their teaching. The peer-group strategy used in the League strengthened and encouraged teachers to share their innovative ideas for organizing classrooms and developing technical skills. Included are chapters for the teacher new to individualization, for those who wish to personalize learning, for those interested in developing a "resource room" or classroom interest centers, and for team and cooperative teaching.

Tye, Kenneth A., and Jerrold M. Novotney: *Schools in Transition: The Practitioner as Change Agent,* McGraw-Hill, New York, 1975 (|I|D|E|A Reports on Schooling).
Chapter 3, "The School as a Social System," provides a framework for investigating systemic change, discussing improved organizational processes needed for successful change, such as communication, decision making, and conflict management. The authors offer a concise review of present change strategies and a summary of emerging strategies which they feel hold promise.

Williams, Richard C., Charles C. Wall, W. Michael Martin, and Arthur Berchin: *Effecting Organizational Renewal in Schools: A Social Systems Perspective*, McGraw-Hill, New York, 1974 (|I|D|E|A| Reports on Schooling).
Report of a study made in eight of the League schools which views the school as a social system within the framework of the Getzels-Guba model. The book addresses itself to the relation between the leader behavior of the principal and the school's organizational renewal ranking; the role-personality conflict and adaptation dimension in the school; and the relations among the values of the teachers, the principals, and the parents involved.

Willis, Charles L.: *What We Have Learned About the |I|D|E|A| Change Program for Individually Guided Education: An Interim Report*. A Charles F. Kettering Foundation Program, |I|D|E|A|, Dayton, Ohio, 1974.
Describes briefly the guidelines and processes of implementation of |I|D|E|A|'s Change Program for Individually Guided Education (IGE) which stem from the Study of Educational Change and School Improvement (SECSI). Reports in detail the methods used to evaluate the program and the findings to date.

Films

Institute for Development of Educational Activities, Inc.: *The League*, |I|D|E|A|, Melbourne, Fla., 1971.
Film reports on the |I|D|E|A| Research Division's Study of Educational Change and School Improvement in cooperation with the League of Cooperating Schools in southern California. Part I: The Strategy, Part II: A Matter of Trust, Part III: Try It Sometime, and Part IV: I Just Wanted to Let You Know How Well Rhonda Is Doing in School. Also, three excerpts: Case History of a Teaching Team, Staff Meeting, and Why Visit Another School?

B. Other Case Studies

Alschuler, Alfred: "Toward a Self-Renewing School," *Journal of Applied Behavioral Science*, vol. 8, no. 5, September/October 1972, pp. 577–600.
In describing the use of OD strategies in a school setting, the author cites the combination of three factors contributing to the successful intervention: favorable historical antecedents, the nature of the intervention, and continuous leadership by key administrators before and after the intervention. Concludes that the decision to work only on the system immediately beyond the classroom—the school—was a good one.

Argyris, Chris: *Behind the Front Page: Organizational Self-Renewal in a Mertopolitan Newspaper*, Jossey Bass, San Francisco, 1974.

Uses behavioral science to diagnose and propose ways to overcome obstacles to organizational change. Outlines method for aiding change in other organizations. Staff relationships and organizational development are examined in detail.

Centre for Educational Research and Innovation (CERI/OECD): *Case Studies of Educational Innovation,* Organisation for Economic Co-operation and Development, Paris, 1973. 4 vols.
Three of the four volumes compile cases illustrating the processes of innovation at the central level, regional level, and school level of school systems in member countries of the OECD. Volume IV, "Strategies for Innovation in Education," by Per Dalin, summarizes and draws conclusions and implications based on the earlier volumes.

Charters, W. W., Jr., et al.: *The Process of Planned Change in the School's Instructional Organization,* Center for the Advanced Study of Educational Administration, University of Oregon, Eugene, 1973. CASEA Monograph, No. 25.
Describes attempts made to implement staff organization plans at the grass roots level of school and school district. Discusses the reasons for failure of implementation of differentiated staffing in one district in both a high school and an elementary school. Problems of implementing a collaborative staffing model in four multiunit schools in Wisconsin are also analyzed.

Colgate University, Kettering Colgate Project: *A Study of Innovation and Change in Education: The Regional University-Schools Research and Development Program.* An Action-Research Project sponsored by the Charles F. Kettering Foundation and Colgate University, 1967–1971, Office of Educational Research, Colgate University, Hamilton, N.Y., 1971.
A detailed description of all the elements of the project. Appendix E compares |I|D|E|A|'s League of Cooperating Schools, directed by John I. Goodlad, with this project.

Fullan, Michael, and Glenn Eastbrook: *School Change Project: Interim Report of Findings,* Department of Sociology, The Ontario Institute for Studies in Education, Toronto, Canada, April 1973.
Describes in detail a study conducted in forty-six Ontario schools in order to increase understanding of the educational change process at the school level and to contribute to research knowledge of the innovative process. Examines (1) participation of students in decision making, (2) forms and levels of parent involvement in schools, (3) interpersonal relationships, communication, and decision making among teachers and between teachers and administrators, and (4) adoption of styles and processes of implementation of major innovations.

Gross, Neal, Joseph B. Giacquinta, and Marilyn Bernstein: *Implementing Organizational Innovations: A Sociological Analysis of Planned Educational Change,* Basic Books, New York, 1971.

A telling account of an attempt to effect change in a school setting with a searching analysis of factors which spelled success and failure. Details the methodology used to study the innovations and provides theoretical, research, and practical implications of it.

Hilfiker, Leo R.: *A Profile of Innovative School Systems,* Center for Cognitive Learning, Wisconsin Research and Development, University of Wisconsin, Madison, 1971.
Reports the relationship of innovation to selected dimensions of interpersonal behavior in eight school systems, especially openness, trust, and adaptiveness. A report from the Models for Planned Educational Change Project.

Pellegrin, Roland J.: *Some Organizational Characteristics of Multi-unit Schools,* Center for the Advanced Study of Educational Administration, University of Oregon, Eugene, 1970.
Describes the interdependence relationships in multiunit and control schools; authority, decision-making processes, and influence; division of labor in the multiunit schools; operational goals of teachers and job satisfaction and environmental climate. Appends sociometric charts. See also John S. Packard, "Changing to a Multiunit School," in *The Process of Planned Change in the School's Instructional Organization,* by W. W. Charters, Jr., et al., University of Oregon, Eugene, 1973, CASEA Monograph No. 25, pp. 105–121.

Schmuck, Richard, et al.: *Consultation for Innovative Schools: OD for Multiunit Structures,* Center for Educational Policy and Management Eugene, Ore., 1975.
Describes research on techniques of organization development and analyzes their application in six elementary schools.

————, and Philip J. Runkel: *Organizational Training for a School Faculty,* University of Oregon Press, Eugene, 1970.
Describes the CASEA experiment at Highland Park Junior High School in Beaverton, Oregon, designed to increase the organizational problem-solving ability of a school faculty by training in aspects of organizational renewal, especially in the improvement of communication skills.

Smith, Louis M., and Pat M. Keith: *Anatomy of Educational Innovation: An Organizational Analysis of an Elementary School,* Wiley, New York, 1971.
An in-depth ecological study of attempted change in a single school with the process of change closely examined and subsequently analyzed.

PART IV. REVIEWS OF THE LITERATURE

Baldridge, J. Victor: *Organizational Change Processes: A Bibliography with Commentary,* Stanford Center for Research and Development in Teaching, Stanford University, Stanford, Calif., 1970.

The first section, "General Problems of Analyzing Organizational Change," discusses neglect by theorists, action by authorities organizational conflict as a promoter of change, and the interrelations of organizational subsystems. The second section discusses (1) changing organizations by changing individuals, (2) partisan groups of agents of change, (3) system changes by authorities, (4) technology as a source of change, and (5) the organization and its environment.

Chin, Robert, and Loren Downey: "Changing Change: Innovating a Discipline," *Second Handbook of Research on Teaching*, Robert M. W. Travers (ed.), Rand McNally, Chicago, 1973, pp. 513–529. Reviews and analyzes summaries of research findings on change in education.

Drag, Lillian K.: "A Bibliography on the Process of Change," *The Power to Change: Issues for the Innovative Educator*, Carmen M. Culver, and Gary J. Hoban (eds.), McGraw-Hill, New York, 1973, pp. 245–277.
An annotated listing of books, pamphlets, and periodical articles developed during the five-year Study of Educational Change and School Improvement for participants in the League of Cooperating Schools, slanted somewhat for elementary school principals' use. Extended by the "Selected Bibliography on Educational Change" in the present volume.

ERIC Abstracts: *A Collection of ERIC Document Resumes on Organizational Renewal: Change and the School Administrator*, AASA, Washington, D.C., 1971.
Compiled from the ERIC monthly catalog, *Research in Education*, under descriptors: administrative organization, organizational change, and organizational climate. Complete through February 1971.

Eve, Arthur W.: "Variables of Institutional Change at the Elementary and Secondary School Levels," Bureau of Educational Personnel Development, U.S. Department of Health, Education, and Walfare, Washington, D.C., 1971.
In reviewing the literature, the author observes "tinkering" with existing organizations whereas he feels the need for "restructuring of the school organization." He proposes the development of the school as a healthy organization, able to cope with, adjust to, or control its environment.

Fullan, Michael: "An Overview of the Innovative Process and the User," *Interchange*, vol. 3, nos. 2–3, 1972, pp. 1–46.
Elaborates on the premise that in order to understand school change, it is necessary to examine the social relations among all major groups of people who are involved in or affected by the process. Reviews relevant literature.

Havelock, Ronald G., et al.: *Major Works on Change in Education: An Annotated Bibliography with Author and Subject Indices*, Center for Research on Utilization of Scientific Knowledge, University of Michigan, Ann Arbor, October 1969.
A compilation of books and pamphlets dealing with planned change,

innovation, dissemination, and knowledge utilization for practitioner and researcher. Still useful though dated.

IMTEC Bibliography, Issue No. 1, January 20, 1974, Centre for Educational Research and Innovation, Organisation for Economic Co-Operation and Development (CERI/OECD), Paris, 1974.

Originally designed to help participants in International Management Training for Educational Change (IMTEC) courses to get into the literature of change. Contemporary issues, change process, research and development, management and management training are treated. Annotations are done in the form of provocative questions.

Maguire, Louis M., Sanford Temkin, and C. P. Cummings: *An Annotated Bibliography on Administering for Change*, Research for Better Schools, Inc., Philadelphia, 1971.

Extends the earlier Maguire work, *An Annotated Bibliography of the Literature of Change*, R.B.S., 1970. Reflects the thrust of the R.B.S. "Administering for Change Program" with the local school districts. Provides a comprehensive, annotated listing covering: an overview of change literature; organizing, planning, and managing for change; and educational problem solving. See also Maguire's work entitled *Observations and Analysis of the Literature of Change*, R.B.S., 1970.

Oliver, Maurice: *A Review of Literature: Training and the Change Process*, Bureau of Educational Personnel Development, U.S. Department of Health, Education, and Welfare, Washington, D.C., 1971.

In searching for information to make valid recommendations for training change personnel, this reviewer concluded that there is great need for more information of direct use to the practicing school administrator.

Piele, Philip K.: *New Programs for Training School Administrators: Analysis of Literature and Selected Bibliography*, ERIC Clearinghouse on Educational Administration, University of Oregon, Eugene, September 1970.

Focus is on (1) effectiveness of existing alternative approaches to training administrators, (2) emerging training programs, and (3) leads for design of new training programs, materials, and approaches.

APPENDIX A

OTHER STUDIES RESULTING FROM THE STUDY OF EDUCATIONAL CHANGE AND SCHOOL IMPROVEMENT

Approximately forty doctoral candidates working in several departments at UCLA served in various capacities—mostly as research assistants—from the time the League was created into the period of preparing final reports. Undoubtedly, what they experienced contributed significantly to their advance preparation for subsequent careers. While other dissertations undoubtedly drew from or dealt with various aspects of these experiences, the following were relatively closely linked to the Study of Educational Change and School Improvement and added to our general knowledge of the entire enterprise.

Elizabeth F. Barry, "Relationship between Propensity toward Self-directed Change in School Faculties and Selected Factors in the School's Subculture," University of California, Los Angeles, 1974.

Arthur Berchin, "Congruency of Values among Teachers, Principals, and Parents and Its Relationship to the Goal-attaining Process," University of California, Los Angeles, 1970.

James M. Bishop, "Organizational Work Context, Informal Organization, and the Development of Occupational Ideologies among Elementary Teachers: A Comparatve Study of 24 Public Schools," University of California, Los Angeles, 1972.

Ann Liebermann, "The Effects of Principal Leadership on Teacher Morale, Professionalism and Style in the Classroom," University of California, Los Angeles, 1969.

W. Michael Martin, "Role Conflict and Deviant Adaptations as Related to Educational Goal Attainment: A Social Systems Approach," University of California, Los Angeles, 1970.

Barbara Peterson, "Adoption of Educational Innovations: A Social System Approach," University of California, Los Angeles, 1969.

Roger L. Rasmussen, "The Adult Social System of the Elementary School and Sixth-Grade Achievement of Basic Skills," University of California, Los Angeles, 1974.

Robert L. Sinclair, "Elementary School Educational Environment: Measurement of Selected Variables of Environmental Press," University of California, Los Angeles, 1968.

George D. Thayer, "Some Relationships between School and Classroom Organizational Climate," University of California, Los Angeles, 1971.

Charles C. Wall, "Perceived Leader Behavior of the Elementary School Principal as Related to Educational Goal Attainment," University of California, Los Angeles, 1970.

A LEAGUE OF COOPERATING SCHOOLS: A PROPOSAL FOR THE STUDY AND ADVANCEMENT OF AMERICAN SCHOOLING (JANUARY 1966)

Reproduced below is the document describing what was intended in the creation of the League of Cooperating Schools and the agreements called for by the participating institutions. This was prepared by John I. Goodlad to convey to all concerned parties what appeared to him to be a reasonable summary of discussions among potential participating institutions which had taken place since May 1965. It conveys a much greater participation on the part of UCLA than what ultimately emerged. Subsequently, communication between the vice chancellor of UCLA and the vice president of the Kettering Foundation resulted in the Research Division of |I|D|E|A being located off-campus and organized entirely independently of UCLA. The linkage between the two institutions was provided by an agreement entered into regarding the joint appointment of Goodlad, the utilization of facilities, the provision of opportunities for doctoral students, and so forth. A Kettering Foundation Account was established at UCLA and certain funds were channeled through this account for specific expenditures related to the League of Cooperating Schools over subsequent years.

The School of Education, University of California, Los Angeles, proposes the development of a cooperative agreement with selected school districts of Southern California to create a League of Cooperating Schools. The League will be an alliance of fifteen to twenty school systems located throughout Southern California and the University wherein the unique resources of each participating unit are to be combined for innovation, experimentation, and research in the study and advancement of American schooling. Each district will designate one elementary school as an innovating educational center to be a member of the League. The University will designate the University Elementary School as its cooperating member.

PURPOSES

The general purposes of the League of Cooperating Schools are to stimulate innovative approaches to schooling and to study the effectiveness of innovations in school practice. Specific purposes include the following:

1   To provide a laboratory for studying educational practices and ideas, the change process, and process of dissemination.

2   To provide a research base for educational decision making.

3   To provide a setting for the appraisal of existing and long established educational practices as well as ideas for change prior to possible research or testing in one or more cooperating schools.

4   To facilitate the initial trial of school practices which already have stood some tests of experimentation but have not yet received widespread adoption in the United States.

5   To develop schools which increasingly can serve as models of good educational practices.

6   To effect such communication among participating schools that the experiences of any one school in effecting educational change can be brought quickly to the attention of others within the League and subsequently to schools outside the League.

7   To provide settings where teachers may be stimulated and supported in their efforts to use modern pedagogical practices in the educational process.

8   To provide settings for the preparation of highly skilled educational leaders.

9   To evaluate and develop curriculum materials, aids, and instruments of evaluation of common interest to participating schools.

THE ESTABLISHMENT AND ORGANIZATION OF THE LEAGUE

The University's Commitment

To administer and coordinate the League's activities, the University will take initial responsibility in securing a grant for the establishment of a Central Office with funds, facilities, and staff to support the following activities:

1   The recruitment of short-term and long-term consultants for projects undertaken by League Schools.

2   The publication and dissemination of illustrative educational practices and research findings through print, film, and television.

3   The conduct of seminars, institutes, and conferences contributing to the implementation of the League's activities.

4   The support of selected doctoral students who will have specific research and development responsibilities in the League while continuing their graduate studies.

5   The establishment of effective means of communication and self-assistance among League Schools through a newsletter, exchange of

personnel, visitations, and other activities designed to bring all schools into a close working relationship.

6   The partial financial support of selected school leaders who will serve as short-term consultants to the League while having an opportunity for mid-career refreshment.

7   The preparation of requests for outside financial aid for major enterprises the League decides to undertake.

8   The establishment of communication with pilot schools in other areas and the utilization of resources from other existing projects or organizations.

The Central League Office will be the connecting link among the members of the League and provide direct assistance in the implementation of the League enterprises. An Advisory Council composed of the superintendents or their representatives from each cooperating school district and representatives of the School of Education, UCLA, will be established. This council, meeting at least semi-annually, will serve to promote a full partnership among the members of the League, to raise and clarify problems associated with League participation, to review the progress of League projects, and to advise on directions and general policies for the functioning of the League.

The ongoing activities of the League will be coordinated by a council of principals composed of the administrator of each League school and the staff of the Central Office of the League. This council will meet regularly, perhaps twice monthly, to communicate and report progress of projects, to consider problems encountered in specific projects, to assist in the development of studies, and to explore ideas for school improvement. In addition, it is expected that each League member will establish or clarify internal patterns and structures of communication so that each principal can function effectively in promoting a close relationship among League schools and the activities of all schools in the district he represents.

The School District's Responsibilities and Commitments

In Joining the League, participating districts agree to the following:

1   To designate, for a period of three years, one school as its representative unit for innovation and research.

2   To secure Board approval for the project and establish community understanding and acceptance of the school district's participation in the League.

3   To facilitate the designated school's participation in the League by deviating where desirable and feasible from general school district policies.

4   To clarify or establish procedures internally which will facilitate par-

ticipation by the staff of the League school and promote communication, harmony, and support within the district for the League's activities.

5   To provide released time for the principal and staff of the League school when necessary so that they can participate in the League's activities. The responsibility of the League school staff in the study project should be considered as a part of the normal work load rather than as an additional commitment. Where possible, other duties of the staff should be lessened to compensate for the work load of League participation.

In addition to these commitments, districts will have a limited financial responsibility. Initially, this responsibility will be to provide funds for the travel and necessary expenses of the participating school staff, for the employment of substitute teachers in excess of normal to free staff for work sessions, for the employment of additional secretarial help, and for the cost of additional resources which may be demanded by the nature of the project chosen by the League school. These funds could be budgeted as an allocation for in-service teacher education.

Later, however, it is assumed that a cooperating school district, through the leadership of its designated school, will identify problems requiring resources beyond those normally available in the school district. To support these projects, the school district with the assistance and cooperation of the League Office will negotiate joint requests for foundation or other funds to support the special interests of the school district. In the request for such funds, it is anticipated that a percentage amount would be included to be allocated to the League Office for its support and continued operation.

Although the University anticipates securing funds for the initial establishment of the League without any contribution from participating districts, the League can be self-sustaining only if future joint grants between the League Office and its members provide allocations for its continuation. Therefore, in time, funding for the League might well consist of University and school contributions of personnel, a central coordinating grant, a variety of sub-grants devoted to the unique problems of cooperating districts, and allocations from joint sub-grants for continuation of the Central League Office.

These commitments made by both the University and the participating districts are in no way intended to restrict other projects or involvements which might be carried on by either party apart from the League. Participation should stimulate many activities in general educational improvement. Ideas and projects implemented in a League school might well be utilized throughout a district; other schools of the districts will wish to continue as usual with special projects; districts will wish to work with other University departments or other institutions; and the University will have commitments and involvements with other schools and school districts. But the members of the League will maintain a close relationship demanding mutual commitments if the purposes of the League are to be attained.

ACTIVITIES AND PROJECTS

Hopefully, the problem chosen by a League school will arise directly from its own needs and interests and yet fit into one of the League's major emphases. Initially, it is anticipated that focal points of attention will include problems in the selection and use of new curriculum materials, the development of nongraded school structures, the utilization of cooperative or team teaching, and aspects of pedagogy. Schools, no doubt, will deviate in their approach to problems or projects falling within this agreed upon realm of activity and will be highly selective in their areas of participation. In this way, there will be opportunities for cooperating schools to observe and test alternatives.

As the League develops and additional resources are secured, the initial guidelines may well be broadened to include other areas for educational inquiry. But then, as now, the decision for a school to participate in a specific League activity will rest with the cooperating district.

COMPOSITION OF THE LEAGUE

League schools will be selected cooperatively by the district and the League staff to represent a wide range in size and socio-economic levels, a reasonable spread of geographic location, inclusion of the racial and ethnic groups found in Southern California, and virtually all of the problems inherent in the American educational enterprise.

Some of the schools in the League are probably not yet built. The challenge here is to plan with the district in creating the program and the building. Others schools might be very old and present unusual problems in adapting to current needs. Hopefully, each school will fit into the composition of the total League in such a way as to provide breadth of representation. Taken together, the schools of the League will present visitors and observers with a cross section of schools, educational problems, and programs of self-improvement and study.

SUMMARY

A League of Cooperating Schools representing a wide range of types of schools and educational problems provides a laboratory, constructed in manageable proportions, for the study and advancement of American schooling.

Envision, then, very different schools, including the University Elementary School, in very diverse school districts located throughout Southern California tied together in a cooperative agreement designed to ultilize as effectively as possible the mutual interests and collaborative resources of all the cooperating educational units. Assume each school is working on problems which are common to the total array of the districts represented and in fact to the total array of school systems in the United States. Assume, also, that this League relationship has made possible the recruitment, at least on a temporary basis, of the best resources available in the United States for the particular problem under study. Envision over all of this a research enterprise designed to examine processes of change and to evaluate special projects. Then begin to think about the possibilities for League schools to stimulate similar activities in many schools; for providing an unusual setting for the education of teachers; for finding out more about how best to conduct the educational enterprise; for the exchange of personnel and ideas; and for training research workers and educational leaders. This is the concept of the proposed League of Cooperating Schools.

THE LEAGUE OF COOPERATING SCHOOLS RENEWAL AGREEMENT (FEBRUARY 1969)

The renewal agreement, prepared in February 1969, more accurately reflects the participating roles of UCLA and |I|D|E|A|. The operating office or hub was conducted through |I|D|E|A|, although UCLA certainly was a legitimatizing agency, along with the Kettering Foundation. The fact that all funds came from the latter and were administered through its affiliate, |I|D|E|A|, placed administrative responsibility clearly with the Foundation and the cooperating schools. Consequently, some of the advisory bodies specified in the initial agreement did not materialize.

The League of Cooperating Schools is an education enterprise of partners. Through a tripartite agreement, eighteen public school districts in eight Southern California counties, UCLA, and the Research and Development Division of the Institute for Development of Educational Activities, Inc. (an Affiliate of the Charles F. Kettering Foundation) have joined to create a vast laboratory for research, study, and advancement of American schooling. Launched officially on May 11, 1966, the League in its present structure is a new institution created from a combination of existing institutions in such a way as to capitalize on interests and to bring into a new relationship resources of component units. It is an effort to strengthen the school as an agent of change. It serves as a laboratory for conceptualization about and research in educational change. The League seeks to implement a strategy for change based upon the assumption that the single school unit is a viable agent for change, given certain supportive conditions. Our assumptions are not yet proven but are to be tested in the real laboratory of schooling.

PURPOSES

The general purposes of the League of Cooperating Schools are to stimulate educational change and to study the processes of bringing about change in schools. Specific purposes include the following:

1 To provide a laboratory for studying the processes of educational change and educational decision making.

2 To facilitate the initial trial of school practices which already have stood some test of experimentation but have not yet received widespread adoption in the United States.

3 To improve the quality of educational practices in particular schools.

4 To effect such communication among participating schools that the experiences of any one school in effecting educational change can

be brought quickly to the attention of others within the League and subsequently to schools outside of the League.

5 To provide settings where teachers may be stimulated and supported in their efforts to improve instructional practices in the educational process.

6 To provide settings for the preparation of educational leaders.

7 To evaluate and develop evaluation techniques and instruments which may be of great interest to participating schools.

THE ESTABLISHMENT AND ORGANIZATION OF THE LEAGUE

|I|D|E|A|'s Commitment

To administer and coordinate the League's activities, |I|D|E|A| will maintain a central office with funds, facilities, and staff to support the following activities.

1 The employment of a small field staff to work with League schools in their endeavors to improve the quality of the educational program.

2 The publication and dissemination of illustrative educational practices and research findings through film, print, and television.

3 The conduct of seminars, institutes, and conferences contributing to the implementation of League activities.

4 The support of selected doctoral students who will have specific research and development responsibilities in the League while continuing their graduate studies.

5 The establishment of effective means of communication and self-assistance among League schools through a newsletter, exchange of personnel, visitations, and other activities designed to bring all schools into a close working relationship.

6 The establishment of a Materials Center to effect communication with pilot schools in other areas and to provide resources from other existing projects or organizations.

The central League office, the Research and Development Division, |I|D|E|A|, will be the connecting link among the members of the League and provide direct assistance in the implementation of the League enterprise. |I|D|E|A| will report from time to time to cooperating school district superintendents, or their representatives, on the progress and developments of League projects and activities. Further, |I|D|E|A| will seek to promote a full partnership among the members of the League. It will confer with superintendents, or their representatives, to seek advice and counsel on (a) problems associated with League participation and (b) directions and general policies for the functioning of the League.

The ongoing activities of the League will be coordinated by the principals of each League school and the staff of the central office of the League. This group will meet regularly to communicate and report progress on projects, to consider problems encountered in specific projects, to assist in the development of studies, and to explore ideas for school improvement.

The School District's Responsibilities and Commitments

In continuing as a member of the League, participating districts agree to the following:

1 To designate for a period of two years (June 1969–June 1971) the current League school as its representative unit.

2 To secure board approval for the project and establish community understanding and acceptance of the school district's continued participation in the League.

3 To facilitate the designated school's participation in the League by approving its deviation where desirable and feasible from general school district policies.

4 To clarify or establish procedures internally which will facilitate participation by the staff of the League school and promote communication, harmony, and support within the district for the League's activities. It is expected that the League district will establish or clarify patterns and structures of communications so that each principal can function effectively in promoting a close relationship among League schools and the activities of all schools in the district.

5 To provide released time for the principal and staff of the League school when necessary so they can participate in the League's activities. The responsibility of the League school staff in the study project should be considered as a part of the normal work load rather than as an additional commitment. Where possible, other duties of the staff should be lessened to compensate for the work load of League participation.

In addition to these commitments, districts will have a limited financial responsibility. This responsibility will be to provide funds for the travel and necessary expenses of the participating school staff, for the employment of substitute teachers in excess of normal to free staff for work sessions, for the employment of additional secretarial help, and for the costs of additional resources which may be demanded by the nature of the program developed by the League school.

These commitments made by both |I|D|E|A| and the participating districts are in no way intended to restrict other projects or involvements which might be carried on by either party apart from the League. Participation should stimulate many activities in general educational improvement. Ideas and projects implemented in a League school might well be utilized throughout a district; other schools of the district will wish to continue as usual with special projects; districts will wish to work with other university departments or other insitutions; and |I|D|E|A| will have commitments and involvements with other schools and other districts. But members of the League will maintain a close relationship demanding mutual commitment if the purposes of the League are to be attained.

ACTIVITIES AND PROJECTS

Initial program thrusts by League schools have been in three major areas: curriculum, school organization, and instruction. Schools have deviated in their approaches to these areas and in the initial focal points of attention. Some efforts have been focused on the utilization of cooperative or team teaching. Others have focused on development of school organizational structures which permit greater flexibility in ways of grouping pupils. Still others have focused on the instructional processes, such as individualizing instruction. Increasingly, school staffs are engaging in dialogue focused on the improvement of the quality of school programs. Questions are being asked. What would a school be like if the focus were on individual needs and differences among learners? What types of teaching tactics, materials, and pupil activities are appropriate and necessary in individualizing instruction? What are alternatives to grading if continuous progress is the goal? What are diagnostic procedures for providing meaningful data for structuring the learning setting? How can schools create improved learning environments? In these and other ways teachers and principals of the League schools are taking a new look at their programs.

With eighteen schools, several alternatives can be tried and tested. As an individual school introduces new forms and substances on its own, it also looks toward whatever practices, processes, and insights emerge from member schools. A participating League member then, in effect, has eighteen innovating centers from which to choose and utilize the most appropriate practices in terms of resources for its own program development. Teachers have partners in many classrooms from whom they can gain stimulation and tried ideas. However, the decision for a League school to develop and participate in a specific program activity rests within the school and the cooperating district as they consider resources, purposes, and environmental press.

COMPOSITION OF THE LEAGUE

League schools were selected cooperatively by the district and the League staff to represent a wide range in size and socio-economic levels, a reasonable spread of geographic location, inclusion of the racial and ethnic groups found in Southern California, and virtually all the problems inherent in the American educational enterprise. One district in the League enrolls about 2,000 pupils; another enrolls over 700,000. The smallest school in the league enrolls 250 students; the largest enrolls over 1,200. One school was built in 1925; another just opened its doors within the past year. Almost 80% of the student population of one school is Mexican-American; in still another the distribution is 37% Caucasian; 27% Negro; 13% Oriental; and 23% Mexican-American, Cuban, Puerto Rican, and other. Faculties range not only in terms of experience but in terms of size, length of working together, backgrounds, and preparation. Each school, then, fits into a composition of the total League in such a way as to provide breadth of representation. Together, the schools of the League present visitors and observers with a cross section of schools, educational problems, and programs of self-improvement and study.

IN CONCLUSION

The League of Cooperating Schools, representing a wide range of types of schools and educational problems, provides a laboratory constructed in manageable proportions for the study and advancement of American schooling.

These schools in very diverse school districts located throughout Southern California are tied together with |I|D|E|A| and UCLA in a cooperative agreement designed to utilize as effectively as possible the mutual interests and collaborative resources of all the cooperating educational units. Hopefully, all of us will come to know more about the factors likely to hamper or enhance the role of the individual school as a change agent and about the viability of the League as a strategy for educational change. We are proceeding with the confidence that at least eighteen schools, whatever their present stage of evolution, will become exceedingly productive places for the good human work that is education.

INDEX

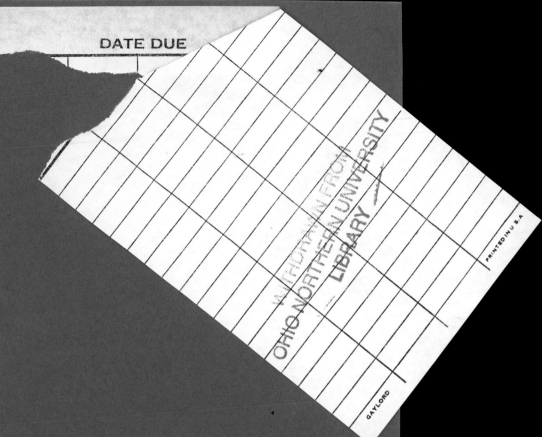